Rabbi Yitzḥak Frank

GRAMMAR FOR GEMARA
& TARGUM ONKELOS

AN INTRODUCTION TO ARAMAIC

≈

Based on
Grammar for Gemara
(Second Edition)

≈

Ariel United Israel Institutes
Maggid Books

Grammar for Gemara and Targum Onkelos
Published 2003
Third Edition, 2016

Maggid Books
An imprint of Koren Publishers Jerusalem Ltd.

POB 8531, New Milford, CT 06776-8531, USA
& POB 4044, Jerusalem 9104001, Israel
www.korenpub.com

Ariel United Institutes
HaPisga 5
POB 16002
Jerusalem, Israel

Copyright © Yitzhak Frank, 2003, 2016

Production and Design:
Leshon Limudim Ltd.
POB 4282, Jerusalem, Israel

Comments and suggestions concerning the contents of
this book are welcome. They should be addressed to
Rabbi Yitzhak Frank at yitzfrank@gmail.com

ISBN 978-1-59264-452-0, *hardcover*

A CIP catalogue record for this title is
available from the British Library

Printed and bound in Israel

I dedicate this work
to the revered memory
of my first Aramaic teacher

HaRav Dr. Michael Bernstein
הרב מיכאל בן אפרים וטובה ז"ל

whose integrity, intellectual honesty,
and dedication to Torah learning
made an indelible impression upon me.
He passed away on 23 Teveth, 5741.

Grammar for Gemara and Targum Onkelos
was originally prepared during the year of mourning for
my beloved mother

Sylvia Frank
שרה רבקה בת אריה לייב וחיה יענטא ז"ל

who passed away on 13 Kislev, 5762.
A woman of unusual perseverance and commitment,
she advanced my two sisters and me
along the path of Torah and mitzvoth
under trying circumstances.

In memory of
my beloved father

Abraham S. Frank
אברהם שניאור בן צבי דוב וצפורה ז״ל

A remarkably humble and gentle person
who passed away on 26 Adar II, 5744.

In memory of
my dear father-in-law

Dr. Benjamin L. Davis
דוב אריה בן חיים מנחם וליבא ז״ל

A distinguished scientist
dedicated to his fellow Jews
and to the State of Israel
who passed away on 25 Iyyar, 5753.

In memory of
my dear mother-in-law

Adele B. Davis
אֶדל בתיה בת משה יצחק ורבקה רחל בסין ז״ל

A staunch supporter of Jewish education
for her family and for all the children of Israel,
who excelled in hospitality and acts of loving-kindness.
She passed away on 10 Sivan, 5765.

MAY THEIR MEMORIES CONTINUE TO INSPIRE US.

TABLE OF CONTENTS

RABBI NATHAN KAMENETZKY
9/B SOROTZKIN ST., JERUSALEM 94423

28th of Adar II, 5752

בס״ד

Since this book is a companion to *The Practical Talmud Dictionary*, the reader is referred to my letter of approbation in that volume in order to perceive my enthusiasm for works of this kind by my worthy colleague Rabbi Yitzhak Frank.

With regard to grammar, I note that my revered father זצ״ל held that its study is included in the מצוה of תלמוד תורה because its knowledge is crucial for reaching correct Halakhic conclusions. He cited a grammatical error which led a well-intentioned author to propose building a מקוה in every Jewish home. Ignorance of the gender of the noun אצבע in רמב״ם הלכות ספר תורה פ״ט ה״ט had led that individual to advocate מקוואות that were undersized and invalid; their use would have resulted in massive איסורי כרת. Knowledge of grammar is thus not פרפראות לחכמה, which the תוספות יו״ט defines as studies undertaken to enhance knowledge — also not to be denigrated — but גופי הלכות, studies that affect Halakha.*

In one sense this new book is more fulfilling than the earlier one. While *The Practical Talmud Dictionary* is only a reference book for occasional use when the student comes across a word or expression which needs clarification, *Grammar for Gemara* can be studied, mastered and then put aside on the student's bookshelf for just the periodic review. Rabbi Frank, an experienced teacher, has made Talmudic grammar accessible to everyone; he has handed over the key to an unjustifiedly arcane discipline, so that a lover of Torah can now simply open the door to a neglected compartment of the Talmudic treasurehouse.

נתן בהגר״יי קמנצקי

---

* עיין תוספות יום טוב מס׳ אבות פ״ג מי״ח ד״ה תקופות.

USING THE VERBAL TABLES

The verbal tables in Chapters 3, 4 and 5 should be useful to the student. Chapter 3 now presents a comprehensive paradigm for the regular Aramaic verb, containing practically all the forms of the common *binyanim*. Chapter 4 features the complete conjugations of thirty important verbs from the Babylonian Talmud, while Chapter 5 has thirty-two verbs from Targum Onkelos (twenty-four of which are the same verbs whose Babylonian Aramaic forms are presented in the previous chapter). Chapters 4 and 5 record only those verbal forms that *actually occur* in the Talmud or in Targum Onkelos, respectively.

If the student can determine that the verb appearing in the text he is studying is regular (i.e., all three root-letters seem to be intact), the *paradigms* in Chapter 3 should be adequate to help him. Otherwise, he should try to locate a verb whose conjugation in Chapter 4 (for Talmud) or Chapter 5 (for Onkelos) can serve as a *paradigm* for the verbal form that confronts him, since they have been selected so that Aramaic verbs of every type are represented. An index of the verbs conjugated in Chapters 4 and 5 appears on the front and back inside covers of this volume.

For further assistance, see the full (artificial) paradigms for regular verbs in the Babylonian Talmud (pp. 258-262) and for regular vebs in Targum Onkelos (pp. 268-270) and the index of all the verbal roots in Targum Onkelos (pp. 271-290).

NOTE: A SYNOPSIS OF THE REGULAR VERBAL CONJUGATION IN THE BABYLO-NIAN TALMUD appears near the beginning of Chapter 5 (pp. 146-147), followed by A SYNOPSIS OF THE REGULAR VERBAL CONJUGATION IN TARGUM ONKELOS (pp. 148-149). They are followed by a table of DIFFERENCES BETWEEN VERBS IN THE TWO DIALECTS (p. 150).

PREFACE TO *GRAMMAR FOR GEMARA* (1ˢᵗ EDITION)

For some people, the words grammar and *Gemara* hardly go together. The study of Torah in general and *Gemara* in particular constitutes a fundamental mitzva in Judaism, valued as much as the sum total of all the commandments.[1] Although *grammar* is certainly less important, Rambam considered the study of Hebrew — the language in which the Torah has been transmitted — a mitzva in its own right.[2] Furthermore, Rashi and Ramban (and other classical commentators on the Torah) were masters of the Hebrew language and serious students of grammar. These Torah giants, whose place among *gedolei Yisrael* of all time is indisputable, drew upon their knowledge of Hebrew grammar in order to clarify the meaning of the Torah text.[3] It stands to reason that a working knowledge of Aramaic grammar could help us cope with the text of the Talmud. In fact, the author of *Peri Megadim*, one of the important halakhic works of the 18th century, wrote: "... the science of grammar is a cornerstone of the Torah, and when studying a lesson in *Gemara*, one should also have grammar books in front of him...."[4]

The student who has a grasp of Babylonian Aramaic grammar can achieve a more precise understanding of a Talmudic passage. Let us consider, for example, the common Talmudic term לֵימָא כְּתַנָּאֵי. Through a false analogy with Hebrew, many students assume that the ־ל indicates an infinitive form, *to say*, and they fumble. Familiarity with the Aramaic verb אמר reveals that לֵימָא is really

---

1   See Rambam, *Mishnei Torah*: Laws of Talmud Torah III:3.

2   Rambam, *Commentary on the Mishna*: Avoth II:1.

3   There are numerous discussions of grammatical points in the classical Torah commentaries of Rashi, Ibn Ezra, Rashbam, and Ramban. See many examples in E. Z. Melamed's מפרשי המקרא (Jerusalem: Magnes, 1975), Vol. 1, pp. 398-414, and Vol. 2, pp. 965-967.

4   So writes Rav Yosef Teumim in paragraph 16 (טז) of the first of two letters to a teacher, printed in the introduction to his *Peri Megadim* on *Shulḥan Arukh, Oraḥ Ḥayyim*. It is quoted by S. Isseroff in the preface to his *Introduction to Rashi's Grammatical Explanations in the Book of Genesis* (Torah Education Department, W.Z.O., 1985), p. III.

in the future tense, and thus the expression means: *Shall we say [it is] like the tannaim?*[5]

Let us look at a somewhat more complicated example from the Talmud. We freely admit that it is quite possible for some students to get an approximate sense of an Aramaic statement such as (עירובין כט, א) אֲנָא אֲמַרִיתָא נִיהֲלֵיה אַמַּתְנִיתִין, without knowing Aramaic grammar. He will get a much clearer picture, however, if he recognizes the following points:

(1) The verbal form אֲמַרִיתָא is a combination of אֲמַרִית, *I said*, the first-person singular of the verb אמר in the past tense — together with the pronoun suffix אָ- (= הָ-), expressing the direct object, *it*.

(2) The pronoun נִיהֲלֵיה serves as an indirect object, meaning *to him*.

(3) The Aramaic prefix אַ-, the equivalent of the Hebrew עַל, means *on* or *with reference to*[6].

Thus, the proper translation is: *I said it to him with reference to our mishna.*

Sometimes, the correct understanding of a particular grammatical form is crucial. In order to illustrate this point, we will briefly consider several different forms that are derived from the verbal root קני in conjunction with two Talmudic passages. In the simple conjugation (*binyan* קַל), קני means *acquire* or *buy*; in the passive conjugation (*binyan* אִתְפְּעֵל), it means *be acquired* or *bought*; and in the causative conjugation (*binyan* אַפְעֵל) it means *transfer* or *sell*. At the bottom of בבא מציעא מז, א, the Talmud quotes the *legal* formula בְּמָנָא דְכָשֵׁר לְמִקְנְיָא בֵּיה, *with a utensil with which it is proper to acquire*. At the top of the next page, an amora points out that the use of the infinitive from the simple conjugation לְמִקְנְיָא,[7] *to acquire (from someone)*, expresses the purchaser's perspective. According to this

---

5   In Babylonian Aramaic, the לְ- prefix is used in the future — usually for the third-person masculine singular, *he* or *one*, and occasionally for the first-person plural, *we*; therefore, the correct translation here is either *shall one say* or *shall we say*. The Aramaic infinitive, *to say*, would be לְמֵימַר.

6   For a full listing of the definitions of this prefix, see the very first entry in *The Practical Talmud Dictionary* (Jerusalem: Ariel: 1991; Maggid-Koren 2016).

7   In his Talmudic commentary, Rashi took the trouble to explain that the Hebrew translation of the Aramaic לְמִקְנְיָא is לִקְנוֹת, *to acquire*, rather than לְהַקְנוֹת, *to transfer*.

amora, this form was deliberately chosen — instead of the causative form לְאַקְנוֹיֵי,[8] *to transfer* (*to someone*) — in order to emphasize a *halakha*: In the mode of transfer referred to as קְנְיַן סוּדָר or קְנְיַן חֲלִיפִין, it is the *purchaser's* object (e.g., a handkerchief) that is handed over to the seller, rather than the other way around.

Secondly, consider the following passage from the tractate *Kiddushin*: אִשָׁה בְּפָחוֹת מִשָׁוֶה פְּרוּטָה לָא **מקניא** נַפְשַׁהּ (קידושין ג,א). According to the printed editions of the Talmud and according to the manuscript Rashi used, the verbal form מקניא means *she sells* or *she lets be acquired*. It should be vocalized מַקְנְיָא, the feminine singular of the active participle from the causative אַפְעֵל conjugation. Thus, the English translation of the whole statement is: *A woman **would** not **let herself be acquired** for less than the value of a peruta.* According to Rabbenu Tam, however, מִקְנְיָא is a participle from the אִתְפְּעֵל conjugation with a passive meaning, *acquired*, and the word נַפְשַׁהּ does not appear in what he considered to be the correct version of the Talmudic text. As a result, the meaning of the statement is: *A woman **may** not **be acquired** for less than the value of a peruta.* The difference between these two interpretations is of considerable halakhic significance, as Tosafoth and other commentaries on that Talmudic passage explain.

Let us not overstate the case. We freely grant that many people learn *Gemara* successfully without knowing Aramaic grammar. Some individuals have been served well by their intuitive powers; others somehow manage to "muddle through." For many students, however, an awareness of grammatical points, such as the ones mentioned above, can make their learning more accurate and more efficient.

Grammar for Gemara is not a comprehensive grammar, but it is mostly a collection of paradigms of the grammatical forms that confront the student of the Talmud Bavli. This work is a companion

---

8   לְאַקְנוֹיֵי, with an א representing the causative אַפְעֵל *binyan*, is the correct spelling according to most authoritative sources. R. Shemuel Strashun (רש"ש) comments that the spelling לַקְנוֹיֵי, with the א omitted, in our standard editions should be vocalized with a *pathaḥ* under the ל prefix (since it is the equivalent of לְאַקְנוֹיֵי).

volume to *The Practical Talmud Dictionary*, which was recently published by the Ariel Institute. The author composed the present work with the intention of providing the dictionary with an appendix that would facilitate its use. Mr. Yaakov Feldheim recommended that *Grammar for Gemara* be published as a separate volume because of the length of the work and because of his conviction that many students of the Talmud are hungry for a taste of Babylonian Aramaic grammar. If this work expedites the process of deciphering the Talmudic text ("making a *laining* on a *blatt Gemara*") for even one student, the effort invested in its composition will have been worthwhile.

Grammar for Gemara presumes that the student has a basic familiarity with Biblical Hebrew. In fact, the tanna Yehuda b. Tema (in *Avoth* 5:20) allocated five years of a child's Torah education to Biblical study before he would undertake the study of Mishna. The *first* chapter of this work deals with the language of the Mishna. It summarizes the main features of Mishnaic Hebrew that distinguish it from Biblical Hebrew. In the *second* chapter, the reader is introduced to the Aramaic language.

The bulk of *Grammar for Gemara* is devoted to the Aramaic verb, since it is the most crucial part of speech in the language. The *third* chapter explains the Aramaic *binyanim* and the tenses. The longest and probably the most useful chapter, the *fourth*, presents conjugations of eighteen important Aramaic verbs, including all their forms that actually occur in the Babylonian Talmud. The recognition of these verbal forms and their meanings will be of assistance to the student who is grappling with a Talmudic text. The next chapter, the *fifth*, analyzes some of the forms of the eighteen verbs that are homographs and/or homonyms which are likely to be a source of confusion.

The *sixth* chapter consists of paradigms for Aramaic nouns and adjectives. Pronouns — both independent words and suffixes attached to prepositions, nouns, and verbs — are the subject of the *seventh* chapter. The *eighth* chapter presents all the forms of Aramaic numbers that are found in the Talmud, including cardinal numbers, ordinal numbers, and fractions. The *ninth* chapter explains three important aspects of Talmudic syntax that might mislead the uninitiated. *Grammar for Gemara* concludes with several exercises based on eight passages from the Talmud, containing thirty of the verbal forms recorded in the conjugations in Chapter 4.

Special thanks are due to the following individuals who helped *Grammar for Gemara* become a reality: to my teacher, HaRav Ezra Zion Melamed, for his assistance in the creation of this work; to Dr. Aryeh Siegel, for his critical reading of the manuscript and his many useful suggestions; to Professor Moshe Bar-Asher of Hebrew University, Dr. Moshe Bernstein of Yeshiva University, Rav Nathan Kamenetsky and Rav Menachem Davis for their corrections and suggestions; to Professor Howard Harrison [ז"ל], for contributing his expertise in English style and form; to the publisher, the Ariel Institute — especially Rav Yeḥezkel Fogel, the Director General, and Naḥum Wengrov, proofreader; to the Girls' Town Computer Project at Kfar Chasidim and its director Rav David Landesman; and, above all, to my wife Marcia for her patience, her constructive criticism, and her invaluable aid in producing the manuscript. I would also like to take this opportunity to thank the Memorial Foundation for Jewish Culture and the State of Israel's Ministry of Religious Affairs for helping make the publication of this work possible. Finally, we thank the Holy One Blessed Be He for granting us the strength to complete this volume.

Yitzḥak Frank
Jerusalem, Iyyar 5752

Between the publication of the first and second editions of *Grammar for Gemara*, my beloved teacher, HaRav Professor Ezra Melamed, died in Jerusalem on the 26th of Adar, 5754. May the memory of the righteous be a blessing. Such a close bond was formed between Rav Melamed and me over the years that his demise, which occurred precisely on the 10th anniversary of the death of my own father ז"ל, was a great personal loss. Ezra Zion Melamed זצ"ל was first and foremost a great מַתְמִיד. There is no English term that can begin to describe the *pious diligence* and *diligent piety* that characterized his dedication to Torah learning and scholarship.

Yitzḥak Frank
Jerusalem, Sivan 5755

PREFACE TO *GRAMMAR FOR GEMARA* (2nd EDITION)

I have never harbored the illusion that *Grammar for Gemara* would gain a wide readership. It was obvious to me that this volume belongs to a genre of literature that is not particularly exciting for most people. In fact, most of the students who are turned on by the study of Talmud tend to approach the text with a mixture of awe and adoration — may the Lord bless them and keep them — but they are not attuned to grammar books and dictionaries. For many of them, the very attempt to be systematic smacks of the Enlightenment or of academia.

It has come as a pleasant surprise to me and to my publisher that several thousand copies of this work have actually been purchased. Apparently there are some people out there who subscribe to two propositions upon which *Grammar for Gemara* is based:

(1) Just as the knowledge of the grammar of any language helps one comprehend the literature written in that language, some acquaintance with Babylonian Aramaic grammar can expedite the study of the Talmud.

(2) The use of grammar to help one understand the Talmud text does not in any way detract from the sanctity of the Talmud.

In addition to correcting a few misprints here and there, this new edition features two major advances beyond the first edition:

(1) GRAMMATICAL FORMS FOR TARGUM ONKELOS AND TARGUM YONATHAN

Since the Talmud's dictum (*Berakhoth* 8b) that a Jew read the weekly Torah portion together with its Aramaic translation has conferred upon *Targum Onkelos* a unique status in Jewish life, we have attempted to make this edition serviceable for the Aramaic of *Targum Onkelos* to the Torah and *Targum Yonathan* to the Prophets as well. Although the authors of both *targumim* presumably lived in Eretz Yisrael, their Aramaic is remarkably similar to the language of the Babylonian Talmud, but not identical — especially with regard to some inflected forms of verbs and pronouns. Therefore, in

Chapters 3, 6 and 7 of this edition, we have indicated the forms that occur in *Targum Onkelos* according to the Yemenite tradition, which is generally considered to be the most reliable.

(2) CONJUGATIONS OF TWELVE ADDITIONAL VERBS

The guts of *Grammar for Gemara* remains Chapter 4, which presents every form conjugated from certain important Aramaic verbal roots that actually occurs in the Babylonian Talmud. In the first edition of this work, eighteen verbs were presented, and in this edition twelve more conjugated verbs have been added — (6A) נחת, (7A) שאל, (8A) ילף (8B) יהב / נתב, (8C) יתב (8D) תוב, (9A) אכל, (12A) גלי, (12B) אסי, (13A) שתי (17A) נוח, and (19) הימן — making a total of thirty. These additional verbs were selected because each one of them has a special feature that is not exemplified by any of the original eighteen. These thirty paradigms provide a more complete picture of the Babylonian Aramaic verb. I thank Rav Tzvi Heilpern, a *rosh kollel* in the Boro Park section of Brooklyn, New York, for his suggestion that the number of verbs in Chapter 4 be increased.

Yitzḥak Frank
Jerusalem, Sivan 5755

PREFACE TO (FIRST EDITION OF)
GRAMMAR FOR GEMARA AND TALMUD ONKELOS

Grammar for Gemara was designed to be primarily an aid to Talmud study and a complement to *The Practical Talmud Dictionary*. The second edition, written more than seven years ago, made a modest attempt to introduce some Aramaic of Targum Onkelos — both for its own sake, to facilitate understanding of the Targum, and for the purpose of comparison with Babylonian Aramaic. In the current edition, the treatment of the Aramaic of Onkelos has been significantly expanded by the addition of a whole new chapter, Chapter 5, which presents the conjugations of thirty-two prominent verbs from the Targum. This chapter is modelled after Chapter 4 and its conjugations of verbs from the Babylonian Talmud. The subsequent chapters have been retained from the previous edition, but they have now been renumbered as Chapters 6, 7, etc.

Furthermore, this edition has been upgraded in other ways:

◊   Chapter 3 has been expanded to include a more comprehensive paradigm of the regular Aramaic verb in all the common *binyanim*. Much of the chapter — particularly the sections about the infinitive and the gerund — has been rewritten under the guidance of my learned friend, Alan Smith, for whose assistance I am grateful.

◊   The paradigms in Chapter 4 have been somewhat restructured: Now, for example, all the participles — active, passive and reflexive — are generally presented side by side.

◊   The typography of this complicated book was entirely redone by Donny Finkel of *Leshon Limudim*, Jerusalem — with exceptional patience, perseverance and dedication to excellence. The improvement in design together with the enhanced clarity of presentation is largely due to his diligent work — coupled with several apt suggestions from my brother-in-law, Rav Menachem Davis; some perceptive remarks from our talented proofreader, Eli Handel; and the invaluable advice of my devoted wife, Marcia (who has also spent many hours proofreading). I sincerely express my gratitude to all of them for their cooperation.

I would also like to take this opportunity to acknowledge the consistent support and encouragement that I have received from our friend Mrs. Els Bendheim תבל״ח and from my mother-in-law, Mrs. Adele B. Davis ל״ז.

◊   Above all, I thank the Almighty for enabling us to complete this project in the midst of these troubled times, and I hope that even this small contribution to *Talmud Torah* be counted among the cumulative merits of our people. May He thwart all the attacks of our enemies and all their efforts to destroy us and to seize our homeland, and may He speedily bring about the complete Redemption in our time.

For whatever competence I have gained over the years in handling Talmudic texts, I owe thanks to my *Gemara* teachers: (in chronological order) Rav Joseph J. Gold ל״ז, rabbi of the Orthodox Jewish community in Worcester, Massachusetts; Hyman Steinberg ל״ז, principal of the Worcester Ivriah School and its Hebrew High School program; and Atty. Arnold J. Miller ז״ל, senior instructor in that program; HaRav Dr. Moshe D. Tendler יבל״ח, HaRav Joseph Weiss יבל״ח and HaRav Yeruḥam Gorelick ז״ל at Yeshivath Rabbenu Yitzḥak Elḥanan, Yeshiva University, in New York; HaRav Ḥayyim Stein ז״ל and HaRav Mordechai Gifter ז״ל at the Telshe Yeshiva in Wickliffe, Ohio; HaRav HaGaon Dr. Joseph B. Soloveitchik ז״ל at the Semicha Program of Yeshiva University and especially HaRav Dr. Aharon Lichtenstein [ז״ל] at the Kolelim of Yeshiva University, both in New York and Jerusalem. In addition, I want to express my gratitude to my friends who learned with me extensively in a *havrutha* framework during my formative years: (in chronological order) Yitzḥak Pechenik ז״ל and Rabbi Jay Miller [ז״ל] at Yeshiva University, and יבל״ח Rabbis Avraham Grossman and Michael Levy at the Telshe Yeshiva, and Rabbis Melech Press, Elimelech Hecht, Shemuel Boylan and Michael Fine after my return to Yeshiva University.

Yitzḥak Frank
Jerusalem, Kislev 5763

PREFACE TO (SECOND EDITION OF)
GRAMMAR FOR GEMARA AND TALMUD ONKELOS

Besides improvements and corrections, this new edition has a detailed table of contents and adds compact presentations of the basic Aramaic *binyanim* (Appendix A for the Babylonian Talmud and Appendix C for Targum Onkelos). The most significant addition to this book is Appendix D, which contains an index of all the verbal roots in the Targum. The two new exercises that comprise Appendix E are designed to enhance the learner's recognition of Aramaic verbal forms and acquaint him with Onkelos' approach to translation.

This edition was prepared with assistance from my wife Marcia, my son Uriel and my associate Leor Jacobi — for which I am grateful. Special thanks are also due to my scholarly colleague, Dr. Yoel Elitzur, for the improvements he has inspired (especially on p. 219) and to my perceptive friend, Alan Smith, for his valuable counsel.

Yitzḥak Frank
Jerusalem, Sivan 5771

1

MISHNAIC HEBREW[1] (לשון חז״ל)

The language of the Mishna and the *baraithoth* is almost exclusively Hebrew.[2] However, post-Biblical Hebrew is so different from Biblical Hebrew that it is regarded as a different dialect called *Mishnaic Hebrew* or לְשׁוֹן חֲכָמִים.[3] This dialect, which developed from Biblical Hebrew, was spoken in Eretz Yisrael throughout the Mishnaic period (at least). Aramaic influence is so pervasive that some scholars have suggested that Mishnaic Hebrew be classified as a "mixed language." In this chapter, we will point out some of the features of Mishnaic Hebrew that distinguish it from Biblical Hebrew.

1.1 THE MASCULINE PLURAL

In Mishnaic Hebrew, the *masculine-plural suffix* is often ין – rather than the form ים – that almost always occurs in the Bible.

Example: (משנה שבת פי״ג מ״א) חוּטִין, *threads*

---

1   This chapter is based on the section on Mishnaic Hebrew by E. Y. Kutscher in the article, "Hebrew Language," *Encyclopedia Judaica* (Jerusalem, 1971), Vol. XVI, pp. 1590-1607, and in his book, *A History of the Hebrew Language*, ed. Raphael Kutscher (Jerusalem: Magnes, 1982), pp. 115-147. See also A. Sáenz-Badillos, *A History of the Hebrew Language* (tr. J. Elwolde, Cambridge, England: Cambridge University Press 1993), "Rabbinic Hebrew", especially pp. 172-173. The two-volume collection of Moshe Bar-Asher's studies, מחקרים בלשון חכמים (Jerusalem: Bialik Institute, 2009), is a very valuable resource.

2   For an example of an Aramaic mishna, see משנה אבות פ״א מי״ג; for a baraitha with Aramaic, see the famous Ḥanukka baraitha (שבת כא, ב).

3   R. Yoḥanan, the greatest halakhic authority of his time, stressed the distinction between these two forms of Hebrew, and declared:
לְשׁוֹן תּוֹרָה לְעַצְמָהּ; לְשׁוֹן חֲכָמִים לְעַצְמָן (עבודה זרה נח, ב; חולין קלז, ב)
The language of the Torah is unique; the language of the ḥakhamim is unique.

1.2 THE CONSTRUCT STATE

The Hebrew language uses a special form of the noun to express a close relationship, often possession, between a noun and the next word. This construction is called סְמִיכוּת in Hebrew, and such a noun is said to be נִסְמָךְ, *in the construct state.* For example, the noun בֵּית (rather than the usual form בַּיִת) appears in the construct state in the phrase בֵּית הָאִישׁ, *the man's house.* For some nouns the form of the construct state is identical with that of the absolute state. Thus, בֶּגֶד is *a cloak,* and בֶּגֶד הָאִישׁ means *the cloak of the man* or *the man's cloak.*

◇   The construct state usually expresses this relationship in Biblical Hebrew, but sometimes the phrase -אֲשֶׁר לְ occurs instead, for example, הַצֹּאן אֲשֶׁר לְאָבִיהָ (בראשית כט, ט), *the flock which (belongs) to her father* (= צֹאן אָבִיהָ, *her father's flock*). In Mishnaic Hebrew, the parallel form -שֶׁל (originally a prefix and later a separate word שֶׁל, *of*)[4] is used in the following two constructions (which are still in use today in contemporary Israeli Hebrew):

1) הַבַּיִת שֶׁל הָאִישׁ, *the house of the man*

2) בֵּיתוֹ שֶׁל הָאִישׁ, *his house, (that) of the man*

In בֵּיתוֹ שֶׁל הָאִישׁ, the personal-pronoun suffix וֹ-, *his,* refers to the noun הָאִישׁ, *the man.* Thus, the וֹ- suffix is said to *anticipate* הָאִישׁ.[5] This construction is also found in Biblical Hebrew, in the phrase מִטָּתוֹ שֶׁלִּשְׁלֹמֹה (שיר השירים ג:ז) — *his bed, that of Shelomo.*

◇   Certain pairs of nouns are regularly used together — with the first in the construct state — to express a single matter or concept.

Examples: בֵּית כְּנֶסֶת, *synagogue;* בֵּית דִּין, *court.*

In the plural, both nouns are pluralized in Mishnaic Hebrew.

Examples: בָּתֵּי כְנֵסִיּוֹת, *synagogues;* בָּתֵּי דִינִין, *courts.*

In modern Hebrew, however, the forms בָּתֵּי כְנֶסֶת and בָּתֵּי דִין are used — with only the first noun in the plural.

---

4   In many manuscripts, -שֶׁל appears as a prefix to the noun it precedes (שֶׁלְּאִישׁ, *of a man,* or שֶׁלָּאִישׁ, *of the man,* with a *kametz* indicating the definite article), rather than as a separate word (in שֶׁל אִישׁ or שֶׁל הָאִישׁ), as it is written today.

5   Similarly, לוֹ, *to him,* anticipates לְר׳, *to R. ...,* in the common Talmudic formula: אָמַר לוֹ ר׳... לְר׳, *R. ... said to him, [that is] to R. ...* See below Chapter 10:2, "The Anticipatory Pronoun Suffix," pp. 253-254.

1.3 PRONOUNS

The first-person *independent personal pronouns* in Mishnaic Hebrew differ from the Biblical Hebrew forms:

MISHNAIC HEBREW	BIBLICAL HEBREW	ENGLISH
אֲנִי	אֲנִי ; אָנֹכִי	*I*
אָנוּ	אֲנַחְנוּ ; נַחְנוּ	*we*

◇   The *possessive-pronoun suffixes* of the second-person singular of both genders in Mishnaic Hebrew differ from those in Biblical Hebrew in their vocalization:

MISHNAIC HEBREW	BIBLICAL HEBREW	ENGLISH
ךָ- (as in דְּבָרָךְ)[6]	ךָ - (as in דְּבָרְךָ)	*your* (m.)
־יִךְ (as in דְּבָרִיךְ)	ךְ- (as in דְּבָרֵךְ)	*your* (f.)

◇   There are also differences between the two dialects in the feminine singular and in the plural of the *demonstrative pronoun*.

MISHNAIC HEBREW	BIBLICAL HEBREW	ENGLISH
זֶה	זֶה	*this* (m.)
זוֹ[7]	זֹאת ; זֹה	*this* (f.)
אֵלּוּ[8]	אֵלֶּה	*these*

6   Compare נַקְדִּישָׁךְ וְנַעֲרִיצָךְ in the Sephardic *Kedusha*.

7   For example, at a Jewish wedding the groom recites to the bride the formula: הֲרֵי אַתְּ מְקֻדֶּשֶׁת לִי בְּטַבַּעַת זוֹ, *with this ring you are wedded to me*. For a discussion of the popular pronunciation זו, see Ḥayyim E. Cohen:
"קביעות תקן בלשון – חדשים גם ישנים", בתוך: 250 שנות עברית חדשה
(Jerusalem: Academy of the Hebrew Language, 5766), pp. 39-46.

8   Sometimes אֵלּוּ has a different function: the plural of the *interrogative* אֵיזֶה, as in אֵלּוּ מְצִיאוֹת שֶׁלּוֹ? (ב"מ פ"ב מ"א), *Which* found objects are his (= the finder's)?

◇   Mishnaic Hebrew sometimes uses אֶת as a *demonstrative pronoun*.[9]

Example:

those who are in front of the bier   אֶת שֶׁלִּפְנֵי הַמִּטָּה (משנה ברכות פ"ג מ"א)

אֶת is also used in Mishnaic Hebrew with third-person pronoun suffixes to form אוֹתוֹ or אוֹתָהּ, a *demonstrative adjective* that is placed before the noun it modifies.

Example:

that day (or: *the same day*)   אוֹתוֹ הַיּוֹם (משנה מכות פ"א מ"ד)

◇   The noun עֶצֶם (lit. *"bone"*), with personal-pronoun suffixes attached, serves as a *reflexive pronoun* in Mishnaic Hebrew, so that עַצְמִי means *myself*; עַצְמוֹ, *himself*; etc. (like the Aramaic גַּרְמֵיהּ).

Example:

he acquires himself   קוֹנֶה אֶת עַצְמוֹ (משנה קידושין פ"א מ"ב)

◇   Mishnaic Hebrew uses the prefix ־שֶׁ, *that, which* or *who*, as the *relative pronoun* instead of the Biblical אֲשֶׁר, which it retains only in Biblical quotations.[10]

Example:

Do not look attentively at the   אַל תִּסְתַּכֵּל בַּקַּנְקַן אֶלָּא בַּמֶּה שֶׁיֵּשׁ
*container but at that **which** is*   בּוֹ! (משנה אבות פ"ד מ"כ)
contained within it!

It also uses ־שֶׁ, as a *conjunction*, meaning *because* or *for*, instead of Biblical כִּי.

Example:

and prepare yourself to study Torah   וְהַתְקֵן עַצְמָךְ לִלְמוֹד תּוֹרָה שֶׁאֵינָהּ
for it is not [given as] an inheri-   יְרֻשָּׁה לָךְ (שם פ"ב מי"ב)
tance to you

---

9   For Biblical precedents, see ויקרא ה:טז; קהלת ד:ג.
10 The prefix ־שֶׁ occurs occasionally in Biblical Hebrew — mostly in שיר השירים, תהלים and קהלת.

1.4 VERBS: *BINYANIM*

In Hebrew, in Aramaic, and in other Semitic languages, a *root* — a grammatical abstraction usually consisting of three consonants — is regarded as the basis of each verb. The root expresses a general idea that may be given different shades of meanings through special vocalization, the addition of certain prefixes or both. The different patterns thus created are termed *binyanim* in Hebrew and, by some grammarians, "conjugations" in English.

It is often difficult for a native English speaker to understand the concept of *binyanim* — which is of great importance in Semitic languages. The difficulty may be due in part to the absence of the phenomenon in the English verbal system, where different shades of meaning are expressed by separate verbs. For example, the Hebrew verbs לָמַד and לִמֵּד are derived from the same root, but the corresponding English verbs, *learn* and *teach*, are completely independent. Nevertheless, the phenomenon of *binyanim* is not altogether foreign to English: The intransitive verbs *sit, fall, lie* and *rise* differ from the transitive verbs *seat, fell (a tree), lay* and *raise,* respectively, only in terms of their vowels. In other words, different vocalization expresses different shades of meaning. A native English speaker who is aware of this phenomenon in his own tongue should be a bit more comfortable with the concept of *binyanim* in Hebrew and Aramaic.

◊ The *binyanim* that occur commonly in Biblical Hebrew are presented in the following table, with explanations, examples (in the third person, masculine singular of the past tense) and translations of the examples into English:

BINYAN	EXPLANATION	EXAMPLE	TRANSLATION
קַל	the simple conjugation	כָּתַב	*he wrote*
נִפְעַל	passive/reflexive of the simple	נִכְתַּב	*it was written*
פִּעֵל	the intensive[11] conjugation	קִדֵּשׁ	*he sanctified*
פֻּעַל	passive of the intensive	קֻדַּשׁ	*it was sanctified*
הִתְפַּעֵל	reflexive (of the intensive)	הִתְקַדֵּשׁ	*he sanctified himself*
הִפְעִיל	the extensive[11] conjugation	הִקְדִּישׁ	*he dedicated*
הָפְעַל	passive of the extensive	הָקְדַּשׁ	*it was dedicated*

◇ In Mishnaic Hebrew, the system of *binyanim* has undergone some changes. The most significant developments are the following:

◇ The פֻּעַל *binyan* is used only in the participle, like מְקֻדָּשׁ, *sanctified*.

◇ The past tense of the הִתְפַּעֵל *binyan* is usually נִתְפַּעֵל, and its participle is occasionally נִתְפַּעֵל instead of the Biblical מִתְפַּעֵל.[12]

Sometimes its meaning is reflexive (as in נִסְתַּפֵּג, *he dried himself*), and sometimes it is passive (as in נִתְגַּלָּה, *it was revealed*). In the latter sense, it replaces the Biblical פֻּעַל.

---

11 The grammatical terms *intensive* and *extensive* both refer to the form of the verb. In the פִּעֵל, the middle root-letter of the verb is usually doubled ("intensified") by means of a *dagesh* (as in קִדֵּשׁ). In the הִפְעִיל, the root is "extended" by the addition of a prefix (as in הִקְדִּישׁ). As for meaning, the פִּעֵל is used in a variety of senses, while the הִפְעִיל usually expresses causative action — as in הִלְבִּישׁ, *he dressed (someone else)*.

12 Bar-Asher (above, p. 1 note 1), vol. 2, pp. 4-5, 131-137.

◊   "New *binyanim*" occur in Mishnaic Hebrew:[13]

The שִׁפְעֵל *binyan* has a causative meaning.

Example: שִׁחְרֵר

> *he caused to be free, he liberated*

The נִשְׁתַּפְעַל *binyan* serves as its reflexive and passive.

Example: נִשְׁתַּחְרַר

> *he freed himself* or *he was liberated*

1.5 VERBS: TENSES

In Mishnaic Hebrew, several important changes have occurred in
the verbal system. Some regular Biblical Hebrew forms are absent
from Mishnaic Hebrew (except for Biblical quotations). One of the
forms that is missing is the so-called "conversive *vav*" (הַוָּ"ו הַמְהַפֶּכֶת)
which supposedly "changes the tense" in Biblical Hebrew — either
from future to past (as in וַיִּכְתֹּב, *and he wrote*) or from past to future
(as in וְכָתַבְתִּי, *and I will write*).[14] Furthermore, some of the Biblical
forms that are retained in Mishnaic Hebrew — such as the
participles presented in the table on the next page — function
somewhat differently.

◊   Here is a summary of the tense system that has evolved in
Mishnaic Hebrew:[15]

---

13 However, see Bar-Asher (ibid., p. 24), who points out that such forms should
    not be regarded as constituting "new *binyanim*." They should rather be
    understood as products of quadriliteral (=four-letter) roots. With regard to
    Aramaic verbs, cf. pp. 59, 221 and 223 below, and especially p. 289 note 10.
14 Grammarians have had difficulty in explaining the apparent switch of the
    tenses with the "conversive *vav*", which is almost unique to Biblical Hebrew.
    In fact, some modern scholars avoid the old term and call it the "*vav*
    consecutive*" instead, since it is used in sequences of verbs in Biblical narrative.
    See the analysis by S. R. Driver in his *The Use of the Tenses in Hebrew*, 3rd ed.
    (London: Oxford University Press, 1969), pp. 70-73; 114-121.
15 For additional details, see Kutscher (above, p. 1 note 1), p. 131.

"TENSE"	TYPE OF ACTION	EXAMPLE	TRANSLATION
past	past	דַּע מֵאַיִן בָּאתָ[16]	*Know from where* **you came**
active participle	present or future	וּלְאָן אַתָּה הוֹלֵךְ[14]	*and where you* **are going**
עָתִיד followed by ־ל with a gerund[17]	clear-cut future	וְלִפְנֵי מִי אַתָּה עָתִיד לִיתֵּן דִּין וְחֶשְׁבּוֹן![14]	*and before Whom you* **are destined to give** *an accounting!*
passive participle	present, future, or sometimes present perfect (indicating the present out-come of a past action)	מְקֻבָּל אֲנִי[18]	*I* **have received** *(a tradition)*
הָיָה with a participle	continual or repeated action	הוּא הָיָה אוֹמֵר[19]	*he* **used to say**
future	future; desired or intended action	כָּל מִי שֶׁיּוֹדֵעַ לוֹ זְכוּת, יָבֹא[20]	*[As for] anyone who knows some merit in his behalf,* **let him come [forward]!**
imperative	commands	דַּע מֵאַיִן בָּאתָ[14]	*know from where you came*

16 משנה אבות פ"ג מ"א
17 See discussion of "The Gerund and the Infinitive," Chapter 3, pp. 43-46.
18 משנה פאה פ"ב מ"ו
19 משנה אבות פ"א מי"ג ועוד
20 משנה סנהדרין פ"ו מ"א

8

◇   Mishnaic Hebrew often uses the past tense to portray the case about which a halakhic ruling is issued. When translating this use of the past tense into English, it is best to supply the conjunction *if* or *when*, as in the following example:

*If the court alone **sighted it*** (= the "new" moon), two [of the judges] should rise and testify before them (= the rest of the judges)...	רָאוּהוּ בֵית דִּין בִּלְבַד, יַעַמְדוּ שְׁנַיִם וְיָעִידוּ בִּפְנֵיהֶם... (ראש השנה פ"ג מ"א)

◇   Mishnaic Hebrew often uses the present tense in formulating a halakhic ruling that imposes an obligation or grants permission:

Example 1:

*On Pesaḥ [we] **must read** [in the Torah] the portion about holidays...*	בְּפֶסַח קוֹרִין בְּפָרָשַׁת מוֹעֲדוֹת... (מגילה פ"ג מ"ה)

Example 2:

*[If a blaze has broken out on the Sabbath, we] **may save** [enough] food for three meals...*	מַצִּילִין מְזוֹן שָׁלֹשׁ סְעוּדוֹת... (שבת פט"ז מ"ב)

◇   According to the Babylonian Talmud, the use of the *past* tense in Mishnaic Hebrew may also indicate an *after-the-fact* (דִּיעֲבַד) perspective towards an act that should *not* have been performed in the first place. The *present* tense, however, indicates a *before-the-fact* (לְכַתְּחִילָה) perspective towards a perfectly permissible act.[21] This distinction has been presented in the following Talmudic passage:

Does [the tanna] state חוֹלֵץ *(in the present tense, "he may perform the ḥalitza")?! [No], he states* חָלַץ *(in the past tense "[If] he has per-formed the ḥalitza) — after the fact (hence the mishna does not advocate ḥalitza in such a case.)!*[22]	מִי קָתָנֵי "חוֹלֵץ"?! "חָלַץ" קָתָנֵי — בְּדִיעֲבַד! (יבמות נג, א)

21   See the entries דִּיעֲבַד and לְכַתְּחִילָה in *The Practical Talmud Dictionary* (above, p. ix note 6).

22   Nevertheless, when a present-tense form (i.e., a participle) is prefaced with the definite article (-ה), it is understood in the Talmud as indicating an *after-the-fact* perspective. Example: הָרוֹחֵץ — דִּיעֲבַד, אִין; לְכַתְּחִילָה, לָא! , *the one who bathes [on the Sabbath] — after the fact, yes; in the first place, no* (= he should not be bathing)!

1.6 VERBS: SPECIFIC FORMS

Certain verbal forms in Biblical Hebrew have undergone significant changes in Mishnaic Hebrew. Here are some examples:

BIBLICAL	MISHNAIC	ENGLISH TRANSLATION
לֵאמֹר	*לוֹמַר[23]	to say
*לָשֶׁבֶת	לֵישֵׁב[21]	to sit
*לָתֵת	לִיתֵּן[21]	to give
*לָרֶדֶת	לֵירֵד[21]	to descend
*לִקְרֹא	לִקְרוֹת	to read
*קוֹרְאִים	קוֹרִין	reading
*מָצָאנוּ	מָצִינוּ	we found
נָדוֹן	*נִדּוֹן	it was judged
הֵחֵלוּ	*הִתְחִילוּ	they began
מַדֹּתִי	*מָדַדְתִּי	I measured
*יָצְאָה	יָצֵאת, יָצְתָה	she went out
*בָּאָה	בָּאת	she came
תֹּאכַלְנָה	*יֹאכְלוּ	they (f.) will eat

* The forms with the asterisk (*) are the ones currently used in Modern Hebrew.

1.7 VOCABULARY[24]

The vocabulary of Mishnaic Hebrew differs considerably from that of Biblical Hebrew. It has been estimated that about half of the lexical material is different, with many foreign words borrowed from Aramaic, Akkadian, Persian, Greek and Latin.

23 In the first four examples of Mishnaic Hebrew, the infinitive/gerund has become similar to the future tense. For example, לֵישֵׁב resembles the future יֵשֵׁב.
24 For details, see Kutscher (above, p. 1 note 1) pp. 132-141.

2

THE ARAMAIC LANGUAGE[1]

The Aramaic language is not primarily a Jewish language, but — as its name implies — it is the language of the ancient Arameans. Indeed, two words in the Torah that are definitely Aramaic were spoken by Lavan, the Aramean: (בראשית לא:מז) יְגַר שָׂהֲדוּתָא, *a mound of testimony*.

Later, this language became a medium of communication between other peoples in the Middle East, including the Jews. For many years, it served as an international language. For example, the Bible relates that during the period of the first *Beth HaMikdash* officials of the kingdoms of Judah and Assyria spoke to each other in Aramaic (מלכים ב יח:כו). Aramaic is also the only language other than Hebrew in which parts of the Bible are written.[2]

2.1 ARAMAIC AND HEBREW CONSONANTS

Aramaic is similar to Hebrew in many ways. Its consonantal and vocalic systems consist of precisely the same consonants and vowels that are used in Hebrew. Because of their different linguistic development, however, there are certain consonants in one language that sometimes correspond to different consonants in the other language. Here is a table of these consonantal shifts with illustrations. It must be emphasized that this table does *not* imply that *every* Aramaic ד, for example, corresponds to a Hebrew ז.

---

1   For a full discussion of the Aramaic language, see E. Y. Kutscher, "Aramaic," *Encyclopedia Judaica* (Jerusalem, 1971), Vol. III, pp. 259-287.
2   See: ירמיה י:יא; דניאל ב:ד-ז:כח; עזרא ד:ה-ו:יח; ז:יב-כו.

ARAMAIC		HEBREW		ENGLISH
Consonant	Example	Consonant	Example	Translation
ד	דְּהַב	ז	זָהָב	*gold*
ת	תְּלָת	שׁ	שָׁלֹשׁ	*three*
ע	אַרְע	צ	אֶרֶץ	*land*
ט	עֵטָא	צ	עֵצָה	*advice*

Furthermore, an Aramaic consonant sometimes corresponds to a different consonant in Hebrew that is pronounced in a similar manner, i.e., from the same point of articulation. Consider, for example, the Aramaic noun נַהְמָא, *bread* — the cognate of the Hebrew noun לֶחֶם. Phonetically, the Aramaic נ is parallel to the Hebrew ל, and the Aramaic ה is parallel to the Hebrew ח: The former pair of consonants are both pronounced with the tongue, while the latter pair are both pronounced deep in the throat. Similarly, the Aramaic פַּרְזְלָא, *iron*, is the equivalent of the Hebrew בַּרְזֶל, with the פ parallel to the Hebrew ב, since both consonants are pronounced with the lips.

The same kinds of consonantal shifts sometimes occur within the Hebrew language: For example, Ramban contends that the noun דָּבְאֶךָ (in דברים לג:כה) is the equivalent of זָבְאֶךָ, with the Hebrew ד replacing the Hebrew ז.[3] According to Rashi (on ויקרא יט:טז), the Hebrew root רכל is the equivalent of the Hebrew רגל, since the כ and the ג are phonetically similar.

---

3   See also Ramban's commentary on שמות טו:י, בראשית מא:מז and ויקרא יט:כ. For additional sources in Ramban's writings, see the index at the end of the second volume of Ḥ. D. Chavell's כתבי הרמב"ן (Jerusalem: Mosad HaRav Kook, 1963), under the entry אותיות.

2.2 ARAMAIC AND HEBREW VOWELS

In the vocalic system, there is a tendency for Aramaic vowels to be shorter than their Hebrew counterparts. For instance, in the Aramaic noun שְׁלָם — the cognate of the Hebrew שָׁלוֹם — a sh^eva is placed under the שׁ instead of the Hebrew *kametz,* and a *kametz* is placed under the ל instead of the Hebrew *holam.*

2.3 ARAMAIC DIALECTS

The Aramaic language includes a variety of dialects that are written in a variety of scripts. Syriac, for example, the language of the Bible translation known as the *Peshitta,* is a non-Jewish dialect that is written in any one of three different scripts. The dialects used by Jews, however, are written in the same script as Hebrew. Here is a list of the major Jewish dialects:

1) *Biblical Aramaic* (the language of the Aramaic parts of Ezra and Daniel, and Yirmeyahu 10:11)

2) *Palestinian or Galilean Aramaic* (the language of the Talmud Yerushalmi, the aggadic Midrashim and the Palestinian Targumim)

3) *Onkelos-Yonathan Aramaic* (the language of Targum Onkelos on the Torah and Targum Yonathan on the Prophets)

4) *Babylonian Aramaic* (the language of the Babylonian Talmud and of some Gaonic texts)

This volume focuses on the latter two dialects, but much of the information provided does apply to Aramaic in general.

2.4 VOCALIZATION AND PRONUNCIATION

What is the correct way to *vocalize* (= to mark with vowels) the Aramaic of the Babylonian Talmud? Nobody knows for sure. In contrast to the Biblical text whose vocalization has been handed down to us with very few controversies, the standard editions of both the Mishna and the Talmud have no vowels. For Mishna, a scholarly vocalized edition has been published that is based upon some vocalized manuscripts and oral reading traditions.[4] The situation with respect to the Aramaic of the Babylonian Talmud, however, is more fuzzy: Little vocalized material is available in manuscript, and the reading traditions among the various Jewish communities are widely divergent. There is no easy solution.

The most scientific way to handle the problem would be to "play it safe" and not vocalize at all. Such an approach would save us from some scholarly criticism, but it would at the same time cause confusion for the *student* for whom this volume has been produced. In our view it is better to furnish the student with a reasonable vocalization — which may be dubious or even erroneous in some of its details — rather than to leave the student in the lurch, without any vocalization.

At first glance, one might assume that Biblical Aramaic should be a guide for the vocalization of the Aramaic of the Talmud, since the books of Ezra and Daniel both have an authoritative vocalized text. Babylonian Aramaic, however, is a different dialect. Just as it would be a mistake to equate Mishnaic Hebrew with Biblical Hebrew,[5] it is a mistake to equate Talmudic Aramaic with Biblical Aramaic.

The Aramaic of Targum Onkelos,[6] which was referred to in Babylonia as (קידושין מט, א) תַּרְגּוּם דִּידַן, *"our Targum,"* is certainly closer to Babylonian Aramaic and would seem to be a more reliable guide. Indeed, a careful vocalization of Targum Onkelos has been painstakingly preserved by Yemenite Jews in their manuscripts and books.[7] Recent studies of the Yemenite reading tradition, however,

---

4   Ḥanokh Albeck (commentator) and Ḥanokh Yalon (vocalizer), ששה סדרי משנה (Jerusalem: Bialik Institute, 1958). See also מבוא לניקוד המשנה by Yalon (Jerusalem: Bialik Institute, 1964).

5   See Chapter 1.

6   Onkelos lived in Eretz Yisrael, but according to some scholars (e.g., J. N. Epstein, E. Y. Kutscher) at least the final editing and the vocalization of his Targum are of Babylonian origin. When quotations from Targum Onkelos are quoted in the Babylonian Talmud, they are almost always introduced by the word וּמְתַרְגְּמִינָן, *and we (= Babylonian Jews) translate.* Later, the Geonim of Babylonia regularly called it תַּרְגּוּם דִּידַן, *our Targum.*

7   See Alexander Sperber, *The Bible in Aramaic* (Leiden: E. J. Brill, 1959), vol. 1.

have shown that their pronunciation of the Babylonian Aramaic of the Talmud differs from their own pronunciation of Targum Onkelos.[8] Furthermore, to vocalize in accordance with the Yemenite tradition would be impractical, since most of the students who will use this volume are non-Yemenites who study in non-Yemenite institutions of learning where the reading tradition of the Talmud differs markedly from the Yemenite pronunciation.

Grammar for Gemara, like *The Practical Talmud Dictionary,*[9] adopts a somewhat eclectic approach towards this problem. On the one hand, an attempt is made to vocalize the Aramaic in a manner that makes sense grammatically and historically — sometimes in the face of the popular pronunciation.[10] For example, the common form מִיפַּלְגִי is vocalized in that manner, since no way was found to justify the popular pronunciation מִיפָּלְגִי. In such cases, a different vocalization based upon the popular pronunciation is mentioned in a note, so that the student will recognize what he hears. On the other hand, *whenever justifiable,* the popular pronunciation is recorded. For example, the traditional pronunciation תָּנוּ is preserved alongside תְּנוּ and the Yemenite תְּנוּ.

8   Shelomo Morag, אַרמית במסורת תימן: לשון התלמוד הבבלי...ותצורת הפועל (Jerusalem: Ben Tzvi Institute, 1988) pp. 41-45.

9   Jerusalem: Ariel, 1991; Maggid-Koren 2016. See the section on "Vocalization," pp. XVI-XVII in the introduction.

10   Besides Morag's work (see note 8), particularly useful have been: J. N. Epstein, דקדוק ארמית בבלית, ed. by E. Z. Melamed (Jerusalem: Magnes; Tel-Aviv: Dvir, 1950) and the critical review of the work by E. Y. Kutscher, reprinted in his מחקרים בעברית ובארמית (Jerusalem: Magnes, 1977), pp. 226-255.

We fully realize that the fine points of pronunciation and vocalization are often insignificant for the understanding of the Talmudic text. In Judaism, there is a basic difference between the study of תּוֹרָה שֶׁבִּכְתָב and the study of תּוֹרָה שֶׁבְּעַל פֶּה. While a Jew can fulfill the mitzvah of learning Torah by reading mechanically from the text of Scripture, reading תּוֹרָה שֶׁבְּעַל פֶּה mechanically — without at least trying to *understand* the content — does *not* fulfill any mitzvah.[11] Reading the words properly is important only as a means to enhance understanding but not as an end in itself. Indeed, my revered teacher, HaRav Dr. Michael Bernstein, of blessed memory, used to say: *Know* the correct pronunciation of the *gemara*, but *read* the *gemara* in the traditional way!

---

11 *Shulḥan Arukh (HaRav), Hilkhoth Talmud Torah* (Brooklyn, New York: "Kehot" Publication Society, 1968), Chapter 2: par. 12-13, p. 1680. See also *Magen Avraham* on *Oraḥ Ḥayyim* 50 and Rashi's distinction between מקרא and משנה in his commentary on ברכות ה, א. This point was stressed by our master, HaRav Dr. Joseph B. Soloveitchik, זצ"ל, on several occasions.

3

THE ARAMAIC VERB

The paradigms that are presented in this chapter are *artificial*, in that they contain the forms from a specific root that are appropriate for each person, number, and gender — even if some of those particular forms do not actually occur in the text of the Babylonian Talmud or the Targumim.[1]

◇   Generally, the spelling of the verbal forms that predominates in the paradigms is *plene* (= full), with the vowel-letters יand וthat frequently occur in the Talmud in such forms as תִּיכְתּוֹב. Nevertheless, this editorial decision is *not* intended to delegitimize *defective* spelling — without the vowel-letters — which is also fairly common in many texts of the Talmud and the Targumim.

◇   The vowels *tzerei* and *ḥirik* are sometimes interchangeable; thus, vocalizations of some forms as a פַּעֵל pattern instead of פְּעֵל, as אַפְעֵל instead of אַפְעֵל and as אִתְפְּעֵל instead of אִתְפְּעֵל are also legitimate, even if not noted specifically in the paradigms below.

---

1   The Aramaic dialect of Targum Onkelos to the Torah and Targum Yonathan ben Uziel to the Prophets is in some ways closer to the language of the Babylonian Talmud than to that of the Jerusalem Talmud. Although both Targumim were apparently composed in Eretz Yisrael, it is likely that the final editing was done in Babylonia. For a summary of the differences between the Targumim and the Babylonian Talmud in the conjugation of verbs, see the table on page 150.

3.1 A SURVEY OF THE ARAMAIC *BINYANIM*

In Aramaic, as in Hebrew,[2] the verb is by far the most complex part of speech. The basic idea is expressed by three-letter roots,[3] while a system of *binyanim* (verbal patterns) is employed to indicate different shades of meaning. In the first chapter of this work, we have discussed the Hebrew *binyanim*. The following table presents the Aramaic *binyanim* together with illustrations (from the third-person masculine singular of the past tense), their *Mishnaic* Hebrew parallels and English translations. The first three *binyanim* פְּעַל, קַל and אַפְעֵל are the primary patterns and they are all in the *active* voice, whereas *binyanim* אִתְפְּעֵל, אִתְפַּעַל and אִתַּפְעַל, which are essentially *reflexive* (like the Hebrew הִתְפַּעֵל), usually function in a *passive* sense.[4]

ARAMAIC *BINYAN*	HEBREW *BINYAN*	ARAMAIC EXAMPLE	HEBREW PARALLEL	ENGLISH TRANSLATION
פְּעַל (קַל)	פָּעַל (קַל)	כְּתַב	כָּתַב	*he wrote*
פַּעֵל	פִּעֵל	קַדֵּישׁ	קִדֵּשׁ	*he sanctified*
אַפְעֵל	הִפְעִיל	אַפְקֵד	הִפְקִיד	*he deposited*
אִתְפְּעֵל	נִפְעַל	אִתְכְּתֵיב	נִכְתַּב	*it was written*
אִתְפַּעַל	נִתְפַּעַל[5]	אִתְקַדַּשׁ	נִתְקַדֵּשׁ	*it was sanctified*
אִתַּפְעַל	הָפְעַל	אִתַּפְקַד	הָפְקַד	*it was deposited*

2 See Chapter 1 above, pp. 5-10, for a brief discussion of the verb in Biblical and Mishnaic Hebrew.

3 The theory of a verbal "root" is a useful but artificial construct invented by grammarians. According to the most popular opinion, most roots are triliteral.

4 Cf. the Hebrew binyan נִפְעַל, as explained by Kutscher (above, p. 1 note 1), pp. 36-37. At least one of his arguments for the *reflexive* nature of the נִפְעַל – that in a true passive *binyan* (like the Hebrew פֻּעַל and הֻפְעַל) the imperative is absent – could easily be applied to the Aramaic *binyanim* אִתְפְּעֵל and אִתְפַּעַל as well.

5 In Mishnaic Hebrew, נִתְפַּעַל is the proper pattern, according to M. Bar-Asher, cited above in Chapter 1 (p. 1, note 11).

◊   In addition to the *binyanim* mentioned in the above table, the Babylonian Talmud and Targum Onkelos also feature four-letter roots — some of which derive from the שַׁפְעֵל *binyan* (like שַׁעְבֵּיד, *he subjugated*) and its reflexive/passive, the אִשְׁתַּפְעַל *binyan* (like אִשְׁתַּעְבַּד, *he was subjugated*). These Aramaic *binyanim* are parallel, respectively, to the *binyanim* שִׁפְעֵל and נִשְׁתַּפְעַל in Mishnaic Hebrew.[6]

◊   The six Aramaic *binyanim* in the table are similar — but not identical — to Hebrew *binyanim*, both in form and in function. The next six paragraphs describe the Aramaic *binyanim* and compare them with their Hebrew counterparts in the conjugation of the *strong* verb (whose root-letters always remain intact). Chapters 4 and 5 present paradigms of many *weak* verbs from the Babylonian Talmud and Targum Onkelos, respectively.

קל) פְּעַל)

The chief distinction between the form of the Aramaic *binyan* קל and that of the Hebrew קל is the vowel under the first root-letter. In the past tense, the Aramaic form is vocalized פְּעַל with a *sheva*, whereas the Hebrew is vocalized פָּעַל with a *kametz*; in the active participle, the Aramaic form is פָּעֵיל with a *kametz*, while the Hebrew form is פּוֹעֵל with a *holam* (except for some participles that are פָּעֵל, mostly those that express a state — rather than an action — like יָשֵׁן, *sleeping*).

פַּעֵל

Like the Hebrew *binyan* פִּעֵל, the Aramaic intensive *binyan* פַּעֵל features a *dagesh* in the middle root-letter, as in קַדֵּישׁ, *he sanctified*. The Aramaic *binyan* differs from the Hebrew with regard to the vowel under the first root-letter in the *past* tense: *pathaḥ* in Aramaic (קַדֵּישׁ) versus *ḥirik* in Hebrew (קִדֵּשׁ). In the other tenses, the vowel is generally *pathaḥ* in both languages.

אַפְעֵל

The אַפְעֵל is the *extensive binyan* in which the root is *extended* by a prefix. Like the Hebrew parallel הִפְעִיל, it usually has a *causative* meaning. In the past tense, in the imperative and in the infinitive, the

6   See above, p. 7 and below, p. 289, note 10.

prefixed consonant is almost always אַ־[7] — rather than the הַ־ in Biblical Hebrew and (to some extent) in Biblical Aramaic. The vowel that appears under the אַ prefix is usually *pathaḥ*, as in אַפְקִיד, *he deposited* — but occasionally a vowel-letter י is found in the Talmud, indicating a *ḥirik* vowel, as in אִיפְלִיג (גיטין כח, א), *he was extraordinary*. Neither the Aramaic א nor the Hebrew ה is retained after the מְ־ prefix in the participle (מַפְקִיד, *depositing*) or after the prefixes in the future tense (אַפְקִיד, *I will deposit*) — apparently due to phonetic factors.[8]

אִתְפְּעֵל (passive and reflexive of פְּעַל)

There is no Aramaic *binyan* that features a נִ־ prefix like the Hebrew נִפְעַל, but it is the *binyan* אִתְפְּעֵל that serves as the passive and reflexive of the קַל. The first root-letter of the אִתְפְּעֵל is vocalized to match the vowel of the first root-letter of פְּעַל, the קַל. Thus, the כְּ in אִתְכְּתִיב, *it was written*, is vocalized with a *sheva* — matching the *sheva* under the כְּ, in כְּתַב, *he wrote*. Some forms, e.g., אִיקְפַּד, have no vowel-letter י between the second and third root-letters; hence, its vowel is probably *pathaḥ*.

אִתְפַּעַל (passive and reflexive of פַּעֵל)

Biblical Hebrew expresses the passive of the intensive פִּעֵל through a vowel change, forming the *binyan* פֻּעַל. In Aramaic this usage occurs only in the passive participle, as in מְפַקַּד, *commanded* — as opposed to the active form מְפַקֵּיד, *commanding*. Otherwise, the אִתְפַּעַל *binyan* serves as the passive or reflexive of the פַּעֵל *binyan*. In form, it is similar to the Biblical Hebrew הִתְפַּעֵל — except for its אִתְ־ prefix instead of הִתְ־ and the *pathaḥ* vowel which usually appears under its middle root-letter instead of the *tzerei*, which is more common in Hebrew. Example: אִתְקַדַּשׁ, *it was sanctified*.

אִתַּפְעַל (passive and reflexive of אַפְעֵל)

Like the passive of פַּעֵל, only in the passive participle is the passive of אַפְעֵל expressed by means of a vowel change, as in מְפְקַד,

---

7   The notable exception is the ה prefix of the root ידע. See pp. 81-82 in Chapter 4 and pp. 185-187 in Chapter 5.

8   In Biblical Aramaic, however, the ה prefix is sometimes retained, as in מְהָקֵים (דניאל ב:כא).

deposited — as opposed to the active participle מַפְקִיד, *depositing*. Otherwise, Aramaic uses the rare אִתַּפְעַל *binyan*, which is a contraction of the prefix אֶת־ plus אַפְעֵל, as the passive or reflexive of *binyan* אַפְעֵל, as in אִתַּפְקַד, *it was deposited.*

3.2 THE PAST TENSE

In the Aramaic past tense, the third-person masculine-singular form is the *groundform* to which suffixes are appended to create the rest of the paradigm. In *binyan* קַל the groundform is vocalized with *sh\u1e17va* under the initial consonant and (as in Hebrew) usually *pathaḥ* under the middle consonant, as in כְּתַב, *he wrote.* Thus, כְּתָבִית means *I wrote.* Nevertheless, in many Aramaic verbs — mostly those expressing a state of being or an intransitive action — the middle letter is vocalized with *tzerei* or *ḥirik*, as in תְּקֵיף, *it became sour,* and סְלִיקוּ, *they went up,* and a few verbs have *shuruk,* as in דְּמוּךְ, *he slept.*

◇　　Phonetic considerations affect the vocalization of the conjugation. For example, when the third-person masculine singular form ends in the vowel-letter א or ה, the preceding vowel is *kametz,* as in בְּעָא, *he asked,* and הֲוָה, *he was.* When suffixes are appended, the vowel-letter י is used instead, as in חֲזֵית, *you saw,* and הֲוֵינַן, *we were.*

◇　　In the following artificial paradigms of the past tense, the five common Aramaic *binyanim* are represented: first, three active *binyanim,* קַל, פַּעֵל and אַפְעֵל; and then two אֶת־ *binyanim,* אִתְפְּעֵל and אִתְפַּעַל, that are used in a passive or reflexive sense. The third אֶת־ *binyan* אִתַּפְעַל has been omitted here, since it is not so common, but its paradigm for Targum Onkelos is presented on page 270.

These paradigms list, from left to right, on the following chart:

1)　　the suffixes that are added to the groundform of the past tense

2)　　the forms that appear in Babylonian Aramaic

3)　　the forms that appear in Targum Onkelos (and Targum Yonathan)

4)　　Hebrew parallels

5)　　English translations

		בִּנְיָן קַל[9]		
ARAMAIC SUFFIX	TALMUD BAVLI ARAMAIC	ONKELOS ARAMAIC	HEBREW PARALLEL	ENGLISH TRANSLATION
‐ִית, ‐ִי	כְּתַבִית, כְּתַבִי	כְּתַבִית	כָּתַבְתִּי	*I wrote*
‐ְתָּ, ‐ְתָּא	כְּתַבְתְּ	כְּתַבְתְּ, כְּתַבְתָּא	כָּתַבְתָּ	*you (m.) wrote*
‐ְתְּ	כְּתַבְתְּ	כְּתַבְתְּ	כָּתַבְתְּ	*you (f.) wrote*
	כְּתַב	כְּתַב	כָּתַב	*he wrote*
‐ָה, ‐ָא, ‐ַת	כְּתַבָה, כְּתַבָא, כְּתַבַת	כְּתַבַת	כָּתְבָה	*she wrote*
‐ַן, ‐ְנָא, ‐ִינַן, ‐ֵן	כְּתַבְנַן, כְּתַבְנָא, כְּתַבִינַן, כְּתַבַן	כְּתַבְנָא	כָּתַבְנוּ	*we wrote*
‐תּוּן, ‐ִיתוּ	כְּתַבְתּוּן, כְּתַבִיתוּ	כְּתַבְתּוּן	כְּתַבְתֶּם	*you (m.pl.) wrote*
‐תִּין	כְּתַבְתִּין	כְּתַבְתִּין	כְּתַבְתֶּן	*you (f.pl.) wrote*
‐וּ, ‐וּ	כְּתַבוּ, כְּתוּב[10]	כְּתַבוּ	כָּתְבוּ	*they (m.) wrote*
‐ָן, ‐ָא	כְּתַבָן, כְּתַבָא	כְּתַבָא	כָּתְבוּ	*they (f.) wrote*

9 As in Hebrew, the vowel under the middle root-letter of the *majority* of regular Aramaic verbs in the past tense, *binyan* קַל is *pathaḥ*, as in this paradigm.

10 In this rare Talmudic form, the sign of plurality וּ is inserted between the second and third root-letters as an *infix* instead of being appended at the end of the root as a suffix.

				בִּנְיַן פְּעַל
ARAMAIC SUFFIX	TALMUD BAVLI ARAMAIC	ONKELOS ARAMAIC	HEBREW PARALLEL	ENGLISH TRANSLATION
־ית, ־י	קַדִּישִׁית, קַדִּישִׁי	קַדִּישִׁית	קַדַּשְׁתִּי	*I sanctified*
־תְּ, ־תָּא	קַדִּישְׁתְּ	קַדִּישְׁתְּ, קַדִּישְׁתָּא	קַדַּשְׁתָּ	*you (m.) sanctified*
־תְּ	קַדִּישְׁתְּ	קַדִּישְׁתְּ	קַדַּשְׁתְּ	*you (f.) sanctified*
	קַדִּישׁ	קַדִּישׁ	קִדֵּשׁ	*he sanctified*
־ָה, ־ַת	קַדִּישָׁה, קַדִּישַׁת	קַדִּישַׁת	קִדְּשָׁה	*she sanctified*
־נָא, ־ַן	קַדִּישְׁנָא, קַדִּישְׁנַן	קַדִּישְׁנָא	קִדַּשְׁנוּ	*we sanctified*
־תּוּן, ־תּוּ	קַדִּישְׁתּוּן, קַדִּישְׁתּוּ	קַדִּישְׁתּוּן	קִדַּשְׁתֶּם	*you (pl.) sanctified*
־וּ, ־וּ	קַדִּישׁוּ, קַדּוּשׁ[11]	קַדִּישׁוּ	קִדְּשׁוּ	*they (m.) sanctified*
־ָן, ־ָא	קַדִּישָׁן, קַדִּישָׁא	קַדִּישָׁא	קִדְּשׁוּ	*they (f.) sanctified*

11 In this rare Talmudic form, the sign of plurality ו is inserted between the second and third root-letters as an *infix* instead of being appended at the end of the root as a suffix.

23

בְּנִין אַפְעֵל				
ARAMAIC SUFFIX	**TALMUD BAVLI ARAMAIC**	**ONKELOS ARAMAIC**	**HEBREW PARALLEL**	**ENGLISH TRANSLATION**
־ית, ־י	אַפְקֵידִית, אַפְקֵידִי	אַפְקֵידִית	הִפְקַדְתִּי	*I deposited*
־תְּ, ־תָּא	אַפְקֵידְתְּ	אַפְקֵידְתְּ, אַפְקֵידְתָּא	הִפְקַדְתָּ	*you (m.) deposited*
־תְּ	אַפְקֵידְתְּ	אַפְקֵידְתְּ	הִפְקַדְתְּ	*you (f.) deposited*
	אַפְקֵיד	אַפְקֵיד	הִפְקִיד	*he deposited*
־ה, ־א, ־ת	אַפְקֵידָה, אַפְקְדָה/א, אַפְקְדַת	אַפְקֵידַת	הִפְקִידָה	*she deposited*
־ינַן, ־ן, ־נָא, ־נַן	אַפְקֵידִינַן, אַפְקְדָן, אַפְקֵדְינַן	אַפְקֵידְנָא	הִפְקַדְנוּ	*we deposited*
־תּוּן, ־יתוּ	אַפְקֵידְתּוּן, אַפְקְדִיתוּ	אַפְקֵידְתּוּן	הִפְקַדְתֶּם	*you (pl.) deposited*
־וּ, ־וּ־	אַפְקֵידוּ, אַפְקַדוּ, אַפְקוּד¹²	אַפְקֵידוּ	הִפְקִידוּ	*they (m.) deposited*
־ן, ־ָא	אַפְקְדָן	אַפְקֵידָא	הִפְקִידוּ	*they (f.) deposited*

12 In this rare Talmudic form, the sign of plurality **ו** is inserted between the second and third root-letters as an *infix* instead of being appended at the end of the root as a suffix.

◇　In the Talmudic paradigms of the next two *binyanim*, the אִתְפְּעֵל and the אִתְפַּעַל, the prefix-letter תָ has been printed smaller and within parentheses in order to indicate that in the Talmud it is often deleted and replaced by a *dagesh* in the next consonant (e.g., אִמְּלִיךְ replaces אִתְמְלִיךְ). In Targum Onkelos, however, the תָ is almost always retained — as it is in the Biblical Hebrew הִתְפַּעֵל.

		בִּנְיַן אִתְפְּעֵל		
ARAMAIC SUFFIX	TALMUD BAVLI ARAMAIC	ONKELOS ARAMAIC	HEBREW PARALLEL	ENGLISH TRANSLATION
־ית, ־י	אִי(תְ)כְּתֵיבִית, אִי(תְ)כְּתֵיבִי	אִתְכְּתֵיבִית	נִכְתַּבְתִּי	*I was written*
־תְ, ־תָּא	אִי(תְ)כְּתַבְתְּ	אִתְכְּתֵיבְתְּ, אִתְכְּתֵיבְתָּא	נִכְתַּבְתָּ	*you (m.s.) were written*
	אִי(תְ)כְּתֵיב	אִתְכְּתֵיב	נִכְתַּב	*it (m.) was written*
־ָא, ־ָה, ־ַת	אִי(תְ)כְּתֵיבָא, אִי(תְ)כַּתְבָא/ה	אִתְכְּתֵיבַת	נִכְתְּבָה	*it (f.) was written*
־ינַן, ־נָא	אִי(תְ)כַּתְבִינַן	אִתְכְּתֵיבְנָא	נִכְתַּבְנוּ	*we were written*
־יתוּ, ־תּוּן	אִי(תְ)כַּתְבִיתוּ	אִתְכְּתֵיבְתּוּן	נִכְתַּבְתֶּם	*you (pl.) were written*
־וּ, ־וּ	אִי(תְ)כְּתֵיבוּ, אִי(תְ)כְּתוּב,[13] אִי(תְ)כַּתְבוּ	אִתְכְּתֵיבוּ	נִכְתְּבוּ	*they (m.) were written*
־ָן, ־ָא	אִי(תְ)כַּתְבָן	אִתְכְּתֵיבָא	נִכְתְּבוּ	*they (f.) were written*

13　In this rare Talmudic form, the sign of plurality וּ is inserted between the 2nd and 3rd root-letters as an *infix* instead of being appended at the end as a suffix.

The paradigms of the intensive *binyanim* (פַּעֵל and אִתְפַּעַל) use as their model the verbal root קדש. In the forms that retain the ת of *binyan* אִתְפַּעַל, e.g., אִיתְקַדַּשׁ, there is no *dagesh* in the initial root-letter (i.e., ק), since it is not one of the consonants (בג״ד כפ״ת) that take a (light) *dagesh* at the beginning of a syllable (as opposed to the כ in אִיתְכְּתֵיב on the previous page). On the other hand, forms from which the ת of *binyan* אִתְפַּעַל has been deleted, e.g., אִיקַּדַּשׁ, do have a (strong) *dagesh* in the letter ק that replaces the missing ת.

בִּנְיַן אִתְפַּעַל				
ARAMAIC SUFFIX	TALMUD BAVLI ARAMAIC	ONKELOS ARAMAIC	HEBREW PARALLEL	ENGLISH TRANSLATION
־ִי, ־ִית	אִי(תְ)קַדַּשִׁי	אִתְקַדְּשִׁית	נִתְקַדַּשְׁתִּי	*I was sanctified*
־ְתְּ, ־ְתָּא	אִי(תְ)קַדַּשְׁתְּ	אִתְקַדַּשְׁתְּ, אִתְקַדַּשְׁתָּא	נִתְקַדַּשְׁתָּ	*you (m.s.) were sanctified*
־ְתְּ	אִי(תְ)קַדַּשְׁתְּ	אִתְקַדַּשְׁתְּ	נִתְקַדַּשְׁתְּ	*you (f.s.) were sanctified*
	אִי(תְ)קַדַּשׁ	אִתְקַדַּשׁ	נִתְקַדַּשׁ	*it (m.) was sanctified*
־ַת, ־ָא, ־ָה	אִי(תְ)קַדַּשַׁת, אִי(תְ)קַדְּשָׁא/ה	אִתְקַדְּשַׁת	נִתְקַדְּשָׁה	*it (f.) was sanctified*
־ַן, ־נָא	אִי(תְ)קַדַּשְׁנַן	אִתְקַדַּשְׁנָא	נִתְקַדַּשְׁנוּ	*we were sanctified*
־ִיתוּ, ־תּוּן	אִי(תְ)קַדַּשִׁיתוּ	אִתְקַדַּשְׁתּוּן	נִתְקַדַּשְׁתֶּם	*you (pl.) were sanctified*
־וּ, ־וּ	אִי(תְ)קַדַּשׁוּ, אִי(תְ)קַדּוּשׁ[14]	אִתְקַדַּשׁוּ	נִתְקַדְּשׁוּ	*they (m.) were sanctified*
־ָן, ־ָא	אִי(תְ)קַדַּשָׁן	אִתְקַדַּשָׁא	נִתְקַדְּשׁוּ	*they (f.) were sanctified*

14 In this rare Talmudic form, the sign of plurality ו is inserted between the second and third root-letters as an *infix* instead of being appended at the end of the root as a suffix.

3.3 THE ACTIVE PARTICIPLE

The participle, the most common verbal form in the Aramaic of the Babylonian Talmud, is essentially a verbal adjective. Like all adjectives, it has four forms: masculine singular, feminine singular, masculine plural and feminine plural. A participle (such as כָּתֵיב, *writing*) can be used in any time context, but it is often convenient to render it in English as a *present* tense (*he is writing*) and sometimes as a *future* tense (*he will write*). Because of its verbal nature, an active participle may take a direct object.

◊   In the active participle of *binyan* קַל of regular verbs, the masculine singular form is כָּתֵיב, and the other three forms are created by appending suffixes to ־כָּתְב.

בִּנְיָן קַל				
ARAMAIC SUFFIX	TALMUD BAVLI ARAMAIC	ONKELOS ARAMAIC	HEBREW PARALLEL	ENGLISH TRANSLATION
	כָּתֵיב[15]	כָּתֵיב	כּוֹתֵב	*writing (m.s.)*
־ָא, ־ָה	כָּתְבָא, כָּתְבָה	כָּתְבָא	כּוֹתֶבֶת, כּוֹתְבָה	*writing (f.s.)*
־ִין, ־ִי, ־וּ	כָּתְבִין, כָּתְבִי, כָּתְבוּ[16]	כָּתְבִין	כּוֹתְבִים	*writing (m.pl.)*
־ָן	כָּתְבָן	כָּתְבָן	כּוֹתְבוֹת	*writing (f.pl.)*

15   According to the Yemenite reading tradition of the Babylonian Talmud, however, the vowel under the initial root-letter of the active participle is *pathaḥ*, as in כַּתֵיב (Morag, [above, p. 15 note 8], pp. 131-32).

16   In the Babylonian Talmud, the masculine-plural participle of verbs with י as the final root-letter often feature an וּ suffix (as in אָתוּ, *coming*), and so do the participles of a few other verbs (such as אָזְדוּ, *going*). In Targum Onkelos, however, the masculine-plural participle of final י verbs has the suffix ־ֶן (as in אָתֶן, *coming*).

27

◇   As in Hebrew, the participles of the other primary (active) Aramaic *binyanim,* the פַּעֵל and the אַפְעֵל feature מ־ prefixes.

בִּנְיַן פַּעֵל				
ARAMAIC SUFFIX	TALMUD BAVLI ARAMAIC	ONKELOS ARAMAIC	HEBREW PARALLEL	ENGLISH TRANSLATION
	מְקַדֵּיש	מְקַדֵּיש	מְקַדֵּשׁ	*sanctifying (m.s.)*
־ָא, ־ָה	מְקַדְּשָׁא, מְקַדְּשָׁה	מְקַדְּשָׁא	מְקַדֶּשֶׁת	*sanctifying (f.s.)*
־ִין, ־ִי, ־וּ	מְקַדְּשִׁין, מְקַדְּשִׁי, מְקַדְּשׁוּ	מְקַדְּשִׁין	מְקַדְּשִׁים	*sanctifying (m.pl.)*
־ָן	מְקַדְּשָׁן	מְקַדְּשָׁן	מְקַדְּשׁוֹת	*sanctifying (f.pl.)*

בִּנְיַן אַפְעֵל				
ARAMAIC SUFFIX	TALMUD BAVLI ARAMAIC	ONKELOS ARAMAIC	HEBREW PARALLEL	ENGLISH TRANSLATION
	מַפְקִיד	מַפְקִיד	מַפְקִיד	*depositing (m.s.)*
־ָא, ־ָה	מַפְקְדָא, מַפְקְדָה	מַפְקְדָא	מַפְקֶדֶת, מַפְקִידָה	*depositing (f.s.)*
־ִין, ־ִי, ־וּ	מַפְקְדִין, מַפְקְדִי, מַפְקְדוּ	מַפְקְדִין	מַפְקִידִים	*depositing (m.pl.)*
־ָן	מַפְקְדָן	מַפְקְדָן	מַפְקִידוֹת	*depositing (f.pl.)*

3.4 THE PASSIVE PARTICIPLE

Like Hebrew, Aramaic also uses a passive participle in any time context, usually in an adjectival sense. In *binyan* קַל, the Aramaic כְּתִיב is the equivalent of the Hebrew passive participle כָּתוּב, *written*. The following paradigms present the passive participles from the three primary (active) Aramaic *binyanim,* the קַל, the פַּעֵל and the אַפְעֵל.

◇ The basic form of the passive participle of *binyan* קַל is כְּתִיב, and the other three forms are created by appending to it the standard suffixes that indicate gender and number.

בִּנְיָן קַל				
ARAMAIC SUFFIX	TALMUD BAVLI ARAMAIC	ONKELOS ARAMAIC	HEBREW PARALLEL	ENGLISH TRANSLATION
	כְּתִיב	כְּתִיב	כָּתוּב	*written (m.s.)*
־ָא, ־ָה	כְּתִיבָא, כְּתִיבָה	כְּתִיבָא	כְּתוּבָה	*written (f.s.)*
־ִין, ־ִי	כְּתִיבִין, כְּתִיבִי	כְּתִיבִין	כְּתוּבִים	*written (m.pl.)*
־ָן	כְּתִיבָן	כְּתִיבָן	כְּתוּבוֹת	*written (f.pl.)*

◇ The passive participles of the other two primary *binyanim,* the פַּעֵל and the אַפְעֵל have מ־ prefixes, like their active participles. The masculine-singular passive forms are respectively: מְקַדַּשׁ, *sanctified* (corresponding to the Hebrew פִּעֵל participle, מְקֻדָּשׁ), and מַפְקַד, *deposited* (corresponding to the Hebrew הֻפְעַל participle, מֻפְקָד). The Aramaic forms differ from their active counterparts in their vocalization, i.e., the *pathah* under their middle root-letters as opposed to the *tzerei* of the active voice. In the other three forms, however, there is no difference between the active and the passive participles, and they are distinguishable from each other only by context.

בִּנְיַן פְּעַל[17]				
ARAMAIC SUFFIX	TALMUD BAVLI ARAMAIC	ONKELOS ARAMAIC	HEBREW PARALLEL	ENGLISH TRANSLATION
	מְקַדַּשׁ	מְקַדַּשׁ	מְקֻדָּשׁ	*sanctified (m.s.)*
־ָא	מְקַדְּשָׁא	מְקַדְּשָׁא	מְקֻדֶּשֶׁת	*sanctified (f.s.)*
־ִין, ־ִי	מְקַדְּשִׁין, מְקַדְּשִׁי	מְקַדְּשִׁין	מְקֻדָּשִׁים	*sanctified (m.pl.)*
־ָן	מְקַדְּשָׁן	מְקַדְּשָׁן	מְקֻדָּשׁוֹת	*sanctified (f.pl.)*

בִּנְיַן אַפְעֵל[17]				
ARAMAIC SUFFIX	TALMUD BAVLI ARAMAIC	ONKELOS ARAMAIC	HEBREW PARALLEL	ENGLISH TRANSLATION
	מַפְקַד	מַפְקַד	מֻפְקָד	*deposited (m.s.)*
־ָא	מַפְקְדָא	מַפְקְדָא	מֻפְקֶדֶת	*deposited (f.s.)*
־ִין, ־ִי	מַפְקְדִין, מַפְקְדִי	מַפְקְדִין	מֻפְקָדִים	*deposited (m.pl.)*
־ָן	מַפְקְדָן	מַפְקְדָן	מֻפְקָדוֹת	*deposited (f.pl.)*

17 Some of the Yemenite sources quoted by Morag (above, p. 15 note 8), p. 151, vocalize *with a kubbutz* — both the first root-letter of the four forms of the פְּעַל passive participle, as in מְקֻדַּשׁ and מְקֻדְּשָׁא (in the manner of the Hebrew פֻּעַל participle), and the מ־ prefix of the אַפְעֵל passive participle, as in מֻפְקַד and מֻפְקְדָא (like the Hebrew הֻפְעַל participle). According to that vocalization, there is always a clear distinction between the active participle and the passive participle in these Aramaic *binyanim*.

3.5 THE ־מִת PARTICIPLE

All the Aramaic *binyanim* that have an אֶת־ prefix in the past tense feature participles with a מִת־ prefix which have a passive or reflexive meaning.[18] The following two tables present the participles from the *binyanim* that are fairly common, אֶתְפְּעֵל and אֶתְפַּעַל.

בִּנְיָן אֶתְפְּעֵל				
ARAMAIC SUFFIX	TALMUD BAVLI ARAMAIC	ONKELOS ARAMAIC	HEBREW PARALLEL	ENGLISH TRANSLATION
	מִ(תְ)כְּתֵיב	מִתְכְּתֵיב	נִכְתָּב	*being written (m.s.)*
־ָא	מִ(תְ)כַּתְבָא	מִתְכַּתְבָא	נִכְתֶּבֶת	*being written (f.s.)*
־ִין, ־ֵי	מִ(תְ)כַּתְבִין, ־בֵי	מִתְכַּתְבִין	נִכְתָּבִים	*being written (m.pl.)*
־ָן	מִ(תְ)כַּתְבָן	מִתְכַּתְבָן	נִכְתָּבוֹת	*being written (f.pl.)*

בִּנְיָן אֶתְפַּעַל				
ARAMAIC SUFFIX	TALMUD BAVLI ARAMAIC	ONKELOS ARAMAIC	HEBREW PARALLEL	ENGLISH TRANSLATION
	מִ(תְ)קַדַּשׁ	מִתְקַדַּשׁ	מִתְקַדֵּשׁ	*being sanctified (m.s.)*
־ָא	מִ(תְ)קַדְּשָׁא	מִתְקַדְּשָׁא	מִתְקַדֶּשֶׁת	*being sanctified (f.s.)*
־ִין, ־ֵי	מִ(תְ)קַדְּשִׁין, ־שֵׁי	מִתְקַדְּשִׁין	מִתְקַדְּשִׁים	*being sanctified (m.pl.)*
־ָן	מִ(תְ)קַדְּשָׁן	מִתְקַדְּשָׁן	מִתְקַדְּשׁוֹת	*being sanctified (f.pl.)*

18 As noted above on p. 18, although these *binyanim* are essentially *reflexive* in nature, they are generally used in a *passive* sense. Consequently, a participle from *binyan* אֶתְפְּעֵל, like מִתְכְּתֵיב, is often similar in meaning to the passive participle of the קַל, כְּתִיב (as in Hebrew where the נִפְעַל participle, נִכְתָּב, is similar to the passive participle of the קַל, כָּתוּב). There may, however, be a slight distinction: The מִת־ participle (such as מִתְכְּתֵיב) tends to be used more like a *verb* (English: *being written*) stressing process — while the passive participle of the קַל (כְּתִיב) tends to be more like an *adjective* (English: *written*).

31

3.6   THE PRESENT TENSE

In the Aramaic of the Babylonian Talmud (but rarely in Targum Onkelos), a *present tense* is formed by adding personal pronouns of the first and second persons as *suffixes* to the masculine singular or plural *active* participle. These suffixes express the *subject* of the participle: *I, you* or *we*. In Mishnaic Hebrew, and in Modern Hebrew too, this usage is employed with certain participles, for example, חוֹשֵׁשׁ, *I am afraid, I am concerned*. In חוֹשֵׁשׁ + אֲנִי = חוֹשְׁשַׁנִי (משנה שבת טז:ז). In the following table, suffixes are added to the active participles in *binyan* קַל.[19]

ACTIVE PARTICIPLE WITH SUFFIXES

ARAMAIC SUFFIX	TALMUD BAVLI ARAMAIC	HEBREW PARALLEL	ENGLISH TRANSLATION
־נָא	כָּתֵיב + אֲנָא = כָּתֵיבְנָא	כּוֹתֵב אֲנִי	*I write*
־ְתְּ	כָּתֵיב + אַתְּ = כָּתְבַתְּ	כּוֹתֵב אַתָּה	*you (s.) write*
־נַן	כָּתְבִי + אֲנַן = כָּתְבִינַן	כּוֹתְבִים אָנוּ	*we write*
־תוּ	כָּתְבִי + אַתּוּ = כָּתְבִיתוּ	כּוֹתְבִים אַתֶּם	*you (pl.) write*

PASSIVE PARTICIPLE WITH SUFFIXES

In like manner, personal pronouns of the first or second persons are sometimes added to the masculine-singular or masculine-plural *passive* participles, as in the Hebrew form סָבוּר+אֲנִי = סְבוּרַנִי, *an opinion is held by me* or *I think*. In the following table, suffixes are added to the passive participles in *binyan* קַל.[20]

---

19 Similarly, the same personal-pronoun suffix that indicates the subject may be appended to the active participles of other *binyanim* in order to create a present tense, e.g., מַשְׁלֵים + אֲנָא = מַשְׁלֵימְנָא (חגיגה ה,א), *I am handing over*.

20 The same suffixes may be appended to passive participles of other *binyanim*.

ARAMAIC SUFFIX	TALMUD BAVLI ARAMAIC	HEBREW PARALLEL	ENGLISH TRANSLATION
־נָא	עָסִיק + אֲנָא = עֲסִיקְנָא[21]	עָסוּק אֲנִי	*I am involved*
־תְּ	עָסִיק + אַתְּ = עֲסִיקַתְּ	עָסוּק אַתָּה	*you (s.) are involved*
־נַן	עֲסִיקִי + אֲנַן = עֲסִיקִינַן	עֲסוּקִים אָנוּ	*we are involved*
־תוּ	עֲסִיקִי + אַתּוּ = עֲסִיקִיתוּ	עֲסוּקִים אַתֶּם	*you (pl.) are involved*

3.7   COMPOUND TENSE: הוי + PARTICIPLE

In both the Babylonian Talmud and in Targum Onkelos, the verb הוי may be used in the past tense as an auxiliary verb together with the participle of another verb to form a compound tense that indicates repeated or continual action.[22]

Examples

*an excellent statement that your father **used to say***	מִלְּתָא מְעַלְּיְתָא דַּהֲוָה אָמַר אֲבוּךְ (סוכה מג, ב)
*whenever he **would tell** them a halakha*	כָּל אֵימַת דַּהֲוָה אָמַר לְהוּ שְׁמַעְתָּא (תענית ט, א)
*when he (= Yosef) **was pleading** to us*	כַּד הֲוָה מִתְחַנַּן לָנָא (תרגום אונקלוס לבראשית מב:כא)
*if he **would say** thus: Your wages will be spotted ones*	אִם כְּדֵין הֲוָה אָמַר נְמוֹרִין יְהֵי אַגְרָךְ (שם לא:ח)

◇   When this construction is used in the first or second person, there is a significant difference in syntax between Targum Onkelos and the Babylonian Talmud.

---

21 Here we did not choose כְּתִיב with suffixes as our example, because the translation of such forms as כְּתִיבְנָא, *I am written*, sounds so strange.

22 See the parallel in Mishnaic Hebrew in Chapter 1, p. 8, and note 17 above.

In the Aramaic of Targum Onkelos, it is the past tense of the auxiliary verb that is conjugated to express the appropriate person, like הֲוֵינָא, *we were*, in the following example:[23]

*when **we were sitting** at the fleshpots*   כַּד הֲוֵינָא יָתְבִין עַל דּוּדֵי בִשְׂרָא

(תרגום אונקלוס לשמות טז:ג)

In the Talmud, on the other hand, a personal-pronoun suffix is appended to the participle, but the auxiliary verb הֲוָה remains stable, as in the following example:[24]

*many times **I would stand** before Rav*   זִמְנִין סַגִּיאִין הֲוָה קָאִימְנָא קַמֵּיהּ דְּרַב

(פסחים קו, רע"ב)

3.8   THE FUTURE TENSE

Like its Hebrew counterpart, the Aramaic future tense features prefixes in all its forms (along with suffixes in some of them). In the Aramaic of Targum Onkelos on the Torah and Targum Yonathan ben Uziel on the Prophets, the prefixes are the same as those used in Hebrew. In *Babylonian* Aramaic, however, there are two departures from the Hebrew paradigm: First of all, the third-person masculine prefix (both singular and plural) is most frequently ־ל, less frequently ־נ, but rarely ־י.[25] Secondly, in the first-person plural of the future, where the prefix both in Hebrew and in Biblical Aramaic is always ־נ, the Babylonian Talmud occasionally has a ־ל prefix, as in the passage:

*Shall **we** get up and penalize him?*   אֲנַן לֵיקוּם וְלִיקְנְסֵיהּ? (גיטין נד, סע"א)

Because of the *homonyms* thus created, the Talmudic context alone determines whether a particular word is functioning as a third-

---

23   This is also the practice in Mishnaic Hebrew, as in: פַּעַם אַחַת הָיִיתִי מְהַלֵּךְ בַּדֶּרֶךְ (משנה אבות פ"ו מ"ט), *once I was walking along the road.*

24   See also the entry הֲוָה אֲמִינָא in *The Practical Talmud Dictionary* (above, p. ix note 6).

25   The ־י prefix is used regularly in such expressions as מִי יֵימַר? , *who can say?* and יְהֵא רַעֲוָא, *may it be [Your] Will,* which may have been influenced by the parallel Hebrew expressions מִי יֹאמַר? and יְהִי רָצוֹן, respectively.

person masculine singular form or as a first-person plural. For example, the verbal form לֵימָא, which frequently occurs in the Talmud, is best translated as *let **him** say* in some cases and as *let **us** say* in other cases.

◇   In the Babylonian Talmud, these prefixes sometimes have full ("plene") spelling with the vowel-letter י added, especially in *binyan* קַל, as in לִיכְתּוֹב. Surprisingly, a vowel-letter is also found occasionally in *binyan* פַּעֵל, as in לִיזַבֵּין (ערכין ל, ב) (instead of לְזַבֵּין), *he should sell*, and in *binyan* אַפְעֵל, as in לִיצְרְכַהּ (יבמות לא, רע״א) (instead of לַצְרְכַהּ), *let him require it.*[26]

◇   In the future of *binyan* קַל of the *strong* verb in Babylonian Aramaic, the vowel-letter ו is usually inserted after the second root-letter, representing either a *holam* (וֹ as in Hebrew), as in our paradigm, or perhaps a *shuruk* (וּ, which is closer to the vowel in Biblical Aramaic). Some verbs, however, especially those whose *third* root-letter is a guttural consonant, have no vowel-letter but a *pathah* vowel under the second letter, as in לִיסְבַּר (שבת סג, א), *let him analyze;* while a few verbs have a vowel-letter י which probably indicates a *tzerei*, as in לֶעֱבֵיד (ברכות י, א), *let him do.*

◇   This Aramaic tense sometimes functions as an ordinary future, e.g., אֵיזִיל (ברכות כד, ב), *I shall go.* Frequently, however, in the course of Talmudic argumentation and discussion, forms with a -ל or a -נ prefix are used in a *jussive* sense (sometimes called a "third-person imperative"). That usage is best translated into English as *let him...*, as in most of the examples cited above and in some of the forms presented on pages 36 to 40. Occasionally, the same form is used with a subjunctive meaning, e.g., דְּלִיזַבֵּין (ערכין ל, ב), *that he (should) sell.*

◇   The following artificial paradigms present the conjugations of the future tense of the regular Aramaic verb in the five common *binyanim*.

---

26 See Epstein (above, p. 15 note 10), p. 32, and Morag (above, p. 15 note 8), pp. 148 and 156. According to Morag, the Yemenite tradition consistently vocalizes the third-person prefix of *binyan* פַּעֵל with *hirik* — whether the vowel-letter י appears in the text or not.

ARAMAIC PREFIX[27]	TALMUD BAVLI ARAMAIC[27]	ONKELOS ARAMAIC	HEBREW PARALLEL	ENGLISH TRANSLATION
אֶ(יִ)-	אֵיכְתּוֹב	אֶכְתּוֹב	אֶכְתֹּב	*I will write*
תְּ(יִ)-	תִּיכְתּוֹב	תִּכְתּוֹב	תִּכְתֹּב	*you (m.) will write*
תְּ(יִ)-	תִּיכְתְּבִין(ן)[28]	תִּכְתְּבִין	תִּכְתְּבִי	*you (f.) will write*
לְ(יִ)-, נְ(יִ)-, יִ-	לִיכְתּוֹב, נִיכְתּוֹב, יִכְתּוֹב[29]	יִכְתּוֹב	יִכְתֹּב	*he will write, let him write*
תְּ(יִ)-	תִּיכְתּוֹב	תִּכְתּוֹב	תִּכְתֹּב	*she will write*
נְ(יִ)-, לְ(יִ)-	נִיכְתּוֹב, לִיכְתּוֹב	נִכְתּוֹב	נִכְתֹּב	*we will write, let us write*
תְּ(יִ)-	תִּיכְתְּבוּן(ן)[28]	תִּכְתְּבוּן	תִּכְתְּבוּ	*you (m.pl.) will write*
תְּ(יִ)-	תִּיכְתְּבָן	תִּכְתְּבָן	תִּכְתֹּבְנָה	*you (f.pl.) will write*
לְ(יִ)-, נְ(יִ)-	לִיכְתְּבוּ(ן)[28], נִיכְתְּבוּ(ן)[28], לִיכְתּוֹב, נִכְתּוֹב[30]	יִכְתְּבוּן	יִכְתְּבוּ	*they (m.) will write, let them write*
יִ-	——	יִכְתְּבָן	תִּכְתֹּבְנָה	*they (f.) will write*

27 Sometimes these future forms appear in the Talmud *without* the vowel-letter י. Consequently, the vowel-letter י has been placed within parentheses in the "Aramaic-Prefix" column, but — for esthetic considerations — the י is presented in the "Talmud-Bavli-Aramaic" column in the full form without parentheses, since generally it does appear in the Talmud.

28 The final ן is often deleted in the Talmud.

29 See above p. 34 note 25.

30 Compare the infixed ו in the form כְּתוּב in the third-person masculine plural of the past tense on p. 22 and note 10 there.

בִּנְיַן פַּעֵל				
ARAMAIC PREFIX	TALMUD BAVLI ARAMAIC	ONKELOS ARAMAIC	HEBREW PARALLEL	ENGLISH TRANSLATION
אֲ־	אֲקַדֵּישׁ	אֲקַדֵּישׁ	אֲקַדֵּשׁ	I will sanctify
תְּ־	תְּקַדֵּישׁ	תְּקַדֵּישׁ	תְּקַדֵּשׁ	you (m.) will sanctify
תְּ־	(ן)תְּקַדְּשִׁי[31]	תְּקַדְּשִׁין	תְּקַדְּשִׁי	you (f.) will sanctify
־(י)לִ, ־(י)נִ, יְ־	לְקַדֵּישׁ, לִיקַדֵּישׁ, נְקַדֵּישׁ, נִיקַדֵּישׁ	יְקַדֵּישׁ	יְקַדֵּשׁ	he will sanctify, let him sanctify
תְּ־	תְּקַדֵּישׁ	תְּקַדֵּישׁ	תְּקַדֵּשׁ	she will sanctify
נְ־, לְ־	נְקַדֵּישׁ, לְקַדֵּישׁ	נְקַדֵּישׁ	נְקַדֵּשׁ	we will sanctify, let us sanctify
תְּ־	תְּקַדְּשׁוּ	תְּקַדְּשׁוּן	תְּקַדְּשׁוּ	you (m.pl.) will sanctify
־(י)לִ, ־(י)נִ, יְ־	לְקַדְּשׁוּ, לִיקַדְּשׁוּ(ן)[31], נְקַדְּשׁוּ, נִיקַדְּשׁוּ	יְקַדְּשׁוּן	יְקַדְּשׁוּ	they (m.) will sanctify, let them sanctify
לְ־, יְ־	לְקַדְּשָׁן	יְקַדְּשָׁן	תְּקַדֵּשְׁנָה	they (f.) will sanctify

31 The final ן is often deleted in the Talmud.

בִּנְיַן אַפְעֵל				
ARAMAIC PREFIX	TALMUD BAVLI ARAMAIC	ONKELOS ARAMAIC	HEBREW PARALLEL	ENGLISH TRANSLATION
־אַ	אַפְקֵיד	אַפְקֵיד	אַפְקִיד	*I will deposit*
־תַּ	תַּפְקֵיד	תַּפְקֵיד	תַּפְקִיד	*you (m.) will deposit*
־תַּ	תַּפְקְדִי	תַּפְקְדִין	תַּפְקִידִי	*you (f.) will deposit*
־לַ, ־לִי, ־נַ, ־יַ	לַפְקֵיד, לִיפְקֵיד, נַפְקֵיד	יַפְקֵיד	יַפְקִיד, יַפְקֵד	*he will deposit, let him deposit*
־תַּ	תַּפְקֵיד	תַּפְקֵיד	תַּפְקִיד	*she will deposit*
־נַ, ־לַ	נַפְקֵיד, לַפְקֵיד	נַפְקֵיד	נַפְקִיד	*we will deposit, let us deposit*
־תַּ	תַּפְקְדוּ	תַּפְקְדוּן	תַּפְקִידוּ	*you (m.pl.) will deposit*
־לַ, ־לִי, ־נַ, ־יַ	לַפְקְדוּ, לִיפְקְדוּ, נַפְקְדוּ	יַפְקְדוּן	יַפְקִידוּ	*they (m.) will deposit, let them deposit*
־לַ, ־יַ	לַפְקְדָן	יַפְקְדָן	תַּפְקֵדְנָה	*they (f.) will deposit*

בִּנְיָן אִתְפְּעֵל

ARAMAIC PREFIX[32]	TALMUD BAVLI ARAMAIC[32]	ONKELOS ARAMAIC	HEBREW PARALLEL	ENGLISH TRANSLATION
אֶ(י)(תְ)-	אִי(תְ)כְּתֵיב	אֶתְכְּתֵיב	אֶכָּתֵב	*I will be written*
תִּ(י)(תְ)-	תִּי(תְ)כְּתֵיב	תִּתְכְּתֵיב	תִּכָּתֵב	*you (m.) will be written*
תִּ(י)(תְ)-	תִּי(תְ)כַּתְבִין[33]	תִּתְכַּתְבִין	תִּכָּתְבִי	*you (f.) will be written*
לִי(תְ)(תְ)-, נִ(י)(תְ)-, יִתְ-	לִי(תְ)כְּתֵיב, נִי(תְ)כְּתֵיב	יִתְכְּתֵיב	יִכָּתֵב	*it (m.) will be written, let it be written*
תִּ(י)(תְ)-	תִּי(תְ)כְּתֵיב	תִּתְכְּתֵיב	תִּכָּתֵב	*it (f.) will be written, let it be written*
נִ(י)(תְ)-, לִי(תְ)-	נִי(תְ)כְּתֵיב, לִי(תְ)כְּתֵיב	נִתְכְּתֵיב	נִכָּתֵב	*we will be written let us be written*
תִּ(י)(תְ)-	תִּי(תְ)כַּתְבוּ	תִּתְכַּתְבוּן	תִּכָּתְבוּ	*you (m.pl.) will be written*
לִי(תְ)-, נִ(י)(תְ)-, יִתְ-	לִי(תְ)כַּתְבוּ(ן), נִי(תְ)כַּתְבוּ	יִתְכַּתְבוּן	יִכָּתְבוּ	*they (m.) will be written, let them be written*
לִי(תְ)-, יִתְ-	לִיתְכַּתְבָן	יִתְכַּתְבָן	תִּכָּתֵבְנָה	*they (f.) will be written*

---

32   Sometimes these future forms appear in the Talmud *without* the vowel-letter י. Consequently, the vowel-letter י has been placed within parentheses in the "Aramaic-Prefix" column, but — for esthetic considerations — the י is presented in the "Talmud-Bavli-Aramaic" column in the full form without parentheses, since generally it does appear in the Talmud.

33   The final ן is often deleted in the Talmud.

בִּנְיָן אִתְפְּעַל

ARAMAIC PREFIX[34]	TALMUD BAVLI ARAMAIC[34]	ONKELOS ARAMAIC	HEBREW PARALLEL	ENGLISH TRANSLATION
־אֶ(י)(תְ)	אֶי(תְ)קַדַּשׁ	אֶתְקַדַּשׁ	אֶתְקַדֵּשׁ	*I will be sanctified*
־תִּ(י)(תְ)	תִּי(תְ)קַדַּשׁ	תִּתְקַדַּשׁ	תִּתְקַדֵּשׁ	*you (m.) will be sanctified*
־תִּ(י)(תְ)	תִּי(תְ)קַדְּשִׁי(ן)[35]	תִּתְקַדְּשִׁין	תִּתְקַדְּשִׁי	*you (f.) will be sanctified*
־לִ(י)(תְ), ־נִ(י)(תְ), יִתְ־	לִי(תְ)קַדַּשׁ, נִי(תְ)קַדַּשׁ	יִתְקַדַּשׁ	יִתְקַדֵּשׁ	*it (m.) will be sanctified, let it be sanctified*
־תִּ(י)(תְ)	תִּי(תְ)קַדַּשׁ	תִּתְקַדַּשׁ	תִּתְקַדֵּשׁ	*it (f.) will be sanctified, let it be sanctified*
־נִ(י)(תְ), ־לִ(י)(תְ)	נִ(תְ)קַדַּשׁ, לִ(תְ)קַדַּשׁ	נִתְקַדַּשׁ	נִתְקַדֵּשׁ	*we will be sanctified, let us be sanctified*
־תִּ(י)(תְ)	תִּי(תְ)קַדְּשׁוּ	תִּתְקַדְּשׁוּן	תִּתְקַדְּשׁוּ	*you (m.pl.) will be sanctified*
־לִ(י)(תְ), ־נִ(י)(תְ), יִתְ־	לִי(תְ)קַדְּשׁוּ(ן), נִי(תְ)קַדְּשׁוּ, לִיקַדּוּשׁ,[36] נִקַדּוּשׁ[36]	יִתְקַדְּשׁוּן	יִתְקַדְּשׁוּ	*they (m.) will be sanctified, let them be sanctified*
־לִ(י)(תְ), יִתְ־	לִי(תְ)קַדְּשָׁן	יִתְקַדְּשָׁן	תִּתְקַדְּשֶׁנָה	*they (f.) will be sanctified*

34　Sometimes these future forms appear in the Talmud *without* the vowel-letter י. Consequently, the vowel-letter י has been placed within parentheses in the "Aramaic-Prefix" column, but — for esthetic considerations — the י is presented in the "Talmud-Bavli-Aramaic" column in the full form without parentheses, since generally it does appear in the Talmud.

35　The final ן is often deleted in the Talmud.

36　Compare the infixed ו in the form כְּתוּב in the third-person masculine plural of the past tense on p. 22 and note 10 there.

3.9   THE IMPERATIVE

As in Hebrew, the forms of the imperative in Aramaic are similar to those of the second-person forms of the future tense — after deleting the תְּ- prefix. The initial א- from the אַפְעֵל, אִתְפְּעֵל and אִתְפַּעַל *binyanim*, which is omitted in the future (because of "assimilation") does appear in the imperative, e.g. in אַפְקֵד. In the following paradigms of the five common *binyanim*, all four forms of the imperative are presented for *binyan* קַל, but for the other *binyanim* the feminine plural form has been omitted because it is hardly ever used.

		בִּנְיָן קַל		
ARAMAIC SUFFIX	TALMUD BAVLI ARAMAIC	ONKELOS ARAMAIC	HEBREW PARALLEL	ENGLISH TRANSLATION
	כְּתוֹב	כְּתוֹב	כְּתֹב	*write! (m.s.)*
־ִי	כְּתוּבִי	כְּתוּבִי	כִּתְבִי	*write! (f.s.)*
־וּ	כְּתוּבוּ	כְּתוּבוּ	כִּתְבוּ	*write! (m.pl.)*
־ִין, ־ָא	כְּתוּבִין	כְּתוּבָא	כְּתֹבְנָה	*write! (f.pl.)*

		בִּנְיָן פַּעֵל		
ARAMAIC SUFFFIX	TALMUD BAVLI ARAMAIC	ONKELOS ARAMAIC	HEBREW PARALLEL	ENGLISH TRANSLATION
	קַדֵּישׁ	קַדֵּישׁ	קַדֵּשׁ	*sanctify! (m.s.)*
־ִי	קַדִּישִׁי, קַדְּשִׁי	קַדִּישִׁי	קַדְּשִׁי	*sanctify! (f.s.)*
־וּ	קַדִּישׁוּ, קַדְּשׁוּ	קַדִּישׁוּ	קַדְּשׁוּ	*sanctify! (m.pl.)*

				בִּנְיָן אַפְעֵל		
ARAMAIC SUFFIX	TALMUD BAVLI ARAMAIC	ONKELOS ARAMAIC	HEBREW PARALLEL	ENGLISH TRANSLATION
	אַפְקֵיד	אַפְקֵיד	הַפְקֵד	*deposit! (m.s.)*
־ִי	אַפְקִידִי	אַפְקִידִי	הַפְקִידִי	*deposit! (f.s.)*
־וּ ־וּ	אַפְקִידוּ, אַפְקְדוּ, אַפְקוּד37	אַפְקִידוּ	הַפְקִידוּ	*deposit! (m.pl.)*

				בִּנְיָן אִתְפְּעֵל		
ARAMAIC SUFFIX	TALMUD BAVLI ARAMAIC	ONKELOS ARAMAIC	HEBREW PARALLEL	ENGLISH TRANSLATION
	אִי(תְ)כְּתֵיב	אִתְכְּתֵיב	הִכָּתֵב	*be inscribed! (m.s.)*
־ִי	אִי(תְ)כְּתִיבִי	אִתְכְּתִיבִי	הִכָּתְבִי	*be inscribed! (f.s.)*
־וּ	אִ(תְ)כְּתִיבוּ	אִתְכְּתִיבוּ	הִכָּתְבוּ	*be inscribed! (m.pl.)*

				בִּנְיָן אִתְפַּעַל		
ARAMAIC SUFFIX	TALMUD BAVLI ARAMAIC	ONKELOS ARAMAIC	HEBREW PARALLEL	ENGLISH TRANSLATION
	אִי(תְ)קַדַּשׁ	אִתְקַדַּשׁ	הִתְקַדֵּשׁ	*sanctify yourself! (m.s.)*
־ִי	אִיתְקַדְּשִׁי	אִתְקַדְּשִׁי	הִתְקַדְּשִׁי	*sanctify yourself! (f.s.)*
־וּ	אִתְקַדְּשׁוּ	אִתְקַדְּשׁוּ	הִתְקַדְּשׁוּ	*sanctify yourselves! (m.pl.)*

---

37 Compare the infixed ו in the form כְּתוּב in the third-person masculine plural of the past tense on p. 22 and note 10 there.

42

3.10   THE GERUND AND THE INFINITIVE

In Aramaic and Hebrew grammar, the terms *gerund* and *infinitive* do not have the same meanings as they do in English grammar, hence native English speakers are hereby warned to proceed with caution. English sometimes uses the gerund and infinitive interchangeably,[38] but in Hebrew and Aramaic their functions are distinct. These functions will first be described with illustrations from Biblical Hebrew, and then the Aramaic forms will be presented on pages 45 and 46.

THE FUNCTIONS OF THE GERUND (שֵׁם הַפֹּעַל)

The *gerund* is a verbal noun. It is frequently brought into close grammatical connection with other elements in the sentence, including prepositional prefixes, personal-pronoun suffixes and other nouns.[39]

◊   The prefixes that are often prefaced to the gerund are בְּ-, *in, at, when, during;* כְּ-, *as;* לְ-, *to* (the most common prefix by far); or מִ-, *from or than.*[40] For example, the לְ- in the Biblical phrase:

to bless the nation   לְבָרֵךְ אֶת הָעָם (דברים ז:יב)

◊   Sometimes, a personal-pronoun suffix is (also) appended.

Example 1

*and during **your** lying down and during **your** arising*   וּבְשָׁכְבְּךָ וּבְקוּמֶךָ (דברים ו:ד)

Example 2

*and to serve **him***   וּלְעָבְדוֹ (שם יא:יג)

In Example 1 the pronoun suffix, ־ךָ, *your,* represents the *subject* of the gerunds, *lying down* and *rising.* In Example 2, however, the suffix ־וֹ, *him,* represents the *direct object* of the gerund, *to serve.*

---

38 I like *walking* (gerund). I like *to walk* (infinitive).

39 It is thus construed (=combined) with other elements in the sentence so as to form a single unit; hence it has also been called the *infinitive construct.*

40 These prefixes are often referred to by the Hebrew anagram בכל״ם.

◊   Like other nouns, the verbal noun is sometimes used as a noun in the construct state and is combined closely with the noun that follows,[41] as in the Biblical phrase:

at **the departing of Israel** from   (תהלים קיד:א) **בְּצֵאת־יִשְׂרָאֵל** מִמִּצְרָיִם
Egypt

◊   Like other verbal forms, it may also take a direct object, as in **לְבָרֵךְ אֶת הָעָם** above.

THE MAJOR FUNCTION OF THE INFINITIVE (מָקוֹר)

The term *infinitive* describes grammatical forms that are "infinite" and "unlimited," in the sense that they are not altered in order to indicate specific tense (or aspect), person, number, or gender — as opposed to "finite" verbal forms, which do change. Thus the Hebrew and Aramaic infinitive is invariable: it is never inflected.[42] Its primary function is to add emphasis to a finite form from the same verbal stem that immediately follows (or precedes) it.[43] The English language, which has no verbal form that can be used in this manner, expresses such emphasis by means of adverbs, such as *completely, firmly, certainly,* and *indeed.*

Examples

*if you will **completely** obey*   (שמות ג:ב) אִם **שָׁמֹעַ** תִּשְׁמַע

*the man **firmly** warned us*   (בראשית מג:ג) **הָעֵד הֵעִד** בָּנוּ הָאִישׁ

*he shall **certainly** be put to death*[44]   (שמות כא:יב) **מוֹת** יוּמָת

---

41   For a discussion of "the construct state" of the noun see p. 231.

42   It has also been termed the *infinitive absolute.*

43   In addition, sometimes the infinitive is used instead of a finite verbal form, especially the imperative, as in (שמות כ:ז) **זָכוֹר** אֶת יוֹם הַשַּׁבָּת, *Remember the Sabbath day.*

44   In the first two examples, the infinitives (שָׁמֹעַ and הָעֵד, respectively) appear in the same *binyan* as the finite verbal forms (תִּשְׁמַע and הֵעִיד, respectively) — as is generally the case with this usage. In the last example, however, a *binyan* קַל infinitive (מוֹת) is used to add emphasis to the future tense (יוּמָת) from a different *binyan*, i.e., the Hebrew הוּפְעַל. The same phenomenon sometimes occurs with the Aramaic infinitive as well, as Morag (above, p. 15 note 8) has pointed out on p. 138, n. 92.

THE ARAMAIC FORMS OF GERUND AND INFINITIVE: *BINYAN* קַל

The gerund and the infinitive forms in the Aramaic *binyan* קַל feature a מ־ prefix that is usually vocalized with a *ḥirik* (often together with the vowel-letter י in the full spelling prevalent in the Talmud), as in (לְ)מִכְתַּב, *to write*. This prefix is almost unknown in Biblical Hebrew, but it occurs in the phrase: לְמִקְרָא הָעֵדָה (במדבר י:ב), *to call together the congregation*.[45]

◇   The Aramaic מ־ prefix becomes an integral part of the gerund and the infinitive: it is never deleted. Thus, when the prepositional prefixes ־בְּ, ־כְּ, or ־לְ are used, they are prefaced to the *full form* of the gerund (with the מ־), as in לְמֵיחַת (תרגום אונקלוס לבראשית מד:כו), *to go down*.

◇   This מ־ prefix must not be confused with the prepositional מִ־ prefix, meaning *from* or *than*, which is quite common in Hebrew. The latter is a contraction of the preposition מִן, whose final ן is represented by a strong *dagesh* in the next consonant (unless that consonant is a guttural letter which cannot take a *dagesh*). When the prepositional מִ־ (=מִן) prefix is used with an Aramaic gerund in *binyan* קַל, it is (surprisingly) followed by a ־ל prefix[46] and then the *full* gerund form, which has been augmented by a מ־. In the ־מִלְמְ combination thus created, it is easy to recognize that the initial מִ־ prefix is a contraction of the preposition מִן.

Examples

and they would not desist from praying	וְלָא הֲווֹ שָׁתְקִי... **מִלְמִיבְעֵי** רַחֲמֵי
	(כתובות קד, א)
don't be afraid of going down to Egypt	לָא תִדְחַל **מִלְמֵיחַת** לְמִצְרַיִם
	(ת"א לבראשית מו:ג)

---

45   In his commentary on this passage, Ibn Ezra concludes (after some hesitation) that לְמִקְרָא is indeed a gerund.

46   So too in Mishnaic Hebrew, as in אֵין מְעַכְּבִין אֶת הַתִּינוֹקוֹת **מִלְתְקוֹעַ** (ר"ה פ"ד מ"ח), *[we] do not prevent children from blowing [the shofar]* — but not in Biblical Hebrew where the prepositional prefix מִ־ is attached directly to the verbal noun, as in the passage אַל תִּירָא **מֵרְדָה** מִצְרָיְמָה (בראשית מו:ג).

◇   The vowel under the middle root-letter of the gerund is regularly *pathaḥ*, as in לְמִיכְתַּב.[47] According to the Yemenite tradition, however, whenever the *infinitive* is used to strengthen a finite verbal form, its middle root-letter is vocalized with a *kametz*.

Example

he is certainly mindful of them   מִדְכָּר דְּכִיר לְהוּ (שבת יב, א)

THE ARAMAIC FORMS OF GERUND AND INFINITIVE: OTHER *BINYANIM*

The gerund and the infinitive in the other Aramaic *binyanim* have no מ־ prefix, but they do feature a distinctive ending — for which there is one predominant pattern in the Babylonian Talmud and a different one in the Targumim.

◇   In Babylonian Aramaic: A full *ḥolam* vowel ־וֹ־ is usually inserted between the second and third root-letters and the suffix ־ִי is appended so that the form ends: ־וֹ־ִי. Thus, in *binyan* פַּעֵל: קַבּוֹלֵי, *(to) receive*; in *binyan* אַפְעֵל: אַשְׁלוֹמֵי, *(to) complete*, etc.[48]

◇   In Targum Onkelos: The ending almost always follows the pattern ־ָ־א. Thus, in *binyan* פַּעֵל: קַבָּלָא, *(to) receive*; in *binyan* אַפְעֵל: אַשְׁלָמָא, *(to) complete*. When a gerund from one of these *binyanim* functions like a noun in the *construct state*[49] or when a personal-pronoun suffix is appended to it, the pattern becomes ־ָ־וּת.

Examples

for meeting Moshe (= to meet Moshe)   לְקַדָּמוּת־מֹשֶׁה (ת״א לשמות ד:כז)

to destroy it   לְחַבָּלוּתַהּ (ת״א לבראשית יט:יג)

---

47 For some verbs, a form with the pattern לְמִיכְתְּבָא is also found in the Talmud.

48 The Yemenite reading tradition of the Babylonian Talmud pronounces the ־וֹ־ infix as a diphthong, ־ַו־, *aw*, for example, קַבַּולֵי. Furthermore, it vocalizes the initial root-letter of some of these forms with *shᵉva* — indicating that they are from *binyan* קַל, for example, תְּנַוּיֵי, *to teach*.

49 See above, p. 43, ''The Functions of the Gerund.''

4

PARADIGMS FOR ARAMAIC VERBS IN THE BABYLONIAN TALMUD

This chapter presents the conjugations of thirty Aramaic verbs that appear frequently in the Babylonian Talmud. (Note: An alphabetical index of the verbs appears on both inside covers of this book.)

1. פלג	7. נחת	13. יתב	19. חזי	25. הוי
2. זבן	8. סלק	14. תוב	20. גלי	26. עלל
3. צרך	9. שאל	15. אזל	21. אסי	27. קום
4. עבד	10. ידע	16. אכל	22. תני	28. נוח
5. הדר	11. ילף (אלף)	17. אמר	23. שתי	29. מות
6. נפק	12. נתב/יהב	18. בעי	24. אתי	30. הימן

The first five verbs are called *strong* verbs (שְׁלֵמִים), since all three root-letters are consonants that are retained in all forms of the conjugation. The others are *weak* verbs, since (at least) one of their root-letters is a *weak* consonant that is deleted in some of the verbal forms. Thus, under certain circumstances, the initial root-letter נ is deleted from the roots נפק and נחת, the middle root-letter ל is deleted from סלק, and the middle א from שאל. The initial י is deleted from the roots ילף, ידע and יהב, while the initial א is deleted from the roots אזל and אכל. In the conjugation of the roots אמר, אסי and אתי, both the initial א and the final root-letter are sometimes missing. The verbs numbered 18 through 25 all feature a י as their final root-letter that affects the preceding vowel; in some verbal forms, the י does not appear. The second and third root-letters of עלל are identical, and one ל is often deleted. The middle root-letter of the ("hollow") verbs — קום, נוח and מות — is the vowel-letter ו which is missing in many forms. The verbs numbered 4, 5, 15, 16, 17,

19, 21, 24, 25 and 26 all begin with a guttural consonant that tends to take a *ḥataf-pathaḥ* (⸗) or a *pathaḥ* (⸗) vowel for phonetic reasons.

◊   A verbal root generates many verbal forms that vary according to person, number, gender, tense, or *binyan*. We have produced the paradigms that follow, according to the following principles:

1) Not every verbal form that could theoretically be generated from each verbal-root does occur in the Babylonian Talmud. In these tables, we record *only* those forms that actually occur in the text of the Talmud. They are presented in large **boldface** type.

2) When a specific form occurs *only* with a pronoun suffix that expresses a direct object, that form is presented in **boldface** except for that suffix which appears in regular type, as in חֲזִיתֵיה, *I saw it.*

3) A long dash (——) is used to indicate that we have found no form of that verb in the Talmud for that particular combination of *binyan*, tense, person, number, and gender — even though theoretically such a form could occur.

4) Some of the forms in the paradigms are presented in regular type, without vowels, and enclosed within angle parentheses, as in <אוקמינן>, *we established.* Those forms are found in current printed editions of the Talmud, but they are absent from important Talmudic manuscripts. These grammatical forms, which are inconsistent with the usual patterns, are somewhat difficult to explain.

5) Other forms are printed in **boldface** type, vocalized and enclosed within square brackets, such as [עֲלָא], *she entered.* These forms appear in manuscripts but not in our editions of the Talmud.

6) In some cases when a form sometimes occurs in the Talmud with the vowel-letter י and sometimes without — or, sometimes with a final ן and sometimes without — we have printed the whole form in **boldface** except for that particular letter, which has been printed in regular type. Two such instances are the first י in the form **לִיפַּלִיגו**, *let them disagree*, and the ן in **יָדְעִיתוּן**, *you know.*

7) We have recorded within braces { } in regular type some of the unique vocalizations that are sometimes found in the Yemenite tradition according to Professor Shelomo Morag's

study.[1] Example: {פַּלְגִי}, *I divided*. In some cases, where just one vowel differs, we have recorded in brackets only the part of the form that has the different vowel, as in {פַ ־} **פָלֵיג**, *dividing*.

8) The Aramaic root appears at the beginning of each paradigm, and the parenthesis to the right of each root indicates which root-letter is troublesome. Before each of the thirty paradigms, a survey of the verb explains the meaning of its *binyanim* and the outstanding features of its conjugation. It also presents in **boldface** any additional forms from *binyanim* not included in the paradigm.

9) When two translations are presented at the top of a column of verbal forms, a *slash* between them indicates two alternatives, and a *comma* indicates that the first translation refers to the first Aramaic form and the second to the next one. An *ellipsis mark* (...) after a (Hebrew) translation applies it to the other Aramaic forms in the columns as well — albeit with a slight grammatical adjustment. *Parentheses* ( ) indicate that a word or letter applies only sometimes.

◊   The following index shows which Aramaic *binyanim* are presented in the paradigms of the various Talmudic verbs.

קַל: All of the triliteral roots except for (14) תוב and (21) אסי

אִתְפְּעֵל: (1) פלג, (3) צרך, (4) עבד, (9) שאל, (16) אכל, (17) אמר, (18) בעי, נוח (28), חזי (19)

פַּעֵל: (2) זבן, (5) הדר, (8) סלק, (9) שאל, (20) גלי, (21) אסי, (25) הוי, (26) עלל, קום (27)

אִתְפַּעַל: (2) זבן, (8) סלק, (20) גלי, (21) אסי, (27) קום

אַפְעֵל: (3) צרך, (5) הדר, (6) נפק, (7) נחת, (8) סלק, (9) שאל, (10) ידע, (11) ילך, עלל (26), אתי (24), תני (22), חזי (19), אכל (16), תוב (14), יתב (13), נוח (28), קום (27)

עבד (4): אִשְׁתַּפְעַל and שַׁפְעֵל   תוב (14) and יתב (13): אִתְפְעַל

These thirty paradigms present every class of verb in Babylonian Aramaic. One of the paradigms will serve as a suitable model for almost any Aramaic verb that confronts the student in the Talmud.

---

1   Morag (above, p. 15, note 8). We have not indicated the diphthongs of the Yemenites described on p. 46, note 47 — except in the case of their special קַל infinitive.

(1) פלג (regular)

The Aramaic root פלג, whose basic meaning is *divide*, parallels the Hebrew root חלק in its various meanings. The common meaning in the Talmud is *disagree* or *argue*, as in the noun פְּלוּגְתָּא, *controversy* (= מַחֲלוֹקֶת in Hebrew). In this sense, it appears frequently in the קַל (the simple *binyan*). In the אִתְפְּעֵל *binyan* (the reflexive/passive of the קַל), the ת is almost always missing — an omission that occurs in the אֶת־ *binyanim* of many verbs.

The verb פלג is occasionally used in other *binyanim* — in the פַּעֵל: as in מְפַלִּיג, *distinguishing*; in the אַפְעֵל: אִיפְלִיג,[2] *he was extraordinary*, and מַפְלִיג, *going afar*; and in its reflexive/passive, the אִתַּפְעַל: אִיתַּפְלַג, *it was distant*. However, these occurrences are not frequent enough to warrant the inclusion of those *binyanim* in this paradigm.

	קַל	אִתְפְּעֵל
	PAST	
	divided/shared חָלַקְתִּי, חָלַקְתָּ...	*disagreed/were divided* נֶחְלַק, נֶחְלְקוּ / נִתְחַלְקוּ
I	פְּלַגִי {פְּלִגִי}	——
you m.s.	פְּלַגְתְּ	——
he/it m.	פְּלַג, פְּלִיג	אִיפְּלִיג
they m.	פְּלַגוּ {פְּלִגוּ}, פְּלוּג,[3] פְּלִיגוּ	אִיפְּלִיגוּ, אִיפַּלְגוּ, אִיפְּלוּג[3] ‹אפלגי›

Code: —— = form not found in Talmud   {Yemenite vocalization}   ‹problematic›   [manuscript]

---

2   See p. 20 (top).

3   In the third-person masculine plural of the past and of the future, ־וּ־ is occasionally found as an *infix* within the root, instead of as a *suffix* after the root.

קַל		אִתְפְּעֵל

PARTICIPLE		
ACTIVE *sharing/ dividing* חוֹלֵק, חוֹלְקִים...	**PASSIVE** *divided/ disagreeing* חָלוּק, חֲלוּקָה...	**REFLEXIVE/PASSIVE** *being divided/ disagreeing* מְחֻלָּק / חָלוּק...
m.s.	**פְּלֵיג** {‑פֶּ}	**פְּלִיג**	‹מִיפְלִיג›
f.s.	——	**פְּלִיגָא**	——
m. pl.	**[פָּלְגִי]** {‑פֶּ} ‹פלגין, פלגו›	**פְּלִיגִי** {‑גֵי} ‹פְּלִיגִין›	**מִיפַּלְגִי**[4] {‑גֵי}
f. pl.	**פָּלְגָאן** {‑פֶּ}	——	——

PARTICIPLE WITH SUFFIX		
ACTIVE *divide* חוֹלֵק אֲנִי...	**PASSIVE** *disagree* חָלוּק אֲנִי...	**REFLEXIVE/PASSIVE** *disagree* חֲלוּקִים אָנוּ...
I	**פְּלֵיגְנָא** {‑פֶּ}	**פְּלִיגְנָא**	——
you m.s.	**פָּלְגַתְּ** {פְּלַגְתְּ}	**פְּלִיגַתְּ** {פְּלֵיגַתְּ}	——
we	**פָּלְגִינַן** {פַּלְגִינַן}	**פְּלִיגִינַן** {פְּלֵיגִינַן}	**מִפַּלְגִינַן**
you m. pl.	‹פלגיתו›	**פְּלִיגִיתוּ** {פְּלֵיגִתוּ}	**מִיפַּלְגִיתוּ**

Code: —— = form not found in Talmud {Yemenite vocalization} ‹problematic› [manuscript]

4 This form is commonly pronounced מִיפְּלְגִי by Ashkenazic Jews.

קַל	אִתְפְּעֵל
FUTURE	
will[5] disagree/divide אֶחֱלִק...	*will[5] disagree* אֶחֱלִק
I [אֶפְלוֹג] {-וּג}	‹איתפליג›
you m.s. תִּיפְלוֹג {-וּג}	—
he/it m. לִיפְלוֹג {-וּג}, נִיפְלוֹג {-וּג}	—
she תִּיפְלוֹג {-וּג}	—
we נִפְלוֹג, לִיפְלוֹג {-וּג} ‹ניפליגן›	—
they m. לִיפְלְגוּ, לִיפְלְגִי {-גִי}, לִיפְלוֹג,[6] נִיפְלְגִי {-גִי}, נִפְלוֹג[6] ‹לפלוגי›	לִיפַּלְגוּ, לִיפַּלְגִי {-גִי}, לִיפַּלוֹג,[6] נִפַּלְגוּ, נִיפַּלְגִי {-גִי}, נִפַּלוֹג[6]
IMPERATIVE	
divide! חֲלוֹק!	
m.s. פְּלוֹג	—
m.pl. פְּלוֹגוּ ‹פליגו›	—
GERUND / INFINITIVE	
(to) share/divide לַחֲלוֹק / חָלוֹק	*(to) disagree* לַחֲלוֹק / חָלוֹק
(לְ)**מִיפְלַג** {מִיפְּלָג} ‹מיפליג, מפליג›	(לְ)**אִיפְּלוֹגֵי** ‹איפליגי›

Code: —— = form not found in Talmud   {Yemenite vocalization}   ‹problematic›   [manuscript]

5   or: *let him...*
6   The ו is *infixed*, as explained on p. 50, note 3.

(2) זבן (initial root-letter sibilant)

The Aramaic root זבן means *buy* in *binyan* קַל, *sell* in the פַּעֵל, and *be sold* in the reflexive/passive of the פַּעֵל, *binyan* אִתְפַּעַל. In the אִתְפַּעַל, the first root letter ז has changed places with the ת from the prefix אֶת-,[7] and the ת has become a ד, producing such forms as אִזְדַּבַּן. The latter change came about through the linguistic process of *assimilation* — whereby the voiced consonant ז caused its neighbor, the unvoiced consonant ת, to become the voiced consonant ד.

קַל	פַּעֵל	אִתְפַּעַל
PAST		
bought קָנִיתִי, קָנִיתָ...	*sold* מָכַרְתִּי, מָכַרְתָּ...	*was sold* נִמְכַּר, נִמְכְּרָה
I זְבַנִי {זְבִנִי}, זְבַנִית ‹זְבִינִי›	זַבִּינִי	—
you m.s. זְבַנְתְּ, זְבִינְתַּהּ	זַבֵּינְתְּ	—
he/it m. זְבַן, זְבֵין	זַבֵּין	אִיזְדַּבַּן ‹איזבן›
she/it f. —	זַבְּנָה, זַבְּנָא, זַבִּינָה [זַבִּינָא]	אִזְדַּבְּנָא
we זְבַנַן {זְבִנַן}	—	—
they m. זְבוּן[8]	זַבִּינוּ ‹זבנו›	—

Code: ——— = form not found in Talmud   {Yemenite vocalization}   ‹problematic›   [manuscript]

7   This phenomenon, called *metathesis*, occurs in the *binyanim* that have an אֶת- prefix when the first root letter is either שׁ ,שׂ ,ס ,ז or צ. Examples: אִשְׁתַּמַּשׁ, *he used*; אִסְתַּכַּל, *he looked at*. In the אִשְׁתַּפְעַל *binyan*, it always occurs. Example: אִשְׁתַּעְבּוּד, *they were subjugated*. The same phenomenon occurs in Hebrew in נִשְׁתַּעְבַּד and הִסְתַּכֵּל, הִשְׁתַּמֵּשׁ.

8   The ו is *infixed*, as explained on p. 50, note 3.

קַל		פַּעֵל		אִתְפַּעַל
PARTICIPLE				
ACTIVE	PASSIVE	ACTIVE	PASSIVE	REFL./PASS.
buying	*bought*	*selling*	*sold*	*being sold*
קוֹנֶה...	קָנוּיָה...	מוֹכֵר...	מְכוּרָה...	נִמְכָּר...

	ACTIVE buying קוֹנֶה...	PASSIVE bought קָנוּיָה...	ACTIVE selling מוֹכֵר...	PASSIVE sold מְכוּרָה...	REFL./PASS. being sold נִמְכָּר...
m.s.	זָבֵין {זַ-}	——	מְזַבֵּין	——	מִיזְדַּבַּן ‹מזדבין›
f.s.	——	זְבִינָא	מְזַבְּנָא, מְזַבְּנָה	מְזַבְּנָא	מִיזְדַּבְּנָא, מִיזַּבְּנָה
m.pl.	זָבְנִי {זַבְנֵי}	מְזַבְּנִי {-נֵי}	מְזַבְּנִי {-נֵי}	מְזַבְּנִי {-נִי}	מִיזְדַּבְּנִי {-נֵי} ‹מיזדבנו›
f.pl.	——	——	——	——	מִיזְדַּבְּנָן

PARTICIPLE WITH SUFFIX		
ACTIVE	ACTIVE	REFL./PASS.
buy	*sell*	*are sold*
קוֹנֶה אֲנִי...	מוֹכֵר אֲנִי, מוֹכֵר אַתָּה...	אַתָּה נִמְכָּר...

	ACTIVE buy קוֹנֶה אֲנִי...	ACTIVE sell מוֹכֵר אֲנִי, מוֹכֵר אַתָּה...	REFL./PASS. are sold אַתָּה נִמְכָּר...
I	זָבֵינָנָא {זַ-} ‹זבנינא›	מְזַבֵּינָנָא, מְזַבֵּינָא ‹מזבנינא›	——
you m.s.	——	מְזַבְּנַתְּ {מְזַבֵּינְתְּ} ‹מזבנית›	מִיזְדַּבְּנַתְּ {-בַּנְתְּ}
we	זָבְנִינַן {זַבְנִינַן}	מְזַבְּנִינַן	מִיזְדַּבְּנִינַן
you m. pl.	זָבְנִיתוּ {זַ-}	——	——

Code: —— = form not found in Talmud   {Yemenite vocalization}   ‹problematic›   [manuscript]

קַל	פַּעֵל	אִתְפַּעַל
FUTURE		
will[9] buy אֶקְנֶה, תִּקְנֶה...	*will[9] sell* תִּמְכֹּר, יִמְכֹּר...	*will[9] be sold* יִמָּכֵר, יִמָּכְרוּ
I **אֶיזְבּוֹן** {בּוּן-}, **[אֶזְבֵּין]**	—	—
you m.s. **תִּזְבֵּין**	**תְּזַבֵּין**	—
he/it m. **לִיזַבֵּין, נִיזַבֵּין, נְזַבֵּין** ‹ליזבון, לזבון›	**לִיזְבּוֹן, נִיזְבּוֹן** {בּוּן-}	**נִיזְדַּבַּן**
we **נִיזְבּוֹן** {בּוּן-}	—	—
you m. pl. **תִּזְבְּנוּן, תִּיזְבְּנוּן**	—	—
they m. **לִיזְבְּנוּ, נִזְבּוּן,[10]** **[נִזְבְּנוּ, נְזְבְּנִי]**	**לִיזַבְּנוּ**	**לִיזְדַּבְּנוּ, יִזְדַּבְּנוּן**

	IMPERATIVE	
buy! קְנֵה!, קְנוּ!	*sell!* מְכֹר!, מִכְרוּ!	*sell yourself!* הִמָּכֵר!
m.s. **זְבוֹן, זְבֵין**	**זַבֵּין**	**אִזְדַּבַּן**
m.pl. **זְבִינוּ**	**זַבִּינוּ** ‹זבנו›	—

	GERUND / INFINITIVE	
(to) buy לִקְנוֹת / קָנֹה	*(to) sell* לִמְכֹּר / מָכֹר	*"be sold"* הִמָּכֵר
(לְ)מִיזְבַּן {מִיזְבָּן}	**(לְ)זַבּוֹנֵי**	**אִיזְדַּבּוֹנֵי**

9   or: *let him...*
10   The ו is *infixed*, as explained on p. 50, note 3.

(3) צרך (initial root-letter emphatic sibilant)

The verb צרך expresses *necessity* in both the קַל and the אִתְפְּעֵל. In the אִתְפְּעֵל (as in the Hebrew הִתְפַּעֵל), the first root letter צ has changed places with the ת from the prefix אִת־[11], and the ת has become a ט — producing such forms as אִיצְטְרִיךְ. The latter change came about through the process of *assimilation*, whereby the emphatic consonant צ caused the neighboring consonant ת to become the emphatic consonant ט.[12] The אַפְעֵל *binyan* has a causative meaning: *make necessary* or *require*.

	קַל	אִתְפְּעֵל	אַפְעֵל
		PAST	
		was required …נִצְרַכְתִּי / הָצְרַכְתִּי	*required* …הָצְרִיךְ
I	——	אִיצְטְרִיכִי	——
he/it m.	——	אִיצְטְרִיךְ	אַצְרְכֵיה
it f.	——	אִיצְטְרִיכָא	——
we	——	——	אַצְרְכִינֵיה
they m.	——	אִיצְטְרִיכוּ \<איצטריכי\>	אַצְרוּךְ, [13] אַצְרְכוּה

Code: —— = form not found in Talmud   {Yemenite vocalization}   \<problematic\>   **[manuscript]**

11   Cf. the survey of the previous verb and note 6 on p. 53.
12   In the traditional pronunciation of some Oriental Jews, especially the Yemenites, צ is still pronounced as an emphatic *s* sound and ט as an emphatic *t* sound.
13   The ו is *infixed*, as explained on p. 50, note 3.

קַל	אִתְפְּעֵל	אַפְעֵל

PARTICIPLE		
PASSIVE *necessary/needed* צְרִיכָה, צְרִיכִים	REFLEXIVE/PASSIVE *necessary/needed* נִצְרָךְ...	ACTIVE *requiring* מַצְרִיךְ...

	PASSIVE *necessary/needed* צְרִיכָה, צְרִיכִים	REFLEXIVE/PASSIVE *necessary/needed* נִצְרָךְ...	ACTIVE *requiring* מַצְרִיךְ...
m.s.	——	מִיצְטְרִיךְ ‹מיצריך›	מַצְרֵיךְ
f.s.	צְרִיכָא	מִיצְטָרְכָא	——
m.pl.	צְרִיכִי {-כֵי}	מִצְטָרְכִי {-כֵי}	מַצְרְכִי {-כֵי}

PARTICIPLE WITH SUFFIX		
PASSIVE *need* אֲנִי צְרִיךְ...	REFLEXIVE/PASSIVE *need* אֲנִי נִצְרָךְ	ACTIVE *require* מַצְרִיךְ אַתָּה...

	PASSIVE *need* אֲנִי צְרִיךְ...	REFLEXIVE/PASSIVE *need* אֲנִי נִצְרָךְ	ACTIVE *require* מַצְרִיךְ אַתָּה...
I	צְרִיכְנָא	מִצְטְרִיכְנָא	——
you m.s.	צְרִיכַתְ {צְרֵיכְתְּ}	——	מַצְרְכַתְ {מַצְרַכְתְּ}
we	——	——	מַצְרְכִינָן
you m. pl.	צְרִיכִיתוּ {צְרֵיכְתּוּ}	——	——

Code: —— = form not found in Talmud   {Yemenite vocalization}   ‹problematic›   [manuscript]

קַל	אִתְפְּעֵל	אַפְעֵל

		FUTURE	

			let us require
			נַצְרִיך
we	—	—	**נַצְרְכַה**
			‹לצרכה, ליצרכה›

		IMPERATIVE	

			require!
			הַצְרֵך!
m.s.	—	—	**[אַצְרְכַה]**

		INFINITIVE	

"be necessary"		*"require"*
צְרוֹך		הַצְרֵך
מִיצְרַך {מִיצְרָך}	—	**אַצְרוֹכֵי**

Code: ——— = form not found in Talmud   {Yemenite vocalization}   ‹problematic›   **[manuscript]**

58

(4) עבד (initial guttural)

The Aramaic verb עבד usually means *do* or *make* in the קַל, like עשׂה in Hebrew — but not like the Hebrew verb עבד, *work* (which is rendered in Aramaic by the verb פלח). The Aramaic *binyan* אֶתְפְּעֵל of עבד, like the נִפְעַל of עשׂה, usually means *become*. The active participle מְעַבֵּד from the rare *binyan* פַּעֵל (not presented in the paradigms below), means *compelling* — like the Hebrew פִּעֵל participle of עשׂה, מְעַשֶּׂה.

Some forms of the Aramaic verb עבד, however, do correspond to the Hebrew עבד. The passive participle מְעַבַּד from *binyan* פַּעֵל (not in the paradigm) means *prepared* or *treated* (like the Hebrew מְעֻבָּד). Forms from *binyan* שַׁפְעֵל (which may also be regarded as a four-letter root שעבד, as on p. 289, n. 10), such as the participle מְשַׁעְבֵּד, *subjugating*, and from the reflexive/passive *binyan* אִשְׁתַּפְעַל, such as the participle מִשְׁתַּעְבַּד, *subjugated*, mean the same as their Hebrew counterparts from the root עבד. Surprising is the expression אִישְׁתַּעְבְּדוּ בְהוּ, *they subjugated them*, from *binyan* אִשְׁתַּפְעַל in the past tense, which seems to have an active meaning (ע"ז ב,ב ועוד).[14]

אִשְׁתַּפְעַל	שַׁפְעֵל	אִתְפְּעֵל	קַל
	PAST (singular)		
	subjugated שֶׁעֲבֵּד...	was done/became נַעֲשָׂה, נֶעֶשְׂתָה	did/made עָשִׂיתִי...
—	—	—	עֲבַדִי {עַבְדִי} ‹עבדית›	I
—	—	—	עֲבַדְתְּ	you m.s.
—	שַׁעֲבֵּיד	אִתְעֲבִיד	עֲבַד, עֲבִיד	he/it m.
—	—	אִתְעֲבִידָא	עֲבַדָא, עֲבַדָה {עַבְדָא/ה}	she/it f.

Code: ――― = form not found in Talmud   {Yemenite vocalization}   ‹problematic›   **[manuscript]**

14   Cf. the uncommon use of the Hebrew *binyan* הִתְפַּעֵל with a transitive meaning (for example, in ויקרא כה:מו and שמות לג:ו).

אִשְׁתַּפְעַל	שַׁפְעֵל	אִתְפְּעֵל	קַל

PAST (plural)			
subjugated/ were subjugated	subjugated		did/made
שֶׁעְבְּדוּ / נִשְׁתַּעְבְּדוּ	שִׁעְבַּדְנוּ		עֲשִׂיתֶם...

	אִשְׁתַּפְעַל	שַׁפְעֵל	אִתְפְּעֵל	קַל
we	—	[שַׁעְבְּדַן]	—	—
you m. pl.	—	—	—	עֲבַדִיתוּ, עֲבִידִיתוּ
they m.	אִישְׁתַּעְבְּדוּ, אִישְׁתַּעְבּוּד־[15] ⟨אישתעבדי⟩	—	—	עֲבַדוּ, עֲבוּד־[15]

ACTIVE PARTICIPLE			
	subjugating		doing/making
	מְשַׁעְבֵּד...		עוֹשֶׂה...

	מְשַׁעְבֵּד... (subjugating)		עוֹשֶׂה... (doing/making)
m.s.	מְשַׁעְבֵּיד		עָבֵיד {עֲ־}
f.s.	מְשַׁעְבְּדָא		עָבְדָא {עֲ־}, עָבְדָה {עֲ־}
m.pl.	מְשַׁעְבְּדִי {־דֵי}		עָבְדִי {עַבְדֵי}, עָבְדִין
f.pl.	—		עָבְדָן {עֲ־}

Code: ——— = form not found in Talmud   {Yemenite vocalization}   ⟨problematic⟩   [manuscript]

15   The ו is *infixed*, as explained on p. 50, note 3.

אִשְׁתַּפְעַל	שַׁפְעֵל	אִתְפְּעֵל	קַל

REFLEXIVE / PASSIVE PARTICIPLE			
becoming subjugated מִשְׁתַּעְבֵּד...	subjugated מְשַׁעְבַּד...	done/ becoming נַעֲשֶׂה...	liable/ used to עָשׂוּי...

	קַל	אִתְפְּעֵל	שַׁפְעֵל	אִשְׁתַּפְעַל
m.s.	עֲבִיד	מִיתְעֲבִיד	מְשַׁעְבַּד	מִשְׁתַּעְבַּד
f.s.	עֲבִידָא	מִתְעַבְדָא	מְשַׁעְבְּדָא	מִשְׁתַּעְבְּדָא
m.pl.	עֲבִידִי {־דֵי}	מִתְעַבְדִין	מְשַׁעְבְּדִי {־דֵי}	מִשְׁתַּעְבְּדִי {־דֵי}
f.pl.	עֲבִידָן	——	מְשַׁעְבְּדָן	——

PARTICIPLE WITH SUFFIX			
ACTIVE am doing עוֹשֶׂה אֲנִי...		REFLEXIVE / PASSIVE become subjugated	
		מְשַׁעְבַּד אֲנִי	מִשְׁתַּעְבֵּד אֲנִי

	ACTIVE		REFLEXIVE / PASSIVE	
I	עָבֵידְנָא {עָ־} ‹עבדינא›	——	[מְשַׁעְבַּדְנָא] ‹שעבדנא›	מִשְׁתַּעְבַּדְנָא
you m.s.	עָבְדַתְּ {עֲבַדְתְּ} ‹עבידת›	——	——	——
we	עָבְדִינַן {עֲבְדִינַן}	——	——	——
you m. pl.	עָבְדִיתוּ {עָ־} ‹עבידתו›, עָבְדִיתוּן {עָ־} ‹עבידתון›	——	——	——

Code: —— = form not found in Talmud   {Yemenite vocalization}   ‹problematic›   [manuscript]

	קַל	אִתְפְּעַל	שַׁפְעַל	אִשְׁתַּפְעַל
	FUTURE			
	will[16] make/do אֶעֱשֶׂה	will[16] become יֵעָשֶׂה / תֵּעָשֶׂה		will[16] be subjugated יִשְׁתַּעְבֵּד
I	**אִיעֱבֵיד**	——	——	——
you m.s.	**תֶּעֱבֵיד** {תִּעְבֵּיד}, **תִּיעֱבֵד** {תִּעְבֵּיד}, **תִּיעֱבֵיד** {תִּעְבֵּיד}	——	——	——
you f.s.	**תַּעַבְדִי** {תִּעְבְּדִי}	——	——	——
he/it. m	**לִיעֱבֵיד** {לְעֱבֵיד}, **נִיעֱבֵיד** {נֶעְבֵּיד}, **יֶעֱבֵיד** {יְעְבֵּיד}	**לִיתְעֲבֵיד,** **לִיעֲבֵד**	——	**לִשְׁתַּעְבֵּיד**
she/it f.	**תִּיעֱבֵיד** {תִּיעֲבֵד}	**תִּתְעֲבֵיד,** **תִּיעֲבֵיד**	——	——
we	**נִיעֱבֵיד** {נֶעְבֵּיד} <ניעבוד, נעבוד>	——	——	——
you m. pl.	**תַּעַבְדוּ** {תִּעְבְּדוּ} <תעבידו>	——	——	——
they m.	**לִיעֶבְדוּ** {לִיעְבְּדוּ} <ליעבדי, לעבדי>, **נִיעֶבְדוּ** {נִיעְבְּדוּ}	——	——	——

Code: —— = form not found in Talmud   {Yemenite vocalization}   <problematic>   **[manuscript]**

16   or: *let him...*

קַל	אִתְפְּעֵל	שַׁפְעֵל	אִשְׁתַּפְעַל

	IMPERATIVE			
	do!/make! ...!עֲשֵׂה			
m.s.	**עֲבֵיד**	——	——	——
f.s.	**עֲבִידִי**	——	——	——
m.pl.	**עֲבִידוּ** ‹עבידי›	——	——	——

	GERUND / INFINITIVE		
	(to) do/make לַעֲשׂוֹת / עָשֹׂה		*"subjugate"* שַׁעֲבֵּד	*"be subjugated"* הִשְׁתַּעֲבֵּד
	(לְ)מִיעֱבַד {מִעְבָּד}	——	**שַׁעֲבוֹדֵי** ‹שיעבודי›	**אִישְׁתַּעֲבוֹדֵי**

Code: —— = form not found in Talmud　{Yemenite vocalization}　‹problematic›　**[manuscript]**

(5) הדר (initial and final guttural)

The Aramaic הדר is the equivalent of the Hebrew verb חזר, *return* — with the Aramaic ה and ד parallel to the Hebrew ח and ז, respectively. The Aramaic verb is used in three *binyanim*: the קַל, the פַּעֵל, and the אַפְעֵל. Like the Hebrew הִפְעִיל, *binyan* אַפְעֵל of this verb means *bring back*, *return* (with a direct object), as opposed to *return* in the sense of *go back* or *come back* in the קַל.

The פַּעֵל, which is used with the preposition אַ־, means *seek (after)* or *pursue (zealously)*. In our printed editions of the Talmud — but not in manuscripts — several forms of the past and the imperative of הדר are spelled as if they were from *binyan* פַּעֵל, even though they have a causative meaning like אַפְעֵל. We have presented them within angle parentheses < > in the פַּעֵל column of our paradigm.

קַל	פַּעֵל	אַפְעֵל
	PAST (singular)	
returned/went back חָזַרְתִּי...	*returned/brought back* הֶחֱזִיר	*returned/brought back* הֶחֱזַרְתִּי...
I ─ הֲדַרִי {הֲדְרִי}	—	אַהְדְּרִי {־דְּרִי}
you m.s. ─ הֲדַרְתְּ	—	אַהְדַּרְתְּ {־דַּרְתְּ}
he/it m. ─ הֲדַר [17] <איהדר>	<הדר>	אַהְדַּר
she/it f. ─ הֲדַרָה, הֲדַרָא {הַדְרָה/הַדְרָא}	—	אַהְדְּרָא

Code:　──── = form not found in Talmud　{Yemenite vocalization}　<problematic>　**[manuscript]**

17　Note: הֲדַר, ostensibly the third-person masculine singular form of the past tense, is often used before another verb as an adverb. In this usage, הֲדַר does not necessarily agree in tense, person, and number with the other verb. Example: הֲדַר פְּלִיגִי (חולין פו, א), *subsequently disagreeing*.

קַל	פְּעַל	אַפְעֵל

PAST (plural)		
returned/went back	*returned/brought back*	*returned/brought back*
חֲזַרְנוּ...	הֶחֱזִירוּ	הֶחֱזִירוּ

	קַל	פְּעַל	אַפְעֵל
we	{הַדְרַן} הֲדַרַן	—	—
they m.	הֲדַרוּ, הֲדוּר[18]	‹הדרוה›	אַהְדְּרוּ {־דְרוּ}, אַהְדּוּר[18]‹אהדרי›
they f.	הֲדַרָן	—	—

PARTICIPLE			
ACTIVE	PASSIVE	ACTIVE	ACTIVE
returning/ going back	*surrounded*	*pursuing (zealously)*	*returning/ bringing back*
חוֹזֵר...	מֻקָּף	מְחַזֵּר...	מַחֲזִיר...

	ACTIVE	PASSIVE	ACTIVE	ACTIVE
m.s.	הָדַר	הָדִיר	מְהַדַּר ‹מיהדר›	מַהְדַּר ‹מיהדר›
f.s.	הָדְרָא {־הַ}, הָדְרָה {־הַ}	—	מְהַדְרָא	מַהְדְּרָא
m.pl.	הָדְרֵי {־הַ} ‹הדרין›	—	מְהַדְרֵי {־רֵי}	מַהְדְּרֵי {־רֵי}, מַהְדְּרִין, מַהְדְּרוּ
f.pl.	הָדְרָן {־הַ}	—	—	—

Code: —— = form not found in Talmud   {Yemenite vocalization}   ‹problematic›   [manuscript]

18   The ו is *infixed*, as explained on p. 50, note 3.

קַל	פַּעֵל	אַפְעֵל

ACTIVE PARTICIPLE WITH SUFFIX		
go back חוֹזֵר אֲנִי...	*pursue* מְחַזֵּר אֲנִי...	*bring back* מַחֲזִיר אֲנִי...

	קַל	פַּעֵל	אַפְעֵל
I	הָדַרְנָא {הַ-}	מְהַדַּרְנָא	מַהְדַּרְנָא
you m.s.	הָדְרַתְּ {הֲדַרְתְּ}	—	מַהְדַּרַתְּ {-דַרְתְּ}
we	—	מְהַדְרִינָן	מַהְדְּרִינַן
you m. pl.	הָדְרִיתוּ {הַ-}	—	מַהְדְּרִיתוּ

FUTURE		
will[19] *go back* אֶחְזֹר...	*will*[19] *seek/go around* יְחַזֵּר / יַקִּיף	*will*[19] *bring back* אַחְזִיר...

	קַל	פַּעֵל	אַפְעֵל
I	אֶיהְדַר {איהדר}	—	אַהְדַר
you m.s.	תֶּהְדַר {תהדר}	—	—
he/it m.	לֶיהְדַר {ליהדר}, נֶיהְדַר {ניהדר}	לִיהַדַּר, נְהַדַּר	לַהְדַּר, לִיהְדַּר, נַהְדַּר, נִיהְדַּר
she/it f.	תֶּיהְדַר {תיהדר}	—	—
we	נֶיהְדַר {נהדר}	—	—
they m.	לֵיהְדְּרוּ, נֵיהְדְּרוּ	—	נַהְדְּרוּ, נִיהְדְּרוּ, לִיהְדְּרוּ

Code: —— = form not found in Talmud   {Yemenite vocalization}   <problematic>   [manuscript]

19   or: *let him...*

קַל	פַּעֵל	אַפְעֵל

	IMPERATIVE		
	return!/go back! ...חֲזֹר!	*return!/bring back!* ...הַחֲזֵר!	*return!/bring back!* ...הַחֲזֵר!
m.s.	הֲדַר	‹הדר›	אַהְדַּר
m.pl.	הֲדַרוּ, הֲדוּר[20]	‹הדרו›	אַהְדְּרוּ {דַּ-ּ}, אַהְדּוּר[20] ‹אהדורו›

	GERUND / INFINITIVE		
	(to) go back לַחֲזֹר / חָזֹר	*to pursue/seek* לְחַזֵּר	*to bring back* לְהַחֲזִיר
	(לְ)מֵיהֲדַר {מִהְדָּר} ‹מיהדרי›	(לְ)הַדּוּרֵי 	(לְ)אַהְדּוּרֵי

Code: ——— = form not found in Talmud   {Yemenite vocalization}   <problematic>   [manuscript]

20   The וֹ is *infixed*, as explained on p. 50, note 3.

(6) נפק (initial נ)

The Aramaic root נפק, whose basic meaning is *go out*, is parallel to the Hebrew root יצא in its various meanings. The verb is used in the קַל and אַפְעֵל *binyanim*. When the first root letter נ has no vowel — in the future and infinitive of the קַל and throughout the אַפְעֵל — it is usually assimilated to the next consonant. In effect, this means that the נ is deleted and represented by the *dagesh forte* in the פ. Thus instead of אֶנְפּוֹק, *I will go out*, the form is אֵיפּוֹק, and instead of אַנְפֵּיק the form is אַפֵּיק in its several meanings.[21]

Besides the forms listed in the tables below, the feminine passive participle, מַפְּקָא, *excluded*, from *binyan* אַפְעֵל, also appears in the Talmud several times.

	קַל	אַפְעֵל
	PAST	
	went out ...יָצָאתִי	*took out* ...הוֹצֵאתִי
I	נְפַקִי {נַפְּקִי}	אַפֵּיקִית
you m.s.	——	אַפֵּיקְתְּ
he/it m.	נְפַק <נפיק>	אַפֵּיק
she/it f.	נְפַקָה, נְפַקָא {נַפְּקה/א}, נָפַקַת	אַפְּקָא, אַפְּקָה
they m.	נְפַקוּ {נַפְּקוּ}, נְפוּק[22]	אַפִּיקוּ, אַפְּקוּ

Code: —— = form not found in Talmud   {Yemenite vocalization}   <problematic>   [manuscript]

21 See Chapter 6, "Homographs and Homonyms," especially p. 226.
22 The ו is *infixed*, as explained on p. 50, note 3.

קַל	אַפְעֵל

	PARTICIPLE		
	ACTIVE *going out* יוֹצֵא...	ACTIVE *taking out* מוֹצִיא...	PASSIVE *excluded* מוּצֵאת
m.s.	נָפֵיק {נַ-}	מַפֵּיק	——
f.s.	נָפְקָא {נַ-}	מַפְּקָא, מַפְּקָה	מַפְּקָא
m.pl.	נָפְקִי {נַפְקֵי}, נָפְקִין	מַפְּקִי {-קֵי}, מַפְּקִין, מַפְּקוּ	——
f.pl.	נָפְקָן {נַ-}	——	——

	ACTIVE PARTICIPLE WITH SUFFIX	
	go out יוֹצֵא אֲנִי...	*take out* מוֹצִיא אֲנִי...
I	נָפֵיקְנָא {נַ-}	מַפֵּיקְנָא
you m.s.	——	מַפְּקַתְּ {מַפַּקְתְּ}
we	נָפְקִינַן {נַפְקִינַן}	מַפְּקִינַן
you m. pl.	נָפְקִיתוּ {נַ-}	——

Code: —— = form not found in Talmud   {Yemenite vocalization}   <problematic>   [manuscript]

קַל	אַפְעֵל
FUTURE	
will[23] go out ...אֵצֵא	will[23] take out ...אוֹצִיא

	קַל	אַפְעֵל
I	אֵיפּוֹק	אַפֵּיק
you m.s.	‹תיפוק›	תַּפֵּיק
he/it m.	לִיפּוֹק, נִיפּוֹק, יְפּוֹק	נַפֵּיק, לַפְקֵיה, לִיפְּקַה
she/it f.	תִּיפּוֹק[24]	תַּפֵּיק
we	נִיפּוֹק	נַפְקֵיה
you m. pl.	——	תַּפֵּיקוּ
they m.	לִיפְּקוּ, לִיפְּקוּן, נִיפְּקוּ, יְפְּקוּן	——

IMPERATIVE	
go out ...צֵא!	take out ...הוֹצֵא!

	קַל	אַפְעֵל
m.s.	פּוּק	אַפֵּיק
m.pl.	פּוּקוּ	אַפִּיקוּ

GERUND / INFINITIVE	
(to) go out לָצֵאת / יְצֹא	(to) take out לְהוֹצִיא / הוֹצֵא

קַל	אַפְעֵל
(לְ)מִיפַּק {מִיפָּק}	(לְ)אַפּוֹקֵי

Code: —— = form not found in Talmud   {Yemenite vocalization}   ‹problematic›   **[manuscript]**

23   or: *let him...*
24   This form (especially) is popularly pronounced תֵּיפוּק by Ashkenazi Jews.

(7) נחת (initial נ, second root-letter guttural)

The Aramaic root נחת has the same meaning as the Hebrew verb ירד, *go down*, and it appears in the *binyan* קַל and in the causative *binyan* אַפְעֵל where it means *bring down*.

	קַל	אַפְעֵל
	PAST	
	went down יָרַד...	*brought down/placed* הוֹרִיד / הִנִּיחַ...
he/it m.	נְחַת, נָחֵית	אַחֵית, אַנְחֲתֵיה
she/it f.	נְחַתַת, [נְחַתָא] ‹נחיתא›	אַחֲתָא
we	——	אַחֲתִינַן
they m.	נְחַתוּ {נְחְ-}, נְחִיתוּ, נָחוּת[25]	אַחִיתוּ
	PARTICIPLE	
	ACTIVE *going down* יוֹרֵד...	ACTIVE *bringing down/ placing* מוֹרִיד / מַנִּיחַ	PASSIVE *brought down/ placed* מוּרָד / מֻנָּח...
m.s.	נָחֵית {נָ-}	מַחֵית	מַחַת, מַחֵית
f.s.	נָחֲתָא, נָחֲתָה	——	מַחֲתָא
m.pl.	נָחֲתִי {-תֵי}, נָחֲתִין ‹נחיתי›	——	מַחֲתִי {-תֵי}
f.pl.	——	——	מַחֲתָן

Code: —— = form not found in Talmud   {Yemenite vocalization}   ‹problematic›   [manuscript]

25 The ו is *infixed*, as explained on p. 50, note 3.

קַל	אַפְעֵל
ACTIVE PARTICIPLE WITH SUFFIX	
go down יוֹרֵד אֲנִי...	*bring down* מוֹרִידִים אָנוּ
I	נָחֵיתְנָא {נַ-}	——
you m.s.	נָחֵיתַתְּ	——
we	נָחֵתִינַן {נַחְתִינַן}	מַחֲתִינַן

קַל	אַפְעֵל
FUTURE	
will[26] go down אֵרֵד...	*will[26] place* יָשִׂים
I	אֵיחוֹת	——
you m.s.	תֵּיחוֹת	——
he/it m.	לִינְחוֹת[27] {לִינְחוֹת}, נֵיחוֹת	[נַחֲתַהּ] ‹נחתיה›
she/it f.	תֵּיחוֹת	——
we	‹ניחות, יחות›	——
you m. pl.	תֵּיחוֹתוּ	——

Code: —— = form not found in Talmud   {Yemenite vocalization}   ‹problematic›   [manuscript]

26   or: *let him...*
27   In this form, the first root-letter נ remains intact!

קַל	אַפְעֵל
IMPERATIVE	
go down! רֵד!, רְדוּ!	*put down!/bring down!* הַנַּח!, הוֹרִידוּ!

	קַל	אַפְעֵל
m.s.	חוּת, נְחֵית	אַחֵית
m.pl.	חוּתוּ	אַחִיתוּן

GERUND / INFINITIVE	
to go down לָרֶדֶת	*(to) bring down* לְהוֹרִיד / הוֹרֵד
(לְ)מֵיחַת >לחות<	(לְ)אַחוֹתֵי

Code: ——— = form not found in Talmud   {Yemenite vocalization}   <problematic>   **[manuscript]**

73

(8) סלק (middle root-letter ל)

The Aramaic root סלק, whose basic meaning is *go up*, is parallel to the Hebrew root עלה in *binyan* קַל and *binyan* אַפְעֵל. The second root-letter ל is usually *assimilated* to the ס in the future, in the imperative and in the infinitive of *binyan* קַל and throughout the entire *binyan* אַפְעֵל. In effect, the ל is deleted and represented by a *dagesh* in the ס, so that instead of אֶסְלַק, *I will go up*, the form is אֵיסַּק,[28] and instead of מַסְלֵיק, *bringing up*, the form is מַסֵּיק. Thus the root סלק behaves as *if* it were נסק.[29]

In the past of the קַל, the vowel *tzerei* or *ḥirik*, followed by a vowel-letter י, is used under the middle root-letter ל (rather than *pathaḥ*), as in סְלֵיק, *he went up*. In *binyan* פַּעֵל, סַלֵּק means *remove*, like סִלֵּק in the Hebrew פִּעֵל, and in the reflexive of פַּעֵל, the אִתְפַּעֵל, it denotes *remove oneself* or *depart*.[30] In the latter *binyan*, the first root letter ס changes places with the ת from the אִתְ- prefix to form אִיסְתַּלַּק, *he departed*, like the Hebrew הִסְתַּלֵּק.

קַל	פַּעֵל	אִתְפַּעֵל	אַפְעֵל
PAST (singular)			
went up עָלִיתִי...	*removed* סִלַּקְתִּי...	*departed* נֶעֱלָה / נִסְתַּלַּק...	*brought up* הֶעֱלֵיתָ...
I סְלֵיקִי {סְלֵי-, סַלְ-}, סְלֵיקִית ‹סליקת›	סַלֵּיקִי	—	—
you m.s. סְלֵיקְתְּ	סַלֵּיקְתְּ	—	אַסֵּיקְתֵּיה
he/it m. סְלֵיק	סַלֵּיק ‹-ליק›	אִיסְתַּלַּק ‹-ליק›	אַסֵּיק
she/it f. סְלֵיקָא	—	אִיסְתַּלְּקָא	אַסְּקָא

28 Compare the Hebrew verbal form אֶסַּק (תהלים קלט:ח).
29 Although it is not at all clear that the root נסק really exists in Aramaic, M. Jastrow's *A Dictionary of the Targumim, the Talmud Babli and Yerushalmi and the Midrashic Literature* (New York 1903) and the C.J. and B. Kasowski's *Concordance* (אוצר לשון התלמוד 42 vols., Jerusalem, 1954-1982) present forms that are missing the ל as part of a separate verbal entry under נסק.
30 Cf. the Biblical Hebrew נַעֲלָה and Rashi's commentary on במדבר ט:יז.

קַל	פַּעֵל	אִתְפְּעַל	אַפְעֵל

		PAST (plural)		
	went up עֲלִינוּ...	*removed* סַלַּקְנוּ...	*departed* נִסְתַּלַּקְתֶּם...	*brought up* הֶעֱלוּ...
we	סְלֵיקִינַן {סַל-}	סַלֵּיקְנָא	—	—
you m. pl.	—	—	[אִסְתַּלְּקִיתוּ] ‹אסתליקתו›	—
they m.	סְלִיקוּ, סָלוּק[31] ‹סקו›	סַלִּיקוּ	אִסְתַּלְּקוּ {-לָקוּ} ‹איסתליקו›, אִיסְתַּלּוּק[31]	אַסִּיקוּ אסוקינהו

		PARTICIPLE		
	ACTIVE *going up* עוֹלֶה...	**ACTIVE** *removing* מְסַלֵּק...	**REFLEXIVE** *departing* מִסְתַּלֵּק	**ACTIVE** *bringing up* מַעֲלֶה...
m.s.	סָלֵיק {סָ-}	מְסַלֵּיק	מִיסְתַּלַּק	מַסֵּיק
f.s.	סָלְקָא {סָ-}	—	—	מַסְּקָא
m.pl.	סָלְקִי {סַלְקִי}, סָלְקִין ‹סלקו›	מְסַלְּקִי {-קִי}	—	מַסְּקִי {-קִי}, מַסְּקוּ
f.pl.	סָלְקָן {סָ-}	—	—	מַסְּקָן

Code: ——— = form not found in Talmud   {Yemenite vocalization}   ‹problematic›   [manuscript]

---

31 The ו is *infixed*, as explained on p. 50, note 3.

	קַל	פַּעֵל	אִתְפְּעַל	אַפְעֵל
	PARTICIPLE WITH SUFFIX			
	ACTIVE *go up* ...עוֹלֶה אֲנִי	ACTIVE *remove* ...מְסַלֵּק אֲנִי	REFLEXIVE *depart* ...מִסְתַּלֵּק אֲנִי	ACTIVE *bring up* ...מַעֲלֶה אֲנִי
I	סָלֵיקְנָא {סְ-}	מְסַלֵּיקְנָא ‹מסלקינא›	מִסְתַּלְּקְנָא	מַסֵּיקְנָא
you m.s.	סָלְקַתְּ {סְלַקְתְּ}	—	—	—
we	סָלְקִינַן {סַלְקִינַן}	מְסַלְּקִינַן	—	מַסְּקִינַן
you m. pl.	—	מְסַלְּקִיתוּ	מִסְתַּלְּקִיתוּ	
	FUTURE (singular)			
	will[32] go up ...אֶעֱלֶה	*will[32] remove* ...אֲסַלֵּק		*will[32] bring up* יַעֲלֶה
I	אֵיסַּק	אִיסַלְּקִינֵיהּ	—	—
he/it m.	לֵיסַּק, נֵיסַּק, יֵיסַּק, לֵיסְלוֹק {-לוּק}, לֵיסְלֵיק	לְסַלְּקִינְהוּ	—	לַסְּקֵיהּ, נַסְּקִינְהוּ
she/it f.	תֵּיסַּק ‹תיסלק›	—	—	—

Code: —— = form not found in Talmud   {Yemenite vocalization}   ‹problematic›   **[manuscript]**

32   or: *let him...*

קַל	פַּעֵל	אִתְפַּעַל	אַפְעֵל

| FUTURE (plural) | | | |
| *will*[33] *go up*
 נַעֲלֶה, יַעֲלוּ | *will*[33] *remove*
 יְסַלְקוּ | *will*[33] *depart*
 יִסְתַּלְקוּ | |

	קַל	פַּעֵל	אִתְפַּעַל	אַפְעֵל
we	**נִיסַק**	——	——	——
they m.	**לִיסְקוּ, נִסְקוּ,** ‹לִיסַלְקוּ›	**לִיסַלְקוּ**	**לִסְתַּלְקוּ**	——

| IMPERATIVE | | | |
| *go up!*
 עֲלֵה! | *remove!*
 ...סַלֵק! | *depart!*
 הִסְתַּלֵק! | *bring up!*
 ...הַעֲלֵה! |

	קַל	פַּעֵל	אִתְפַּעַל	אַפְעֵל
m.s.	**סַק** ‹סְלִיק›	**סַלֵיק**	**אִיסְתַּלַק**	**אַסֵיק**
m.pl.	——	**סַלֵיקוּ**	——	**אַסֵיקוּ**

| GERUND / INFINITIVE | | | |
| *(to) go up*
 לַעֲלוֹת / עֲלֹה | *(to) remove*
 (לְ)סַלֵק | *(to) depart*
 (לְ)הִסְתַּלֵק | *(to) bring up*
 לְהַעֲלוֹת / הַעֲלֵה |

	קַל	פַּעֵל	אִתְפַּעַל	אַפְעֵל
	לְמִיסַק, (לְ)**מִיסְלַק** {מִיסְלָק}	(לְ)**סַלוֹקֵי**	(לְ)**אִיסְתַּלוֹקֵי**	(לְ)**אַסוֹקֵי**

Code: —— = form not found in Talmud　{Yemenite vocalization}　‹problematic›　**[manuscript]**

33　or: *let us, let them.*

(9) שאל (middle root-letter א)

This root means *ask* or *borrow* in *binyan* קַל and *binyan* פַּעֵל. In *binyan* אִתְפְּעֵל, it means *let oneself be questioned*, i.e., before a *ḥakham* in order to be absolved from a vow. In *binyan* אַפְעֵל, the meaning is causative, *lend* (= *cause to borrow*), like the Hebrew הִפְעִיל. The second root-letter א complicates the conjugation: It is represented by the diphthong ‑יִ in some of the forms of *binyan* קַל and *binyan* פַּעֵל, and it is omitted throughout *binyan* אִתְפְּעֵל. The אַפְעֵל features the pattern אוֹשִׁיל, in the manner of hollow verbs like קום (e.g., אוֹקִים) and verbs with initial י like ידע (e.g., אוֹדַע).

קַל	אִתְפְּעֵל	פַּעֵל	אַפְעֵל
PAST			
asked/ borrowed ...שָׁאַלְתִּי	*submitted to questioning* נִשְׁאַלְתִּי, נִשְׁאַל	*asked/ borrowed* שָׁאַל, שָׁאֲלוּ	*lent* הִשְׁאִיל
I	שְׁאֵילִית, שְׁאֵילִי, ‹שׁאלי›	אִיתְשְׁלִי {אִתְשְׁלִי}	——	——
he/it m.	שְׁאֵיל	אִיתְשְׁיל {‑תְּ‑}	שַׁיּילָה ‹שׁייל›	אוֹשְׁלַהּ
we	שְׁאֵילְנָא	——	——	——
you m. pl.	שְׁאֵילְתּוּן	——	——	——
they m.	שְׁאֵילוּ, שָׁאוּל[34] ‹שְׁאֵיל›	——	שַׁיּילוּ	——

Code: —— = form not found in Talmud   {Yemenite vocalization}   ‹problematic›   **[manuscript]**

---

34 The ו is *infixed*, as explained on p. 50, note 3.

	קַל	אִתְפְּעֵל	פַּעֵל	אַפְעֵל

PARTICIPLE

	ACTIVE	PASSIVE	REFLEXIVE	ACTIVE	ACTIVE
	asking/ borrowing שׁוֹאֵל...	*borrowed* שָׁאוּל...	*submitting to questioning* נִשְׁאָל, נִשְׁאָלִים	*asking/ borrowing* שׁוֹאֵל, שׁוֹאֲלִים	*lending* מַשְׁאִיל...
m.s.	שָׁאֵיל {שֶׁ-}, שָׁיֵיל {שֶׁ-}	שְׁאִיל	מִיתְשִׁיל {-תְ-}	מְשַׁאֵיל, מְשַׁיֵיל	מוֹשִׁיל ‹משיל›
f.s.	שָׁיְילָה [שְׁאִילָה]	——	——	——	[מַשְׁיְילָא]
m.pl.	שָׁיְילִי {-לֵי}, שָׁאֲלִי {-לֵי}	——	מִתְשְׁלִין {-תַ-}	מְשַׁיְילִי {-לֵי}	מוֹשְׁלִי {-לֵי}, מַשְׁאֲלִי {-לֵי}

ACTIVE PARTICIPLE WITH SUFFIX

	ask/borrow שׁוֹאֵל אֲנִי, שׁוֹאֲלִים אָנוּ		*ask* שׁוֹאֵל אֲנִי	
I	שָׁאֵילְנָא {שֶׁ-}		מְשַׁיְילְנָא	——
we	שָׁיְילִינַן {-שֶׁ}		——	——

Code: —— = form not found in Talmud   {Yemenite vocalization}   ‹problematic›   **[manuscript]**

אַפְעֵל	פַּעֵל	אִתְפְּעֵל	קַל
FUTURE			
	will[35] ask אֶשְׁאֵל...	will[35] submit to questioning אֶשָׁאֵל, יִשָׁאֵל	will[35] borrow/ will ask יִשְׁאַל, יִשְׁאֲלוּ
I	—	אֱשַׁיְּילֵיה	[אִיתְשִׁיל] {-תְּ-}	—
you m.s.	—	תְּשַׁיְּילֵיה	—	—
he/it m.	—	לִישַׁיְּילֵיה, נְשַׁיְּילֵיה	נִיתְשִׁיל {-תְּ-}	לִשְׁאוֹל
we	—	נְשַׁיְּילֵיה, לְשַׁיְּילֵיה	—	—
they m.	—	לִישַׁיְּילוּ	—	לִשְׁאֲלוּ
IMPERATIVE			
	lend! הַשְׁאֵל!	ask! שְׁאֵל...!	submit to questioning! הִשָׁאֵל!	ask!/ borrow! שְׁאַל...!
m.s.	אוֹשְׁלַן	שַׁיְּילֵיה	אִיתְשִׁיל {-תְּ-}	שְׁאוֹל, שְׁאֵיל
f.s.	—	—	—	שְׁאִילִי
m.pl.	—	שַׁיְּילוּה	—	שְׁאִילוּ
GERUND/INFINITIVE			
	to lend לְהַשְׁאִיל	(to) ask לִשְׁאוֹל / שָׁאוֹל	to submit to questioning לְהִשָׁאֵל	(to) ask/ to borrow לִשְׁאוֹל / שָׁאוֹל
	לְאוֹשׁוֹלֵי	(לְ)שַׁיּוּלֵי	לְאִיתְשׁוּלֵי {-תְּ-}	(לְ)מִישְׁאַל {-אַל}

35   or: *let him…*

(10) יד״ע (initial י and final guttural)

The קַל of the Aramaic verb יד״ע means *know* (or *learn*) as in Hebrew. In the אִתְפְּעֵל, only two forms occur: the past אִיתְיְידַע, *it was known*, and the participle מִתְיְידַע, *it is known*, which have not been included in the paradigm. The causative *binyan*, אַפְעֵל — or occasionally הַפְעֵל, with a ה prefix — means *make known* or *inform*. Its first root-letter י becomes ו, as in the Hebrew הִפְעִיל. The rare form אִשְׁתְּמוֹדַע is explained on p. 183.

קַל		אַפְעֵל / הַפְעֵל
PAST		
knew יָדַעְתִּי...		*made known, informed* הוֹדַעְתִּי...
I	יְדַעִי {יָדְעִי}	הוֹדַעְתִּינְהוּ
you m.s.	יְדַעְתְּ	אוֹדַעְתָּן
he/it m.	יְדַע	אוֹדְעֵיה
she/it f.	יְדַעָה, יָדְעָא {יָדְעָה/א}	——
they m.	——	אוֹדְעוּהוּ
PARTICIPLE		
ACTIVE *knowing* יוֹדֵעַ...	PASSIVE *known* יָדוּעַ...	ACTIVE *informing* מוֹדִיעַ...
m.s.	יָדַע {יַָדַע}	יְדִיעַ {יַָדִיעַ}	מוֹדַע
f.s.	יָדְעָה, יָדְעָא	יְדִיעָא	——
m.pl.	יָדְעִי {יַָדְעִי}, יָדְעִין	יְדִיעִי {יַָדִיעִי}	מוֹדְעִי {יַָדְעֵי}, מוֹדְעוּ, מְהוֹדְעִין

Code: —— = form not found in Talmud   {Yemenite vocalization}   <problematic>   [manuscript]

קַל	אַפְעֵל

ACTIVE PARTICIPLE WITH SUFFIX

	know יוֹדֵעַ אֲנִי...	*inform* מוֹדִיעַ אֲנִי...
I	יָדַעְנָא {-יְ} ‹ידעינא›	מוֹדַעְנָא
you m.s.	יָדַעַתְּ {יְדַעְתְּ}	——
we	יָדְעִינַן {יַדְעִינַן}	מוֹדְעִינַן
you m. pl.	יָדְעִיתוּ {-יַ}, יָדְעִיתוּן {-יַ}	——

FUTURE

	will[36] know יֵדַע	*will[36] inform* יוֹדִיע
he/it m.	לֵידַע, נֵידַע {גם: נִידַע}	לוֹדְעֵיהּ
we	נֵדַע	——
they m.	לֵידְעוּ, ‹לידעי› [נֵידְעוּ]	——

GERUND/INFINITIVE

	(to) know לָדַעַת, יָדוֹעַ	*(to) inform* לְהוֹדִיעַ / הוֹדֵע
	(לְ)מֵידַע {מֵידָע, וגם: מִידָע}	(לְ)אוֹדוֹעֵי

Code: —— = form not found in Talmud   {Yemenite vocalization}   ‹problematic›   [manuscript]

36   or: *let him...*

(11) יְלַף (initial root-letter י)

The Babylonian Aramaic root ילף means *learn* in *binyan* קַל and *teach* in the causative *binyan* אַפְעֵל. In the קַל the initial root-letter י is retained — with the prefix in the future and infinitive vocalized with *tzerei*, rather than the usual *ḥirik*. In the אַפְעֵל, however, the י does not appear, and it is replaced by a strong *dagesh* (as in אַלְפוּהָ, *they taught her*).[37]

קַל		אַפְעֵל
PAST		
learned לָמַדְתִּי		*taught* לְמְדוּ
I	[וְלֵיפִית] ‹יליפת›	—
they m.	—	אַלְפוּהָ

PARTICIPLE		
ACTIVE *learning/deriving* לוֹמֵד...	ACTIVE *teaching* מְלַמֵּד...	PASSIVE *accustomed to* מְלֻמֶּדֶת/רְגִילָה...
m.s.	יָלֵיף {-ְיָ}	‹מלפא›	—
f.s.	יָלְפָא	—	[מַלְפָּא]
m.pl.	יָלְפִי {-ְפֵי}	[מַלְפוּ][37]	‹מלפי›

Code: ——— = form not found in Talmud   {Yemenite vocalization}   ‹problematic›   [manuscript]

37 According to Epstein (p. 69), however, all the forms that we have labeled as *binyan* אַפְעֵל from the root ילף are regarded as *binyan* פַּעֵל forms from the root אלף — as in our Onkelos paradigm on pp. 179-180. Thus the participles מַלְפָּא and מַלְפוּ are contractions of מְאַלְפָא and מְאַלְפוּ, respectively.

קַל	אַפְעֵל

ACTIVE PARTICIPLE WITH SUFFIX	
learn/derive לוֹמֵד אֲנִי...	
I	יָלֵיפְנָא {יְ-} ‹ילפינא›	—
you m.s.	יָלְפַתְ {יְלַפְתְּ}	—
we	יָלְפִינַן {יְלְפִינַן}	—

FUTURE	
will[38] *learn/derive* יִלְמַד...	
he/it m.	לֵילַף, לֵיליף, נֵילַף	—
she/it f.	תֵּילַף, תֵּיליף	—
we	נֵילַף, לֵילַף	—
they m.	לֵילְפוּ, נֵילְפוּ ‹לילפי›	—
they f.	לֵילְפָן	—

Code: ——— = form not found in Talmud   {Yemenite vocalization}   ‹problematic›   [manuscript]

38   or: *let him...*

קַל	אַפְעֵל

	IMPERATIVE
	teach!
	לַמְּדוּ!

m.pl.	——	אַלְפוּהָ

GERUND / INFINITIVE	
(to) learn	*to teach*
לִלְמוֹד / לָמוֹד	לְלַמֵּד
(לְ)מֵילַף {מֵילָף}	לְאַלּוּפֵי

Code: —— = form not found in Talmud   {Yemenite vocalization}   <problematic>   [manuscript]

(12) יהב/נתב (weak initial root-letter)

The Aramaic root יהב means *give*, like the Hebrew root נתן (which occurs rarely in Babylonian Aramaic). The verb יהב is found almost exclusively in *binyan* קַל (except for a few forms in the אִתְפְּעֵל, meaning *it was given*: the masculine form אִיתְיְהִיב and two feminine forms, אִיתְיְהִיבָא and אִיתְיְהִיבַת, which are not listed in the table below). The conjugation of the future tense (and usually of the infinitive) is extraordinary: the Talmud uses forms such as לֵיתֵיב, *let him give*, which are derived from the root נתב (or perhaps יתב), rather than from the root יהב as one would have expected.[39]

	קַל
	PAST
	gave
	נָתַתִּי...
I	יְהַבִי {יְהְבִּי} ‹יהיבי›, **יְהַבִית**
you m.	יְהַבְתְּ ‹יהיבת›
you f.	[יְהַבְתְּ] ‹יהיבית›
he/it m.	יְהַב, יְהֵיב, הַב
she/it f.	יְהַבָה {יַהְבָּה} ‹יהיבה›, **יְהַבַת**
we	יְהֵיבְנָא, יְהֵיבְנַן
they m.	יְהַבוּ, הַבוּ ‹יהבי, יהיבו›

Code: ──── = form not found in Talmud   {Yemenite vocalization}   ‹problematic›   **[manuscript]**

39 The root נתב is apparently a combination of two roots (נתן + יהב). Compare Syriac, where יהב is replaced by נתל (= ל + נתן) in the future (Morag [above, p. 15 note 8], p. 201, note 15). Targum Onkelos, however, uses forms from the root נתן in the future and in the infinitive, as we have recorded in Chapter 5, p. 189.

	קַל	

	PARTICIPLE	
	ACTIVE *giving* ...נוֹתֵן	**PASSIVE** *given* נְתוּנָה
m.s.	יָהֵיב {-יְ}	——
f.s.	יָהֲבָא {יָהֵ-}, יָהֲבָה {יָהֲ-}	יְהִיבָה, יְהִיבָא
m.pl.	יָהֲבִי {יָהֲבֵי} ‹יהבו›	——

ACTIVE PARTICIPLE WITH SUFFIX
give ...נוֹתֵן אֲנִי

I	יָהֵיבְנָא {-יְ} ‹יהבינא›
you m.s.	יָהֲבַתְּ {יָהְבְתְּ}
we	יָהֲבִינַן {יָהְבִּינַן} ‹יהיבנן›
you m. pl.	יָהֲבִיתוּ {יָהְבִיתוּ}

Code: —— = form not found in Talmud   {Yemenite vocalization}   ‹problematic›   **[manuscript]**

קַל

FUTURE
will[40] give
...אֶתֵּן

I	אִיתֵּיב {אִיתֵּיב}
you m.s.	תִּיתֵּיב {תִּיתֵּיב}
he/it m.	לִיתֵּיב {לִיתֵּיב}, נֵיתֵיב {נִיתֵּיב}
we	נֵיתֵיב {נִיתֵּיב} ‹ניתוב, ניתבי›, לִיתְבֵיה {לִיתְבֵיה}
they m.	נֵיתְבוּ {נִיתְּבוּ}, לֵיתְבוּ {לִיתְּבוּ}, [לֵיתְבוּן]

IMPERATIVE
give!
...תֵּן!

m.s.	הַב ‹יהביה›, ‹יהבה›
f.s.	הַבִי
m.pl.	הַבוּ ‹יהבוהו›

GERUND / INFINITIVE
(to) give
לָתֵת / נָתוֹן

| (לְ)מֵיהַב {מֵיהָב}, לְמֵיתַב {לְמֵיתַּב} |

Code: —— = form not found in Talmud　{Yemenite vocalization}　‹problematic›　[manuscript]

40　or: *let him...* Note: These future forms are *homonyms* of the parallel forms of the
　　next verb, יתב.

(13) יתב (initial root-letter י)

The Aramaic root יתב, *sit*, is equivalent to the Hebrew verb ישׁב because of the correspondence ("the consonantal shift") between the Hebrew שׁ and the Aramaic ת. The paradigms below present the two *binyanim* whose conjugation is relatively complete, i.e., the קל and אַפְעֵל. In the past tense of the קל, some of the forms (e.g., יְתֵיב) follow the פְּעֵיל pattern, like סְלֵיק and שְׁאֵיל in verbs 8 and 9 above. In a few forms a prosthetic א occurs (e.g., in אִיתֵיב, *he sat*). In the causative *binyan*, the אַפְעֵל, the vowel letter ו appears after the prefix, instead of the initial root letter י (e.g., אוֹתֵיב, *he seated*) as in the Hebrew הִפְעִיל (e.g., הוֹשִׁיב). The same phenomenon occurs in forms from *binyan* אִתְפְּעַל, such as אִיתּוֹתַב.

Besides the *binyanim* in the paradigm, one form occurs from *binyan* פַּעֵל: the infinitive לְיַתּוּבֵי, *to set at ease*, and several from *binyan* אִתְפַּעַל: for example, the passive participle מְיַתְּבָא, *set at ease*.

	קַל	אַפְעֵל	אִתְפְּעַל
	PAST		
	sat יָשַׁבְתִּי...	*set/placed* הוֹשַׁבְתִּי...	*was established/settled* נִקְבַּע / נִתְיַשֵּׁב
I	{יְתַבִּי} יְתַבִּי	אוֹתֵיבִי	——
you m.s.	[יְתֵיבְתְּ] ,יְתַבְתְּ ‹איתיבת, אותיבת›	——	——
he/it m.	יְתֵיב, אִיתֵיב ‹איתוב›	אוֹתֵיב	אִיתּוֹתַב
she/it f.	{יַתְבָּה} יְתָבָה	——	——
we	——	אוֹתְבִינַיה	——
they m.	‹יתבו› יְתִיבוּ, אִיתִיבוּ ‹אותבי›	אוֹתִיבוּ	——

Code: —— = form not found in Talmud   {Yemenite vocalization}   ‹problematic›   [manuscript]

89

	קַל		אַפְעֵל		אִתַּפְעַל

			PARTICIPLE			
	ACTIVE	PASSIVE	ACTIVE	PASSIVE	PASSIVE
	sitting	*seated*	*placing*	*placed*	*is settled*
	יוֹשֵׁב...	יָשׁוּב / מֻנָּח...	מוֹשִׁיב / מַנִּיחַ...	מֻנַּחַת	מִתְיַשֵּׁב
m.s.	יָתֵיב {יְ-}	יְתִיב	מוֹתֵיב, מֵיתֵיב {מִיתֵּיב}	——	מִיתוֹתַב
f.s.	יָתְבָה, יָתְבָא	[יְתִיבָא]	——	מוֹתְבָא	——
m.pl.	יָתְבִי {-בֵי} ‹יתבו›, יָתְבִין	יְתִיבִי {-בֵי}	מוֹתְבִי {-בֵי}, מֵיתְבִי {מִיתְבֵי}	——	——
f.pl.	יָתְבָן	——	——	——	——

			ACTIVE PARTICIPLE WITH SUFFIX	
	sit	*place*	
	יוֹשֵׁב אֲנִי...	מוֹשִׁיב / מַנִּיחַ אֲנִי...	
I	יָתִיבְנָא {יְ-}	מוֹתִיבְנָא ‹מותבינא›	
you m.s.	יָתְבַתְּ {יְתַבְתְּ}	מוֹתְבַתְּ	
we	יָתְבִינַן {יַתְבִּינַן} ‹יתיבינן›	מוֹתְבִינַן	
you m. pl.	יָתְבִיתוּ {יַתְבִּיתוּ}	מוֹתְבִיתוּ	

Code: —— = form not found in Talmud   {Yemenite vocalization}   ‹problematic›   [manuscript]

קַל	אַפְעֵל	אִתְפְּעַל
FUTURE		
will[41] sit אֵשֵׁב...	will seat/place אוֹשִׁיב...	will be settled תְּתְיַשֵׁב

	קַל	אַפְעֵל	אִתְפְּעַל
I	אִיתֵיב {אִיתֵּיב}	אוֹתְבִינָךְ	——
you m.s.	תֵּיתֵיב {תִּיתֵּיב}		——
he/it m.	לֵיתֵיב {לֵיתֵּיב}, נֵיתֵיב {נֵיתֵּיב}, יְתֵיב, לֵיתוֹב {לֵיתּוּב}	לוֹתִיב, נוֹתְבֵיה	——
she/it f.	תֵּיתֵיב {תֵּיתֵּיב}	——	[תִּיתוֹתַב]
we	נֵיתֵיב {נֵיתֵּיב}	——	——
you m. pl.	תֵּיתְבוּ {תֵּיתְּבוּ}	——	——
they m.	לֵיתְבוּ {לֵיתְּבוּ}, לֵיתְבוּן {לֵיתְּבוּן}, יִתְבוּן[42]	לוֹתְבוּ	——

Code: —— = form not found in Talmud   {Yemenite vocalization}   <problematic>   [manuscript]

41   or: *let him...* Note: The future קַל forms are *homonyms* of the parallel forms of the previous verb, יהב / נתב.

42   This form is found in the Talmud only in a quote from Targum Yonathan.

91

	קַל	אַפְעֵל	אִתְפְּעַל
	IMPERATIVE		
	sit! שֵׁב!, שְׁבוּ!	*seat!, settle!* הוֹשֵׁב!, הוֹשִׁיבוּ!	
m.s.	תִּיב ‹תוב›	אוֹתֵיב	——
m.pl.	תִּיבוּ	אוֹתִיבוּ	——

	GERUND / INFINITIVE		
	(to) sit לָשֶׁבֶת / יָשׁוֹב	*(to) seat/place* לְהוֹשִׁיב / הוֹשֵׁב	
	(לְ)מֵיתַב {(לְ)מֵיתַב, מִיתָב}	(לְ)אוֹתוּבֵי ‹לאותבי›	——

Code: —— = form not found in Talmud   {Yemenite vocalization}   ‹problematic›   **[manuscript]**

(14) תוב ("hollow" verb)

The Aramaic root תוב, *return*, is the equivalent of the Hebrew root שוב because of the correspondence ("the consonantal shift") between the Hebrew שׁ and the Aramaic ת. Surprisingly, in *binyan* קַל of Babylonian Aramaic, only one verbal form, **תַּבְנָא**, *we returned*, has been clearly documented in the Talmud, in a quotation from *Megillath Ta'anith* — besides the adverbial usage of תוּ, *further, again*, a contraction of תוּב.[43] In Babylonian Aramaic, the idea of *return*, i.e., *go back*, is expressed by the verb הדר (verb 5 above) in *binyan* קַל.

Almost all of the forms of the verb תוב in the Talmud are in the causative אַפְעֵל *binyan*, and they bear the meaning *respond* in the sense of *retort* or *object*. As in other hollow verbs in Aramaic (such as קום, verb 17), the vowel letter ו appears after the prefix א, e.g., אוֹתִיבוּ, *they objected*, in the manner of roots with initial י. In fact, a form such as אוֹתִיבוּ is really a homonym, since it could be explained as the אַפְעֵל of either יתב, meaning *they seated*, or תוב, meaning *they objected*, depending upon the Talmudic context. Similarly, אִיתּוֹתַב, past tense of *binyan* אֶתַּפְעַל, the passive of the אַפְעֵל, is a homonym: It could mean either *it was refuted*, from the root תוב, as recorded in this paradigm, or *it was settled* or *established*, from the root יתב, as recorded in the previous paradigm.[44]

---

43 There are a number of occurrences of the form תוּב in current editions of the Talmud, but in the Munich manuscript several appear as תִּיב, *sit*, from the root יתב; one (in עבודה זרה ו,ב) is missing altogether; and the other (in נזיר כ, סע״ב) appears as an adverbial תוּ.

44 See Chapter 6, "Homographs and Homonyms," especially p. 229.

	אַפְעֵל	אִתַּפְעַל

	PAST	
	objected/refuted הֵשַׁבְתִּי (= הִקְשֵׁיתִי)...	*was refuted, were refuted* הוּשַׁב (= הֻקְשָׁה), הוּשְׁבוּ
I	אוֹתֵיבְנָא	——
you m.s.	[אוֹתְבִיתַן] ‹אותיבתן›	——
he/it m.	אֵיתֵיבֵיה {אֵי־}, **אוֹתְבֵיה**	אִיתּוֹתַב
we	אוֹתְבִינֵיה	——
they m.	אוֹתֵיבוּ	אִיתּוֹתְבוּ

	ACTIVE PARTICIPLE	
	objecting/refuting מֵשִׁיב (= מַקְשֶׁה)...	
m.s.	מֵתִיב {מְ־}, **מוֹתֵיב**	
m.pl.	מֵיתִיבִי {מְיתִיבֵי}	

	ACTIVE PARTICIPLE WITH SUFFIX	
	object/refute מֵשִׁיב (= מַקְשֶׁה) אֲנִי...	
I	[מוֹתֵיבְנָא] ‹מותבינא›	
you m.s.	מוֹתְבַתְּ {מוֹתַבְתְּ}	
we	מוֹתְבִינַן	

Code: —— = form not found in Talmud   {Yemenite vocalization}   ‹problematic›   [manuscript]

אַפְעֵל

	FUTURE
	will[45] *object/refute* ...(תָּשִׁיב =) תַּקְשֶׁה
you m.s.	תּוֹתְבֵיה
he/it m.	לוֹתֵיב ‹ליתוב›
we	נְתִיב
you m. pl.	תּוֹתְבוּ

	IMPERATIVE
	object! (הַקְשֵׁה! =) הָשֵׁב!
m.s.	אוֹתֵיב

	GERUND/INFINITIVE
	to object/refute (לְהַקְשׁוֹת =) לְהָשִׁיב
	לְאוֹתוּבֵיה ‹לאותביה›

Code: ——— = form not found in Talmud   {Yemenite vocalization}   ‹problematic›   **[manuscript]**

45   or: *let him...*

(15) אזל (initial root-letter א)

The verb אזל means *go* in a variety of senses, much like הלך in Hebrew. It appears only in *binyan* קַל. In its conjugation, the initial א is deleted in the future tense, in the infinitive and usually in the imperative.

	קַל

	PAST
	went הָלַכְתִּי...
I	אֲזַלִי {אַזְלִי}
you m.s.	אֲזַלְתְּ
he/it m.	אֲזַל, אֲזִיל, [אֲזָא]
she/it f.	אֲזַלָא {אַזְ-}, אֲזַלָה {אַזְ-}, אֲזַלַת
they m.	אֲזַלוּ {אַזְלוּ}, אֲזוּל⁴⁶

	ACTIVE PARTICIPLE
	going הוֹלֵךְ...
m.s.	אָזֵיל {אַ-}
f.s.	אָזְלָא, אָזְלָה {אַ-}
m.pl.	אָזְלִי {אַזְלֵי} אָזְלִין
f.pl.	אָזְלָן {אַ-}

Code: ──── = form not found in Talmud {Yemenite vocalization} <problematic> [manuscript]

46 The ו is *infixed*, as explained on p. 50, note 3.

קַל

	ACTIVE PARTICIPLE WITH SUFFIX
	go הוֹלֵךְ אֲנִי...
I	‹אזלינא› {אֲ-} אָזֵילְנָא
you m.s.	{אֲזַלְתְּ} אָזְלַתְּ
we	{אָזְלִינַן} אָזְלִינַן
you m. pl.	{אֲ-} אָזְלִיתוּ

	FUTURE
	will[47] go אֵלֵךְ...
I	{זֵיל-} אֵיזִיל
you m.s.	‹תיזול› {זֵיל-} תֵּיזִיל
you f.s.	תֵּיזְלִי
he/it m.	{זֵיל-} נֵיזִיל ,יֵיזִיל ,‹ליזול› {זֵיל-} לֵיזִיל
she/it f.	תֵּיזַל ,{זֵיל-} תֵּיזִיל
we	{זֵיל-} לֵיזִיל ,{זֵיל-} נֵיזִיל
you m. pl.	תֵּיזְלוּ
they m.	לֵיזְלוּ

Code: ─── = form not found in Talmud {Yemenite vocalization} ‹problematic› [manuscript]

47 or: *let him...*

	קַל

	IMPERATIVE
	go!
	...לֵךְ!
m.s.	זִיל, אִיזִיל {אִיזֵיל}
f.s.	זִילִי, [אִיזִילִי]
m.pl.	זִילוּ, אִיזִילוּ, [זוּל]

	GERUND / INFINITIVE
	(to) go
	לָלֶכֶת / הָלוֹךְ
	(לְ)מֵיזַל {מֵיזָל}

Code: —— = form not found in Talmud   {Yemenite vocalization}   <problematic>   **[manuscript]**

(16) אכל (initial root-letter א)

Like its Hebrew counterpart, the Aramaic verb אכל means *eat*, and it appears in *binyan* קַל, in its reflexive/passive *binyan* אִתְפְּעֵל and in the causative *binyan* אַפְעֵל. In the אַפְעֵל, this verb — like some other Aramaic verbs with initial root letter א — is usually conjugated in the manner of verbs with י as the first root-letter, e.g., אוֹדַע from ידע.

	קַל	אִתְפְּעֵל	אַפְעֵל
		PAST	
	ate אָכַלְתִּי...		*fed* הֶאֱכִיל
I	{אֲ-} אֲכַלִית, אֲכַלִי	——	——
you m.	אֲכַלְתְּ	——	——
he/it m.	אֲכַל, אֲכֵיל	——	**אוֹכְלֵיהּ**
she/it f.	אֲכַלָה {אַכְלָה}	——	——
we	אֲכַלְנָא, [אֲכַלַן] {אַכְלַן}	——	——
they m.	אֲכַלוּ, אֲכוּל[48]	——	——

Code: —— = form not found in Talmud {Yemenite vocalization} <problematic> [manuscript]

---

48 The ו is *infixed*, as explained on p. 50, note 3.

	קַל	אִתְפְּעֵל	אַפְעֵל

	PARTICIPLE		
	ACTIVE *eating* אוֹכֵל...	**PASSIVE** *eaten* אָכוּל	**REFL./PASS.** *being eaten* נֶאֱכָל...	
m.s.	אָכֵיל {אָ-}	אָכִיל	מִתְאֲכִיל ⟨מתאכל⟩, מִיתְכִיל	—
f.s.	אָכְלָה {אָ-}	—	מִיתְאַכְלָא	—
m.pl.	אָכְלִין, אָכְלִי {-לֵי}, אָכְלוּ	—	מִיתְאַכְלִי {-לֵי}, מִיתַּכְלִי {-לֵי}	—
f.pl.	אָכְלָן	—	מִיתְאַכְלָן	—

	ACTIVE PARTICIPLE WITH SUFFIX		
	eat אוֹכֵל אֲנִי...		*feed* מַאֲכִיל אֲנִי...
I	אָכֵילְנָא {אָ-}		מַאֲכֵילְנָא
you m.s.	אָכְלַתְּ {אֲכַלְתְּ}		—
we	אָכְלִינַן {אָ-}		[מַאֲכֵילִינַן], מוֹכְלִינַן

Code: —— = form not found in Talmud　{Yemenite vocalization}　⟨problematic⟩　[manuscript]

קַל	אִתְפְּעֵל	אַפְעֵל
FUTURE		
will[49] eat אֹכַל...	will[49] be eaten יֵאָכֵל, תֵּאָכֵל	will[49] feed אַאֲכִיל, יַאֲכִיל

	קַל	אִתְפְּעֵל	אַפְעֵל
I	אֵיכוֹל {-וּל}	—	אוֹכְלִיךְ
you m.s.	תֵּיכוֹל {-וּל}	—	—
he/it m.	נֵיכוֹל {-וּל}, לֵיכוֹל, נֵאכוֹל {-וּל}	לִיתְאֲכִיל, נִיתְאֲכִיל	לוֹכִיל
she/it f.	תֵּיכוֹל {-וּל}, תּוֹכְלִיךְ	תִּיתְכִיל	—
we	נֵיכוֹל {-וּל}	—	—
you m. pl.	תֵּיכְלוּן ‹תיכלין›	—	—
they m.	נֵיכְלוּ, לֵיכְלוּ	—	—

IMPERATIVE			
	eat! אֱכֹל!...		
m.s.	אֵיכוֹל, אֱכוֹל	—	—
m.pl.	אֵכְלוּ {אֲכַלוּ}, [אֵיכְלוּ]	—	—

GERUND / INFINITIVE			
	(to) eat לְאֶכֹל / אֱכוֹל		to feed לְהַאֲכִיל
	(לְ)מֵיכַל {מֵיכָל}	—	[לְאוֹכוֹלֵי] ‹לאכולי›

Code: —— = form not found in Talmud   {Yemenite vocalization}   ‹problematic›   [manuscript]

49   or: *let him...*

(17) אמר (initial א and final guttural)

The root אמר, *say* or *state*, in both Aramaic and Hebrew, is the most
common verb in the Talmud. It appears in the קַל and in its passive,
the Aramaic אִתְפְּעֵל, and the Hebrew נִפְעַל. In the conjugation of the
Aramaic verb, the first root-letter א and even the final root-letter ר
are sometimes deleted in the future and in the imperative of the קַל.

	קַל	אִתְפְּעֵל
	PAST	
	said ...אָמַרְתִּי	*was said* ...נֶאֱמַר
I	אָמַרִי {אַמְרִי}, אָמַרִית	—
you m.s.	אָמַרְתְּ	—
he/it m.	אֲמַר	אִתְּמַר, אִתְאֲמַר, [50] אִתֵּימָא, [51] אִתֵּימַר
she/it f.	אָמְרָה	אִתַּמְרָה[50]
we	אָמַרַן {אַמְרַן}, אָמַרְנָא	—
you m. pl.	אֲמַרִיתוּ	—
they m.	אֲמַרוּ {אַמְרוּ}, אָמוּר[52]	—
they f.	—	אִתְאַמְרָן

Code: ——— = form not found in Talmud   {Yemenite vocalization}   <problematic>   [manuscript]

50 The Yemenite tradition pronounces איתמר and איתמרה as if spelled אִיתְאֲמַר
    and אִיתְאַמְרָה, respectively.

51 This form belongs here according to only one of the explanations presented in
    the entry אִתֵּימָא in *The Practical Talmud Dictionary* (Jerusalem: Ariel: 1991;
    Maggid-Koren 2016).

52 The ו is *infixed*, as explained on p. 50, note 3.

קַל	אִתְפְּעֵל

PARTICIPLE

	ACTIVE *saying* אוֹמֵר...	PASSIVE *said* אָמוּר...	REFLEXIVE / PASSIVE *being said* נֶאֱמָר...
m.s.	אָמַר	אֲמִיר	מִיתְּמַר
f.s.	אָמְרָה	אֲמִירָא	מִיתְאַמְרָא, מִתְאַמְרָה
m.pl.	אָמְרֵי {אַמְרֵי}, אָמְרִין	—	—
f.pl.	אָמְרָן {אַ-}	—	—

PARTICIPLE WITH SUFFIX

	ACTIVE *say* אוֹמֵר אֲנִי...	PASSIVE *say* אָמוּר אֲנִי	
I	אֲמֵינָא [53] {אַ-}, אָמַרְנָא	אֲמֵינָא [53]	—
you m.s.	אָמְרַתְּ {אַמַרְתְּ}	—	—
we	אָמְרִינַן {אַמְרִינַן}	—	—
you m. pl.	אָמְרִיתוּן {אַ-}	—	—

Code: ——— = form not found in Talmud   {Yemenite vocalization}   <problematic>   **[manuscript]**

53 It is not certain whether אמינא is an *active* participle with a suffix, vocalized אֲמֵינָא (but cf. Morag, p. 167) – or a *passive* participle (in spite of its active meaning) with a suffix, a contraction of אֲמִיר + אֲנָא vocalized אֲמֵינָא, as it is commonly pronounced today.

קַל	אֶתְפְּעֵל
FUTURE	
will[54] say אֹמַר...	

	קַל	אֶתְפְּעֵל
I	אֵימָא {-מַא} , אֵימַר	—
you m.s.	תֵּימָא {-מַא} , תֵּימְרָא	—
he	לֵימָא {-מַא} , נֵימָא {-מַא} , יֵימַר	—
she	תֵּימָא {-מַא}	—
we	נֵימָא {-מַא} , לֵימָא {-מַא} , נֵימְרִינְהוּ, לֵימְרִינְהוּ	—
you m. pl.	תֵּימְרוּן	—
they m.	לֵימְרוּ, נֵימְרוּ	—

IMPERATIVE		
say! אֱמֹר!...		
m.s.	אֵימָא {-מַא} , אֵימוּר, אֵימַר {-מַר}	—
f.s.	אֵימַרִי	—
m.pl.	אֵימַרוּ	—

GERUND / INFINITIVE		
(to) say לוֹמַר / אָמוֹר		
(לְ)מֵימַר {מֵימָר} , לְמֵימְרָא		—

Code: ——— = form not found in Talmud　{Yemenite vocalization}　<problematic>　**[manuscript]**

54　or: *let him...*

(18) בעי (second guttural and final י)

The verb בעי is used in the Talmud with a variety of meanings — including *ask, request, want,* and *require.* In some forms of its conjugation, the third root-letter י is deleted (e.g., in בְּעַן, *we asked*). Aside from the קַל, this verb is also used in the reflexive/passive אִתְפְּעֵל *binyan*, usually with the ת from the אֶת־ prefix deleted. Some forms are often pronounced as if they were from *binyan* אִתְפַּעַל, for example, אִיבְּעִי for אִיבָּעִי.

	קַל	אִתְפְּעֵל
	PAST	
	asked/required שָׁאַלְתִּי / הָיִיתִי צָרִיךְ...	was required/asked הָיָה צָרִיךְ / נִשְׁאַל / נִתְבַּקֵּשׁ...
I	בְּעַאי, בְּעַי, ‹בְּעַיי›, בְּעֵיתִי	—
you m.s.	בְּעֵית	—
he/it m.	בְּעָא, בְּעִי	אִיבְּעִי[55]
she/it f.	בְּעֲיָא	אִיבַּעְיָא איבעאי
we	בְּעַן, בְּעֵינַן	—
you m. pl.	בְּעֵיתוּ {בְּעִי-}	—
they m.	בְּעוּ[56] ‹בעון›	—

Code: ——— = form not found in Talmud   {Yemenite vocalization}   ‹problematic›   [manuscript]

55   This form is popularly pronounced אִבָּעֵי, with a *kametz* under the ב.
56   In this table and in the conjugations of the seven final י verbs that follow, we have vocalized the suffix of this form וּ, as it is commonly pronounced, even though an וֹ vocalization is supported by the Targumim and by Biblical Aramaic. The evidence from vocalized Talmudic manuscripts is mixed.

קַל	אִתְפְּעֵל
PARTICIPLE	

	ACTIVE *asking/requiring* שׁוֹאֵל / צָרִיךְ...	REFLEXIVE/PASSIVE *required* צָרִיךְ...
m.s.	בָּעֵי {בַּ-}	מִיבְּעֵי {עִי-} 57, מִיתְבְּעֵי {עִי-}
f.s.	בָּעְיָא {בַּ-}	מִיבַּעְיָא
m.pl.	בָּעוּ {בְּ-}, בָּעַן ‹בעין, בעיין› [בָּעְיֵי]	מִיתְבְּעִי, מִתְבְּעוּ [מִתְבְּעִין]
f.pl.	בָּעְיָין	——

	PARTICIPLE WITH SUFFIX	

	ACTIVE *ask/require* שׁוֹאֵל / צָרִיךְ אֲנִי...	REFLEXIVE/PASSIVE *am required* מִתְבַּקֵּשׁ אֲנִי
I	בָּעֵינָא {בְּ-}	מִתְבְּעֵינָא, מִבְּעֵינָא
you m.s.	בָּעֵית {בְּ-}	——
we	בָּעֵינַן {בְּעֵינַן}	——
you m. pl.	בָּעֵיתוּ {בְּעֵי-}, **בָּעִיתוּן** {בְּעֵיתוּן}	——

Code: —— = form not found in Talmud   {Yemenite vocalization}   ‹problematic›   [manuscript]

---

57   This form is popularly pronounced מִיבָּעֵי, with a *kametz* under the ב.

קַל	אִתְפְּעֵל

	FUTURE	
	will[58] ask/require אֶשְׁאַל / אֶהֱיֶה צָרִיךְ...	will[58] be asked/required תִּשָׁאֵל / תְּהֵא צְרִיכָה
I	אֵיבְּעֵי	——
you m.s.	תִּיבְּעֵי	——
he/it m.	לִיבְּעֵי, נִיבְּעֵי	——
she/it f.	תִּיבְּעֵי	תִּיבְּעֵי[59] (תיבעיא)
we	נִיבְּעֵי, לִיבְּעֵי	——
they m.	לִיבְּעוּ	——

	IMPERATIVE	
	ask! שְׁאַל! / בַּקֵּשׁ!...	
m.s.	בְּעִי	——
m.pl.	בְּעוּ	——

	GERUND / INFINITIVE	
	(to) ask/require לִשְׁאֵל / (לְ)בַקֵּשׁ / שָׁאוֹל / צָרוֹךְ	"be asked" נִשְׁאַל
(לְ)מִיבְּעֵי, (לְ)מִיבְּעָא ‹מיבעיא›		אִיבְּעוֹיֵי

Code: —— = form not found in Talmud   {Yemenite vocalization}   ‹problematic›   [manuscript]

58   or: *let him...*
59   This form is popularly pronounced תִּבָּעֵי, with a *kametz* under the ב.

(19) **חזי** (initial guttural and final י)

The Aramaic root חזי, whose basic meaning is *see*, is the equivalent of the Hebrew root ראה in its various meanings. Like its Hebrew parallel, the Aramaic verb is used in *binyan* קַל, in its reflexive/ passive, the אִתְפְּעֵל, where it means *be seen* or *fit*, and in the אַפְעֵל with the causative meaning, *show*. The reflexive/passive of אַפְעֵל, the אִתַּפְעַל, occurs occasionally in the forms **אִיתַּחְזִי**, *it was shown*, **מִתַּחְזִי**, *shown*, and **לִיתַּחְזִי**, *let it be shown*; but it is not common enough to be included in our paradigm. The third root-letter י of this verb (and the next two verbs) is treated like the י in בעי, the previous verb.

	קַל	אִתְפְּעֵל	אַפְעֵל
		PAST	
	saw רָאִיתִי...	*was fit/seen* הָיָה רָאוּי / נִרְאָה...	*showed* הֶרְאֵיתִי...
I	חֲזַאי, חֲזֵינָא, חֲזֵיתִי	——	אַחְזִיתֵיה
you m.s.	חֲזֵית	——	——
he/it m.	חֲזָא	אִיחֲזִי, אִיתְחֲזִי	אַחְזִי
she/it f.	חֲזַאי, חֲזָת, חַזְיָת {חֲזֵית}, חַזְיָא	אִיחַזְיָא, אִיתְחַזְאִי	אַחְזְיָא
we	חֲזֵינַן, חֲזַן, חֲזֵינָא	——	——
you m. pl.	חֲזֵיתוּן {-תוּן}	——	——
they m.	חֲזוּ	אִיחֲזוּ	אַחְזוּ

Code: —— = form not found in Talmud   {Yemenite vocalization}   <problematic>   [manuscript]

	קַל		אִתְפְּעֵל
	PARTICIPLE		
	ACTIVE *seeing* רוֹאֶה...	PASSIVE *fit* רָאוּי...	REFLEXIVE / PASSIVE *seem(s)/becoming fit* נִרְאֶה / רָאוּי...
m.s	חָזֵי {חָ-}	חֲזֵי {חֲזִי}	מִיחֲזֵי {-זִי}, מִיתְחֲזֵי, מִתְחַזְיָא
f.s.	חָזְיָא {חָ-}	חַזְיָא	מִיחַזְיָא, מִיתְחַזְיָא
m.pl.	חָזוּ {חָ-}	חֲזוּ {חֲזוּ}	מִתְחַזְיָין
f.pl.	חָזְיָין {חָ-}	חַזְיָין	מִתְחַזְיָין

	קַל		אַפְעֵל
	PARTICIPLE WITH SUFFIX		
	ACTIVE *see* רוֹאֶה אֲנִי...	PASSIVE *am fit, are fit* רָאוּי אֲנִי, רָאוּי אַתָּה	ACTIVE *show* מַרְאֶה אֲנִי / מַרְאֶה אַתָּה
I	חָזֵינָא {חֲ-}	חֲזֵינָא	מַחֲזֵינָא
you m.s.	חָזֵית {חֲ-}	חֲזֵית	[מַחֲזֵית]
we	חָזֵינַן {חֲזֵינַן}	——	——
you m. pl.	חָזֵיתוּן {חֲ-}	——	——

Code: —— = form not found in Talmud   {Yemenite vocalization}   <problematic>   [manuscript]

קַל	אִתְפְּעֵל	אַפְעֵל

	FUTURE		
	will[60] *see* ...אֶרְאֶה	*will*[60] *be seen* ...יֵרָאֶה	*will*[60] *show* ...תַּרְאֶה
I	אִיחֲזֵי {אֶיחֱזֵי}	—	—
you m.s.	תִּיחֲזֵי {תִּיחֱזֵי}	—	**תַּחְזֵי**
he/it m.	לִיחֲזֵי {לִיחֱזֵי}	לִיתְחֲזֵי	**נִיחֲזֵי**
we	נִיחֲזֵי {נִיחֱזֵי}, לִיחֲזֵי {לִיחֱזֵי}	—	—
you m. pl.	תֶּחֱזוּ {תֶּחְזוּ}	תִּתְחֲזוּ	—
they m.	לִיחֲזוּ {לִיחְזוּ}	—	—

	IMPERATIVE		
	see! ...!רְאֵה	*appear!* !הֵרָאֵה	*show!* !הַרְאֵי
m.s.	חֲזִי	אִיתְחֲזִי	—
f.s.	חֲזִי (חזאי)	—	**אַחְזִי**
m.pl.	חֲזוּ	—	—

	GERUND / INFINITIVE	
	(to) see לְרָאוֹת / רָאֹה	*(to) be seen* לְהֵרָאוֹת / הֵרָאֶה	
(לְ)מִיחֲזֵי, מִיחֱזָא {מִיחְ־} <מִיחזיא>	(לְ)אִיתְחֲזוֹיֵי	—

Code: —— = form not found in Talmud   {Yemenite vocalization}   <problematic>   **[manuscript]**

60   or: *let him...*

(20) גלי (final root-letter י)

The Aramaic root גלי (like its Hebrew parallel גלה) is used in two totally different senses: (1) *exile* and (2) *reveal*. In *binyan* קַל, the verb means *go into exile*, but in the causative *binyan* אַפְעֵל just two forms occur — the past tense אַגְלִי, *he exiled* (= sent into exile) and the infinitive אַגְלוֹיֵי, *to exile*. In *binyan* פַּעֵל, גַּלִּי means *he revealed*, and in its reflexive/passive, the אִתְפַּעֵל, אִיגַּלִּי means *it was revealed*. As in Hebrew, the passive participle of *binyan* קַל also has this latter meaning, e.g., גַּלְיָא (Heb. גְּלוּיָה), *revealed*. As in all such verbs in Aramaic, the third root-letter י is deleted in some of the conjugated forms.

	קַל	פַּעֵל	אִתְפַּעֵל
		PAST	
	went into exile גְּלִיתִי...	*revealed* גְּלִיתָ...	*was revealed* נִתְגַּלָּה...
I	גְּלַאי	—	—
you m.s.	—	גְּלֵית	—
he/it m.	[גְּלָא] ‹גלי›	גַּלִּי	אִיגַּלִּי
she/it f.	—	גַּלְיָא ‹גלייה›	אִיגַּלַּאי, אִיגַּלְיָא, אִיגַּלְיָה
we	גְּלֵינַן	—	—
you m. pl.	גְּלֵיתוּן	—	—
they m.	גְּלוּ	גַּלּוּ	{אִתְגַּלְּיוּ} ‹אתגלין›
they f.	—	—	אִיגַּלְיָיא

Code: ——— = form not found in Talmud   {Yemenite vocalization}   ‹problematic›   [manuscript]

111

	קַל		פַּעֵל		אִתְפַּעַל
	PARTICIPLE				
	ACTIVE *going into exile* גּוֹלֶה, גּוֹלִים	**PASSIVE** *revealed* גְּלוּיָה, גְּלוּיִים	**ACTIVE** *revealing* מְגַלֶּה...	**PASSIVE** *revealed* מְגֻלָּה...	**REFL./PASS.** *revealed* מְגֻלֶּה / מִתְגַּלֶּה...
m.s.	**גָּלֵי** {גַּ־}	——	**מְגַלֵּי**	——	**מִיגַּלֵּי**
f.s.	——	**גַּלְיָא**	**מְגַלְּיָא**	**מְגַלְּיָא**	**מִיגַּלְּיָא**
m.pl.	**גָּלוּ** {גְּ־}	**גַּלְיָן**[61]	**מְגַלּוּ**	<מגלו>	**מִיגַּלּוּ**
f.pl.	——	——	——	**מְגַלְּיָין**	**מִיגַּלְּיָין**

	ACTIVE PARTICIPLE WITH SUFFIX				
			reveal מְגַלֶּה אֲנִי...		
I	——		**מְגַלֵּינָא**		
you m.s.	——		**מְגַלֵּית** <מגלת>		
we	——		**מְגַלִּינַן** {־לֵּי־}		

Code: —— = form not found in Talmud {Yemenite vocalization} <problematic> **[manuscript]**

61 See Morag (above, p. 15 note 8), p. 262.

קַל	פַּעֵל	אִתְפְּעַל
FUTURE		
will[62] go into exile ...אֶגְלֶה	will[62] reveal ...אֲגַלֶּה	will[62] be revealed תִּתְגַּלֶּה

	קַל	פַּעֵל	אִתְפְּעַל
I	אֶגְלֵי	אֶיגַלֵּי	—
you f.s.	—	תְּגַלֵּי	—
he	לִיגְלֵי	לְגַלֵּי, נִיגַלֵּי	—
she/it f.	—	—	תִּיגַלֵּי
we	נִגְלֵי	—	—
you m. pl.	—	תִּיגַלוּ	—
they m.	לִיגְלוּ	—	—

	IMPERATIVE		
	go into exile! !גְּלֵה	reveal! ...!גַּלֵּה	
m.s.	גְּלִי	גַּלִּי	—
f.s.	—	גַּלִּי	—
m.pl.	—	גַּלּוּ	—

	GERUND / INFINITIVE	
	to reveal לְגַלּוֹת / גַּלֵּה	to be revealed לְהִתְגַּלּוֹת
—	(לְ)גַּלוֹיֵי	לְאִיגַּלוֹיֵי ‹אִיגלוייי›

62   or: *let him...*

(21) אָסִי (initial root-letter א and final י)

This Aramaic root, which means *heal* or *cure*, is used in the פְּעַל *binyan* and in its reflexive/passive אִתְפְּעַל. In some of the forms in both *binyanim*, the initial root letter א or the third root letter י is deleted.

פְּעַל		אִתְפְּעַל
PAST		
cured רְפֵּא		*was cured...* נִרְפֵּאתִי...
I	—	אִיתַּסַּאי
he/it m.	אַסִי	אִיתַּסִי
she/it f.	—	אִיתַּסִיאַת, אִתַּסְיָא
they m.	—	אִיתַּסוּ

PARTICIPLE		
ACTIVE *curing* מְרַפֵּא		**REFLEXIVE/PASSIVE** *being cured* נִרְפָּא
m.s.	מַסֵּי	מִיתַּסֵּי
f.s.	מַסְיָא	—
m.pl.	מַסוּ, מַסְיָין[63]	—

Code: ——— = form not found in Talmud   {Yemenite vocalization}   <problematic>   [manuscript]

---

63 See Morag (above, p. 15 note 8), pp. 259 and 278.

פַּעֵל	אִתְפַּעַל

PARTICIPLE WITH SUFFIX	
ACTIVE *am curing* מְרַפֵּא אֲנִי	**REFLEXIVE / PASSIVE** *are being cured* נִרְפָּאִים אֲנַחְנוּ

	פַּעֵל	אִתְפַּעַל
I	**מַסֵּינָא**	——
we	——	**מִתַּסִּינַן** {־סֵי־}

FUTURE	
	will be cured יֵרָפֵא

	פַּעֵל	אִתְפַּעַל
he/it m.	——	**לִתַּסֵּי**

GERUND / INFINITIVE	
to cure לְרַפֵּא	*to be cured* לְהֵרָפֵא

פַּעֵל	אִתְפַּעַל
אַסּוּיֵי, לְאַסָּאָה, [לְאַסָּיָה]	**אִיתַּסּוּיֵי**

Code: —— = form not found in Talmud   {Yemenite vocalization}   <problematic>   [manuscript]

(22) תני (final root-letter י)

The Aramaic root תני is usually parallel to the Hebrew verb שָׁנה in its various meanings: *teach, learn, state, present, recite* and *repeat*. The Talmud uses it very commonly in *binyan* קַל with reference to statements of *tannaim*. In the אִתְפְּעֵל, only two forms occur in the Talmud: the past אִיתְּנִי, *it was repeated*, and the participle מִיתְּנֵי, *it is taught*; hence, we have not included that *binyan* in the paradigm below. We have also omitted the פַּעֵל, since the infinitive תַּנּוּיֵי, *(to) teach*, is apparently the only form from that *binyan*. According to the Yemenite tradition, moreover, even תנויי is not from *binyan* פַּעֵל, but it is an infinitive from the קַל, vocalized תְּנוּיֵי.[64] The suggestion that in some cases the participle מתני should be vocalized מְתַנֵּי from the פַּעֵל, rather than מַתְנֵי from the אַפְעֵל, is not so convincing.[65]

In the אַפְעֵל *binyan*, אַתְנֵי is sometimes parallel to the Hebrew הִשְׁנָה and means *he taught*. In other instances, however, it is parallel to the Hebrew הִתְנָה, meaning *he stipulated*. In both languages, the latter usage is apparently derived from the noun meaning *stipulation*, the Hebrew תְּנַאי and the Aramaic תְּנָאָה, respectively.

Note: The Yemenite vocalization places a *dagesh* in the ת of almost every form of this verb — even in such forms as לִיתְנֵי and מַתְנֵי, but we have not recorded such variations in our paradigms.

---

64   Morag (above, p. 15 note 8), pp. 138, 263 and 334.

65   Wilhelm Bacher presented that suggestion in his ערכי מדרש (translated into Hebrew from German by A.Z. Rabinowitz, Tel Aviv, 5683), pp. 318-319. See also Michael Sokoloff, *A Dictionary of Jewish Babylonian Aramaic of the Talmudic and Geonic Periods* (Ramat Gan, Israel: Bar Ilan University Press, 2002), pp. 1217 and 1221.

	קַל	אַפְעֵל (1)	אַפְעֵל (2)
PAST			
	stated/learned/presented שָׁנִיתִי / לָמַדְתִּי / לִמַּדְתִּי...	*taught* הִשְׁנֵיתִי...	*stipulated* הִתְנָה, הִתְנוּ
I	תְּנַאי, תְּנֵיתַה	אַתְנִיתֵיה	—
you m.s.	תְּנֵית	—	—
he/it m.	תְּנָא, תָּנָא,[66] תָּאנָא {תַּא-}, תּוּנָא[67]	אַתְנִי	אַתְנִי
she/it f.	{תְּנֵייָה} תְּנַיְיה	—	—
we	תְּנַן, תְּנֵינָא, תְּנֵינַן	—	—
you m. pl.	תְּנֵיתוּ	—	—
they m.	תְּנוּ {תְּנוֹ}, תָּנוּ[66]	אַתְנִיוּה	אַתְנוּ
ACTIVE PARTICIPLE			
	stating/learning/presenting שׁוֹנֶה / מְלַמֵּד...	*teaching* מַשְׁנֶה...	*stipulating* מַתְנֶה...
m.s.	תְּנֵי {תְּנֵי} <תנא>, תָּאנֵי {תַּאנֵי}	מַתְנֵי	מַתְנֵי
f.s.	{תַּ-} תְּנַיְיה	—	—
m.pl.	תָּנוּ {תְּנוּ}	מַתְנוּ	מַתְנוּ, מַתְנֵי {-נֵי}
f.pl.	—	מַתְנְיָין	—

Code: ——— = form not found in Talmud {Yemenite vocalization} <problematic> [manuscript]

66 The third-person masculine forms are popularly pronounced תָּנָא and תָּנוּ, respectively, like the Hebrew שָׁנָה and שָׁנוּ.

67 This is the interpretation according to Rabbenu Ḥananel in his commentary, e.g., on בבא מציעא ג, א, but not according to Rashi who, in his commentary on the same passage, explains תּוּנָא as a noun meaning *our tanna*. See תָּנָא תּוּנָא in *The Practical Talmud Dictionary* (Jerusalem: Ariel: 1991; Maggid-Koren 2016).

קַל	אַפְעֵל (1)	אַפְעֵל (2)
ACTIVE PARTICIPLE WITH SUFFIX		
state/learn/present שׁוֹנֶה אֲנִי / מְלַמֵּד אֲנִי...	*teach* מַשְׁנֶה אֲנִי...	
I	תָּנֵינָא {תְּ-}	מַתְנֵינָא	——
you m.s.	——	מַתְנֵית	——
we	——	מַתְנִינַן	——
you m. pl.	תָּנִיתוּ {תְּ-}	מַתְנִיתוּ, מַתְנִיתוּן	——

	PASSIVE PARTICIPLE	
	stated/presented שְׁנוּיָה...		
f.s.	תַּנְיָא	——	——
f.pl.	‹תניין›	——	——

Code: —— = form not found in Talmud   {Yemenite vocalization}   ‹problematic›   **[manuscript]**

קַל	(1) אַפְעֵל	(2) אַפְעֵל
FUTURE		
will[68] *learn/teach* אֶשְׁנֶה...	*will*[68] *teach* אַשְׁנֶה	*will*[68] *stipulate* יַתְנֶה, יַתְנוּ
I — אֶתְנְיֵיה	אַתְנֵי	——
you m.s. — תִּיתְנֵי	——	——
he/it m. — לִיתְנֵי, נִיתְנֵי	——	לַתְנֵי, נִיתְנֵי
we — נִיתְנֵי	——	——
they m. — ——	——	לִיתְנוּ

IMPERATIVE		
state!/teach! שְׁנֵה! / לְמֵד!	*teach!* הַשְׁנֵה!	*stipulate!* הַתְנֵה!...
you m.s. — תְּנֵי	אַתְנֵי	אַתְנֵי
you m. pl. — ——	——	אַתְנוּ

GERUND / INFINITIVE		
(to) learn/state/teach לִשְׁנוֹת / (לְ)לַמֵד / שָׁנֹה	*enabling to learn* הַשְׁנוֹת	*(to) stipulate* לְהַתְנוֹת / הַתְנֵה
(לְ)מִיתְנֵי, (לְ)מִיתְנָא, {(לְ)תָנוּיֵי}	אַתְנוּיֵי	(לְ)אַתְנוּיֵי

Code: —— = form not found in Talmud   {Yemenite vocalization}   <problematic>   [manuscript]

68   or: *let him...*

(23) שתי (initial sibilant and final י)

The Aramaic verb שתי, the equivalent of the Hebrew verb שתה, *drink*, is used only in *binyan* קַל, except for one form in *binyan* אִתְפְּעֵל, מִשְׁתְּתֵי, *fit for drinking*, which is not included in the paradigm. There are two unique elements in its conjugation: (1) In several forms (such as אִישְׁתִּי, *he drank*) a prosthetic א is added, apparently because of the phonetic difficulty presented by the combination of the consonants שׁ and ת at the beginning of a word. (2) Unlike most Aramaic roots with final י, the form used in the third-person masculine singular of the past tense ends with ־ִי (אִישְׁתִּי or שְׁתִי), rather than with ־ָא.

קַל	
	PAST
	drank
	...שָׁתִיתִי
I	שָׁתַאי
you m.s.	שָׁתֵית, אִשְׁתִּיתֵיה
he/it m.	אִישְׁתִּי, שְׁתִי
she/it f.	אִשְׁתְּיָא, שָׁתַאי
they m.	שְׁתוּ

Code: ——— = form not found in Talmud   {Yemenite vocalization}   <problematic>   [manuscript]

קַל	
ACTIVE PARTICIPLE	
drinking שׁוֹתֶה...	
m.s.	שָׁתֵי {שַׁתִי}
f.s.	שָׁתְיָא, שָׁתְיָיא
m.pl.	שָׁתוּ {שְׁ־} <שתי>, שָׁתַין {שַׁתְיָן}
ACTIVE PARTICIPLE WITH SUFFIX	
drink שׁוֹתֶה אֲנִי...	
I	שָׁתֵינָא {שְׁ־}
you m.s.	שָׁתֵית {שְׁ־}
we	שָׁתֵינַן {שְׁתֵינַן}
FUTURE	
will[69] drink אֶשְׁתֶּה...	
I	אִישְׁתֵּי
you m.s.	תִּשְׁתֵּי
he/it m.	לִישְׁתֵּי, נִישְׁתֵּי
she/it f.	תִּשְׁתֵּי
we	נִישְׁתֵּי
you m. pl.	תִּשְׁתּוּן
they m.	לִישְׁתּוּ

69   or: *let him...*

קַל

IMPERATIVE
drink!
שְׁתֵה!, שְׁתוּ!

you m.s.	שְׁתִי, אִישְׁתִּי <אשתי>
you m. pl.	שְׁתוּ, אִשְׁתוּ

GERUND / INFINITIVE
(to) drink
לִשְׁתּוֹת / שָׁתֹה
(לְ)מִישְׁתֵּי, מִישְׁתָּא <משתה>, מִישְׁתְּיָא

Code: ⸺ = form not found in Talmud   {Yemenite vocalization}   <problematic>   **[manuscript]**

(24) אתי (initial א and final י)

אתי, *come*, is a common Aramaic root that is also found in Biblical Hebrew, as in וְאָתָה מֵרִבְבוֹת קֹדֶשׁ (דברים לג:ב). The Aramaic verb is parallel to the Hebrew verb בוא. In the אַפְעֵל, אַיְיתִי (like הֵבִיא in the Hebrew הִפְעִיל) has a causative sense, *bring*. In certain forms of the conjugation, the first root letter א and the third root letter י are sometimes deleted.

Note: Yemenite vocalization places a *dagesh* in the ת of almost every form of this verb — even in such forms as אֲתָא, but we have ignored that phenomenon in our paradigm.

	קַל	אַפְעֵל
	PAST	
	came בָּאתִי...	*brought* הֵבֵאתִי...
I	אֲתַאי, אֲתֵיתִי	אַיְיתֵית [אַיְתַאי] ‹אתאי›
you m.s.	אֲתֵית	אַיְיתֵית
he/it m.	אֲתָא	אַיְיתִי
she/it f.	אֲתַאי, אֲתָת ‹אתיא›	אַיְיתָא, אַיְיתִי, [אַיְיתִיאָה, אַיְיתִיא] ‹אתיא, אתאי›
we	אֲתַאן, אֲתַן, אֲתֵינַן	אַיְיתֵינָא
you m. pl.	אֲתֵיתוּ	——
they m.	אֲתוּ	אַיְיתוּ
they f.	אֲתַיִין, [אֲתַאן] ‹אתן›	——

Code: —— = form not found in Talmud {Yemenite vocalization} ‹problematic› [manuscript]

	קַל	אַפְעֵל

ACTIVE PARTICIPLE

	coming בָּא...	*bringing* מֵבִיא...
m.s.	אָתֵי {אָ-} ‹אתא›	מַיְיתֵי
f.s.	אָתְיָא {אָ-}	מַתְיָא, מַיְיתָא
m.pl.	אָתֵי ,אָתוּ {אָ-} ‹אתי›	מַיְיתוּ {-תֵי}, מַיְיתֵי {-תֵי}, מַיְיתִין
f.pl.	אָתְיָין {אָ-} אתאן	מַיְיתָן, מַתְיָין

ACTIVE PARTICIPLE WITH SUFFIX

	come בָּא אֲנִי...	*bring* מֵבִיא אֲנִי...
I	אָתֵינָא {אֱ-}	מַיְיתֵינָא
you m.s.	אָתֵית {אֱ-}	מַיְיתֵית
we	אָתִינַן {אֲתֵינַן} אתיאן	מַיְיתִינַן {-תֵי-}

IMPERATIVE

	come! בּוֹא...!	*bring!* הָבֵא...!
m.s.	תָּא {תַּא}	אַיְיתִי
f.s.	תָּאִי {תַּאי}	אַיְיתִי
m.pl.	אֵיתוּ, תוּ	אַיְיתוּ

Code: —— = form not found in Talmud   {Yemenite vocalization}   ‹problematic›   **[manuscript]**

124

קַל	אַפְעֵל
FUTURE	
will[70] come אָבוֹא...	will[70] bring אָבִיא...

	קַל	אַפְעֵל
I	אֵיתֵי	אַיְיתֵי
you m.s.	תֵּיתֵי	תַּיְיתֵי
he/it m.	נֵיתֵי, יֵיתֵי, לֵיתֵי	לַיְיתֵי, נַיְיתֵי, יַיְיתֵי
she/it f.	תֵּיתֵי ‹תתיא›	תַּיְיתֵי
we	נֵיתֵי ‹ניתו›	נַיְיתֵי, לַיְיתֵי
you m. pl.	——	תַּיְיתוּ
they m.	לֵיתוּ, נֵיתוּ, יֵיתוּן	לַיְיתוּ, נַיְיתוּ
they f.	——	‹ניתן›

GERUND / INFINITIVE	
(to) come (לְ)בוֹא	(to) bring לְהָבִיא / הָבֵא
(לְ)מֵיתֵי, לְמֵיתָא	(לְ)אָתוֹיֵי {אַ-}, (לְ)אַיְיתוֹיֵי

Code: —— = form not found in Talmud   {Yemenite vocalization}   ‹problematic›   **[manuscript]**

70   or: *let him...*

(25) הוי (initial guttural and final י)

In *binyan* קל the Aramaic root הוי, with a *consonantal vav*, serves as the equivalent to the Hebrew root היה, and its forms are presented in the paradigm below. The conjugation of the future also includes the forms תְּהֵא and יְהֵא (without a consonantal *vav*), which are similar to their Hebrew parallels.

The verb הַוִּי, which is apparently the *binyan* פַּעֵל of this root, is used in the past tense only, meaning *he raised an objection* or *he discussed*. It may have developed from the Biblical Aramaic חַוִּי, *he told*.[71]

	קל		פַּעֵל
	PAST		
	was... הָיִיתִי...		*raised an objection/discussed* הִקְשָׁה / דָּן...
I	**הֲוַאי, הֲוֵיתִי, הֲוֵינָא**		—
you m.s.	**הֲוֵית** (הות, הוות)		—
he/it m.	**הֲוָה**, ‹הֲוִי›		הַוִּי
she/it f.	**הֲוַאי, הֲוָות, הֲוֵית, הֲוַיָא** {הֲוָיָא}		—
we	**הֲוֵינַן** הוא, **הֲוֵינָא**		הַוֵּינַן
you m. pl.	**הֲוֵיתוּן** {־תוּן}		—
they m.	**הֲווֹ**[72]		הַווֹ
they f.	**הֲוַיָין** {הֲוָיָן}, **הֲוַיָא**		—

Code: ——— = form not found in Talmud   {Yemenite vocalization}   <problematic>   [manuscript]

71   See Morag, *Babylonian Aramaic*, p. 267, note 114.
72   Among some Yemenites: הַווֹ. See Morag, (above, p. 15 note 8), p. 254 and note 22 ad loc.

קַל

	ACTIVE PARTICIPLE
	being הֲוָה...
m.s.	הָוֵי {הֲ-}
f.s.	הָוְיָא {הֲ-}
m.pl.	הָווּ {הֲ-}, הָוְיין {הַוְיָן}
f.pl.	הָוְיין {הֲ-}

	ACTIVE PARTICIPLE WITH SUFFIX
	I am... הֲוָה אֲנִי...
I	הָוֵינָא {הֲ-}
you m.s.	הָוֵית {הֲ-}
you m. pl.	הָוִיתוּ {הֲ-}

	FUTURE (singular)
	will[73] be אֶהְיֶה...
I	אֱהֱוֵי {אֲהֲוֵי}
you m.s.	תֵּיהֱוֵי {תִּיהֲוֵי}, תְּהֵא
you f.s.	תֵּיהֱוְיין {תִּיהֲוְיִין}
he/it m.	לֶהֱוֵי {לִיהֱוֵי}, נֶהֱוֵי {נִיהֱוֵי} {יְהֵוֵי} {יְהֵוֵי}, יְהֵא <יהי>, נְהֵי
she/it f.	תֵּיהֱוֵי {תִּיהֲוֵי}, תְּהֵא

73　or: *let him...*

קַל

	FUTURE (plural)
	will[74] be
	נִהְיֶה...
we	‹לִיהוּ› {לִיהֱוֵי} [לִיהֱוֵי]
you m.pl.	{תִּיהְווּ} תֵּיהֱווּ
you f.pl.	{תִּהְוְיָין} תֵּהֱוְיָין
they m.	[וְיָהוֹן] ,{יִיהְווּ} יֶהֱווּ ,{נִיהְווּ} נֶיהֱווּ ,{לִיהְווּ} לֵיהֱווּ
they f.	[תֵּהוֹן] ,{יִהְוְיָן} יֶהֱוְיָן ,{לִיהְוְיָין} לֵיהֱוְיָין

	IMPERATIVE
	be!
	הֱיֵה...!
m.s.	הֲוִי
f.s.	{הֲוַי} הֲוִי
m.pl.	הֲווּ[75]

	GERUND / INFINITIVE
	(to) be
	לִהְיוֹת / הָיָה
	{מִיהְוָה} מֶיהֱוָה ,{מִיהְוֵי} מֶיהֱוֵי(לְ)

Code: ——— = form not found in Talmud   {Yemenite vocalization}   ‹problematic›   [manuscript]

74   or: *let us...*
75   or: הֲווּ, see note 70 above.

(26) עלל ("geminate" root)

The verb עלל means *come in* or *enter* in the Aramaic *binyan* קַל. It should not be confused with the Hebrew verb עלה, which means *go up* — a meaning that Aramaic expresses with the verb סלק, verb 8. In both the פַּעֵל and אַפְעֵל *binyanim*, עלל has a causative sense, *bring in*. There is also one instance of *binyan* אִתְפַּעַל (which is not included in the paradigm) found in the Talmud in the phrase: לָא מִתְעַיֵּיל, *it cannot be brought in*. In the course of this paradigm, one of the letters ל is often deleted — as happens in the paradigms of Hebrew verbs with identical second and third root-letters, like סבב and חנן.

קַל	פַּעֵל	אַפְעֵל
	PAST	
entered	*brought in*	*brought in*
נִכְנַסְתִּי...	הִכְנַסְתִּי...	הִכְנִיס...
I	עַלִית, עַיַילִית {עֲיֵי-}, עַיֵילִי {עֲיֵ-}	עֲיֵילִית	——
you m.s.	עַיֵילְתְ {עֲיֵילְתְּ}	עֲיֵילְתֵּיה	——
he/it m.	עָל, עָאל, עֲיֵיל {עֲיֵיל}	עֲיֵיל [עֲלֵיל]	אֲעֵיל
she/it f.	עַלַת (עלתה), עֲיַילָא {עֲיֵ-}, [עֲלָא, עָאל]	עֲיֵילָא {עֲיֵ-} ‹עיילה›	‹אעיילא›
they m.	עָלוּ, עוּל, [76]עֲיֵילוּ, [עֲיֵיוּל][76]	עֲיֵילוּ {עֲיֵ-}	אֲעֵילוּ

Code: —— = form not found in Talmud   {Yemenite vocalization}   ‹problematic›   [manuscript]

[76] The ו is *infixed*, as explained on p. 50, note 3.

קַל	פַּעֵל	אַפְעֵל

	ACTIVE PARTICIPLE		
	entering ...נִכְנָס	*bringing in* ...מַכְנִיס	
m.s.	עָיֵיל {עָ-}	מְעַיֵּיל	——
f.s.	עָיֵילָא	מְעַיֵּילָא, מְעַיֵּילָה	——
m.pl.	עָיֵילִין, עָיֵילִי {עָיֵילֵי}, עָיֵילוּ	מְעַיֵּילִין, מְעַיֵּילִי {-לֵי}	——
f.pl.	עָיֵילָן	——	——

	ACTIVE PARTICIPLE WITH SUFFIX		
	enter ...נִכְנָס אֲנִי	*bring in* ...מַכְנִיס אֲנִי	
I	עָיֵילְנָא {עָ-}	מְעַיֵּילְנָא	——
you m.s.	עָיֵילַתְּ {עָיֵילְתְּ}	מְעַיֵּילַתְּ {מְעַיֵּילְתְּ}	——
we	עָיֵילִינַן {עָיֵילִינַן}	מְעַיֵּילִינַן	——
you m. pl.	עָיֵילִיתוּ {עָ-, עָיֵילְתוּ}	——	——

Code: —— = form not found in Talmud   {Yemenite vocalization}   <problematic>   [manuscript]

קַל	פַּעֵל	אַפְעֵל

	FUTURE		
	will[77] enter אֶכְנֵס...	will[77] bring in אַכְנִיס...	will[77] bring in תַכְנִיס...
I	אֵיעוֹל {עוּל-}	אַעֲיֵילֵיה	——
you m.s.	——	תְעַיֵיל	תַעֵיל
he/it m.	לֵיעוֹל {עוּל-}, נֵיעוֹל {עוּל-} <נֵיעַל>	נְעַיֵיל, לִיעַיֵיל, לְעַיֵיל	——
she/it f.	תֵּיעוֹל {עוּל-}	——	——
they m.	לֵיעַלוּן {לֵיעְלוּן}, [לִיעַיְילוּ, נֵיעוּל][78]	לִיעַיְילוּ [נְעַיְילוּ] <לְעַיְילִי>	——

	IMPERATIVE		
	enter! הַכָּנֵס!, הִכָּנְסוּ!	bring in! הַכְנֵס!	
m.s.	עוֹל {עוּל}	עַיֵיל	——
m.pl.	עוּלוּ	——	——

	GERUND / INFINITIVE		
	(to) enter (לְ)הִכָּנֵס	(to) bring in לְהַכְנִיס / הַכְנֵס	(to) bring in (לְ)הַכְנִיס
	(לְ)מֵיעַל	(לְ)עַיּוֹלֵי	אַעוֹלֵי

Code: —— = form not found in Talmud   {Yemenite vocalization}   <problematic>   [manuscript]

77   or: *let him...*
78   The ו is *infixed*, as explained on p. 50, note 3.

(27) קוֹם ("hollow" root)

The Aramaic verb קוֹם in *binyan* קַל usually means *stand*, like the Hebrew verb עמד. Occasionally, it has the same meaning as קוֹם in Hebrew, *get up* or *rise*. In *binyan* פַּעֵל, קַיֵּים means *he fulfilled*, and in the אִתְפַּעַל, its passive, אִיקַּיַּים means *it was fulfilled* — like the Hebrew קִיֵּם and נִתְקַיֵּם, respectively. In the אַפְעֵל, אוֹקִים means *he established*, like הֶעֱמִיד from the Hebrew הִפְעִיל. Its passive אִיתּוֹקַם, the אִתְפַּעַל, appears only in the participle, e.g., מִיתּוֹקַם, *established*.

The Aramaic conjugation sometimes deletes the final root-letter ם, as in קָאֵי. The *binyan* אַפְעֵל features a ו after its prefix letter (as in אוֹקִים and מוֹקִים) in the manner of verbs with י as the first root-letter, such as אוֹדַע from ידע.[79]

	קַל	פַּעֵל	אִתְפַּעַל	אַפְעֵל
	PAST			
	stood/rose עָמַדְתִּי / קַמְתִּי...	*fulfilled* קַיָּמְתִּי...	*was fulfilled* נִתְקַיֵּם	*established* הֶעֱמַדְתָּ...
I	[קָמֵית]	קַיְּימִי, קַיְּימִית	—	—
you m.s.	קַמְתְּ	קַיַּמְתְּ	—	אוֹקִימְתָּא
he/it m.	קָם	קַיֵּים	אִיקַּיַּים	אוֹקֵי, אוֹקִים
she/it f.	קַמַת, קָמָה <קמא>	—	—	—
we	[קַמְנַן, קַמְנָא] <קמינן>	קַיְּימְנוּהִי	—	אוֹקִימְנָא <אוקימנן, אוקמינן>
you m. pl.	—	—	—	אוֹקִימְתּוּן
they m.	קָמוּ, קוּם[80]	—	—	אוֹקִימוּ, אוֹקְמוּ
they f.	—	—	—	<אוקמן>

79 Compare the Hebrew verb זול, which in the sense of *cheapen* is conjugated in the הִפְעִיל: הוֹזַלְתִּי, etc., like verbs with the initial root-letter י.

80 The ו is *infixed*, as explained on p. 50, note 3.

קַל	פַּעֵל	אִתְפְּעַל	אַפְעֵל	
PARTICIPLE[81]				
ACTIVE *standing/rising* עוֹמֵד / קָם...	ACTIVE *fulfilling* מְקַיֵּם...	REFL./PASS. *fulfilled* מִתְקַיֵּם...	ACTIVE *establishing* מַעֲמִיד...	PASSIVE *set in place* מָעֳמָדִים...
m.s. קָאִים, קָאֵי {קָאֵי}, קָ־[82] {קָא}	מְקַיֵּים	מִיקַיַּים, מְקַיֵּים	מוֹקִים, מוֹקֵי	—
f.s. {קָיְימָא} קָיְימָא	מְקַיְּימָא	מְקַיְּימָא	מוֹקְמָה	—
m.pl. קָיְימִין, קָיְימִי {קָיְימֵי}, קָיְימוּ	מְקַיְּימִין {מְקַיְּימֵי}	מְקַיְּימִי {מְקַיְּימֵי}	מוֹקְמִי {־מֵי}	[מוֹקְמִי]
f.pl. קָיְימָן	—	—	—	‹מוקמן›

	stand/rise עוֹמֵד אֲנִי...	fulfill מְקַיֵּם אֲנִי...		establish מַעֲמִיד אֲנִי...
ACTIVE PARTICIPLE WITH SUFFIX				
I	קָאִימְנָא {קָ־}	מְקַיְּימְנָא		מוֹקִימְנָא ‹מוקמינא›
you m.s.	קָיְימַתְּ {קָיְימְתְּ}	‹מקיימת›		מוֹקְמַתְּ {מוֹקַמְתְּ, מוֹקֶמְתְּ} מוקמית
we	קָיְימִינַן {קָיְימִינָן}	מְקַיְּימִינַן		מוֹקְמִינַן ‹קיימינא›
you m. pl.	קָיְימִיתוּ {קָ־, קָיְימְתוּ}	מְקַיְּימִיתוּן		מוֹקְמִיתוּ

Code: —— = form not found in Talmud   {Yemenite vocalization}   ‹problematic›   **[manuscript]**

81   In addition to these active forms, there is one common passive participle from *binyan* קַל: **קִים**, *established*. According to Epstein (p. 90), the feminine participle קַיְימָא in the phrase קַיְימָא לָן is also a passive form.

82   קָא or the prefix קָ־ is used before other participles for emphasis, as in קָא אָמַר or קָאָמַר, *he is saying*.

	קַל	פַּעֵל	אִתְפְּעַל	אַפְעֵל
	FUTURE			
	will[83] stand/ rise	will[83] fulfill/ certify	will[83] be fulfilled	will[83] establish
	אֱמֹד / אָקוּם...	יְקַיֵּם...	יִתְקַיֵּם...	אַעֲמִיד...
I	אֵיקוּם, אֵיקוּ	—	—	אוֹקִים ‹אוקי›
you m.s.	—	—	—	תּוֹקְמַה
he/it m.	לֵיקוּם, לֵיקוּ, יְקוּם, נֵיקוּם	לִיקַיֵּים, לְקַיֵּים	לִיקַיַּים	לוֹקִים, לוֹקֵי, נוֹקִים ‹נוקי›
she/it f.	תֵּיקוּם, תֵּיקוּ, {תֵּיקוּ}[84] תְּקוּם	—	תִּתְקַיַּים	—
we	נֵיקוּם, נֵיקוּ, לֵיקוּם, לֵיקוּ	נְקַיֵּים {נְקַיִּים}	—	נוֹקִים
you m. pl.	תְּקוּמוּ	—	—	—
they m.	לֵיקוּמוּ	לְקַיְּימוּ	—	לוֹקְמוּ ‹לוקמי›

Code: ——— = form not found in Talmud   {Yemenite vocalization}   ‹problematic›   [manuscript]

83 or: *let him...*

84 The Yemenite pronunciation distinguishes between תֵּיקוּ, as a technical term that indicates an unresolved controversy, and תֵּיקוּ when used in other senses (Morag [above, p. 15 note 8] p. 213, note 12).

קַל	פַּעֵל	אִתְפַּעַל	אַפְעֵל

		IMPERATIVE		
	stand!/rise! ...!עֲמֹד! / קוּם	*fulfill!/certify!* !קַיֵּמוּ		*establish!* !הַעֲמֵד
m./f.s.	**קוּם**	——	——	**אוֹקִי, אוֹקִים**
m.pl.	**קוּמוּ**	**קַיְּימוּ**	——	——

		GERUND / INFINITIVE		
	(to) stand/rise קוּם / לָקוּם / לַעֲמֹד	*to fulfill* לְקַיֵּם	*to be fulfilled* לְהִתְקַיֵּם	*(to) establish* לְהַעֲמִיד / הַעֲמֵד
	(לְ)**מֵיקָם** {מֵיקַם} <לקיומא>	(לְ)**קַיּוֹמֵי** <לקיומא>	**[לְאִיקַיּוֹמֵי]** <לאיקיומא>	(לְ)**אוֹקוֹמֵי** <אוקמי>

Code: —— = form not found in Talmud   {Yemenite vocalization}   <problematic>   [manuscript]

(28) נוח ("hollow" root with initial נ)

As in its Hebrew counterpart, in the Aramaic verb נוח the initial root-letter נ is retained throughout the conjugation because of its second root-letter ו. The third root-letter ח causes the vowel that precedes it to become *pathaḥ*, as in the participle מַנַח. With regard to meaning, the *binyan* קַל of this verb means *rest*. In most instances, the causative אַפְעֵל is parallel to the Hebrew הִפְעִיל, הִנִּיחַ, *he placed*, but elsewhere the Hebrew הֵנִיחַ (with the *tzerei* vowel under the ה and no *dagesh* in the נ), *he gave rest*, is more appropriate.

The other *binyan* in which this root appears is presented in the middle column below as the אִתְפְּעֵל, as it is usually pronounced אִתְּנַח — even though sometimes it may be better understood as אִתַּנַּח from *binyan* אִתַּפְעַל, the reflexive/passive of the אַפְעֵל.

קַל	אִתְפְּעֵל	אַפְעֵל
	PAST	
rested נָח	was placed, was acceptable הֻנַּח, הוּנְחָה	placed הִנַּחְתִּי...
I ——	——	אַנְחִי
you m.s. ——	——	אַנַחְת {אֲנַחַת} <אנחתת>
he/it m. נָ֫ח	אִתְּנַח	אַנַּח
she/it f. ——	אִיתְּנַחָא	אַנְחַתָּא
we ——	——	אַנַּחְנָא
they m. ——	——	אַנְחוּ

Code: —— = form not found in Talmud   {Yemenite vocalization}   <problematic>   [manuscript]

136

קַל	אִתְפְּעֵל	אַפְעֵל

	PARTICIPLE[85]			
	ACTIVE *resting* נָח...	**REFL./PASS.** *being placed* מֻנָּח / מְנָחִים	**ACTIVE** *placing* מַנִּיח...	**PASSIVE** *placed* מֻנָּח
m.s.	**נָיֵיח** {נַיֵּיח}	**מִתְּנַח** {מַתְּנַח}[86]	**מַנַּח**	**מַנַּח** {גם: מְנַּח :מנח}
f.s.	**נָיְיחָא** {נַיְחָא}	—	**מַנְּחָא**	**מַנְּחָא, מַנְּחָה** <מנחת>
m.pl.	**נָיְיחִי** {נַיְחֵי}	**מִתְּנְחִי** {מַתְּנְחֵי}[86]	**מַנְּחִי** {חֵי-}	**מַנְּחִי** {חֵי-}
f.pl.	**נָיְיחָן** {נַיְ-}	—	—	—

		ACTIVE PARTICIPLE WITH SUFFIX	
		place מַנִּיח אֲנִי...	
I	—	**מַנַּחְנָא**	
you m.s.	—	**מַנַּחַתְּ** {מַנַּחְתְּ}	
we	—	**מַנְּחִינַן**	

Code: ——— = form not found in Talmud   {Yemenite vocalization}   <problematic>   [manuscript]

---

85 In addition to the active forms, there is one common *passive* participle from *binyan* קַל (f.s.): **נִיחָא**, *pleasant* or *convenient*.

86 These Yemenite forms may not belong under the root נוח, *binyan* אִתְפְּעֵל, but they may be passive participles from *binyan* אַפְעֵל of the derivative root תנח (Morag, [above, p. 15 note 8], p. 232).

קַל	אִתְפְּעֵל	אַפְעֵל

FUTURE		
will[87] rest	will[87] be placed	will[87] place
יָנוּחַ, תָּנוּחַ	יְנַּח	יַנִּיחַ...

	קַל	אִתְפְּעֵל	אַפְעֵל
he/it m.	לֵינַח, גֵינַח	לִיתְּנַח	לֵינַח, לַנְחֵיהּ, נַּח
she/it f.	תֵּינַח	——	——
they	——	——	נֵינְחוּ

IMPERATIVE		
		place!
		הַנַּח!, הַנִּיחוּ!

	קַל	אִתְפְּעֵל	אַפְעֵל
m.s.	——	——	אַנַּח
m.pl.	——	——	אַנְּחוּהּ

GERUND / INFINITIVE		
(to) rest	"be acceptable"	to place
לָנוּחַ / נוּחַ	הוּגַּח	(לְ)הָנִיחַ
(לְ)מֵינַח {(לְ)מֵינָח}	אִיתְּנוֹחֵי	(לְ)אַנּוֹחֵי

Code: —— = form not found in Talmud   {Yemenite vocalization}   <problematic>   [manuscript]

87 or: let him...

138

(29) מות ("hollow" root)

This verb has the same meaning as its Hebrew parallel, *die*. It appears only in *binyan* קַל in Aramaic. As in קום, verb 27, the middle root-letter ו does not appear in the past tense or in the participle. In this verb, however, the *ḥirik* is the dominant vowel in the past tense, rather than a *pathaḥ* or a *kamatz*.

קַל

	PAST
	died
	מֵת...
he/it m.	מִית
she/it f.	מִיתַת, מִיתָא [מִיתָה]
they m.	מִיתוּ

	ACTIVE PARTICIPLE
	dying
	מֵת...
m.s.	מָיֵית ‎{מַ-}‎, מָאֵית ‎<מית>‎
f.s.	מָיְיתָא, מִיתָה
m.pl.	מָיְיתִין, מָיְיתִי ‎{-תֵי}‎

Code: ——— = form not found in Talmud   {Yemenite vocalization}   <problematic>   [manuscript]

139

קַל

ACTIVE PARTICIPLE WITH SUFFIX

are dying

מֵת אַתָּה, מֵתִים אֲנַחְנוּ

you m.s.	מָיְתַתְּ {מְיֵיתְתְּ}
we	[מָיְיתִינַן] ‹מיתנן›

FUTURE

will[88] die

אָמוּת...

I	[אֵימוּת]
he/it m.	לֵימוּת, יְמוּת
she/it m.	תְּמוּת
they m.	לֵימוּתוּ ‹ימותו›

GERUND / INFINITIVE

to die

לָמוּת

(לְ)מֵימַת {(לְ)מֵימָת}

Code: ——— = form not found in Talmud　{Yemenite vocalization}　‹problematic›　[manuscript]

88　or: *let him...*

(30) הימן (quadriliteral)

The Aramaic verb הימן, *believe*, is regarded by modern scholars as essentially a four-letter root, with the long vowel *tzerei* under the first root-letter ה together with the vowel letter י (יֵ –) representing an original consonant א.[89] Its conjugation is somewhat similar to *binyan* פַּעֵל. All the forms have an active meaning — except for the unique form **לִיתְהֵימַן**, *let him be believed*, which is not presented in our tables, and the passive participles like מְהֵימַן, *believed*, *trustworthy*.

	PAST
	believed/trusted
	הֶאֱמַנְתִּי...
I	**הֵימַנִי**
you m.s.	**הֵימַנְתֵּיהּ**
he/it m.	**הֵימְנֵיהּ**
they m.	**הֵימְנוּהּ**

	PARTICIPLE	
	ACTIVE	PASSIVE
	believing	*believed/trustworthy*
	מַאֲמִין / מַאֲמִינִים	נֶאֱמָן...
m.s.	**מְהֵימֶן**	**מְהֵימַן**
f.s.	——	**מְהֵימְנָא**
m.pl.	**מְהֵימְנִי** {-נֵי}	**מְהֵימְנִי** {-נֵי}

Code: —— = form not found in Talmud {Yemenite vocalization} <problematic> [manuscript]

89 See Morag (above, p. 15 note 8), p. 284. It is apparently derived from the root אמן *be firm, be true*. Cf. אָמֵן in the Hebrew prayerbook.

PARTICIPLE WITH SUFFIX	
ACTIVE *believing* מַאֲמִין אֲנִי, מַאֲמִינִים אֲנַחְנוּ	**PASSIVE** *believed/trustworthy* נֶאֱמָן אֲנִי, נֶאֱמָן אַתָּה
I am — **מְהֵימְנָא** {מְהֵימֶנְנָא}	**מְהֵימַנְנָא, מְהֵימַנָא** <מהימנינא>
you (s.) are — ——	**מְהֵימַנְתְּ**
we are — **מְהֵימְנִינַן**	——

FUTURE
let him believe יַאֲמִין
he — **לֵיהֵימְנֵיהּ, נְהֵמְנֵיהּ**

GERUND / INFINITIVE
(to) believe לְהַאֲמִין / הַאֲמֵן
לְהֵימוֹנֵיהּ, הֵימוֹנֵי

Code: —— = form not found in Talmud   {Yemenite vocalization}   <problematic>   [manuscript]

5

PARADIGMS FOR ARAMAIC VERBS IN TARGUM ONKELOS

The previous chapter presented conjugations of thirty Aramaic verbs that appear frequently in the Babylonian Talmud — recording only the specific forms that actually occur in that text. Following the same system[1], this chapter presents conjugations of thirty-two verbs that are common in Targum Onkelos, according to the forms that actually occur in the Targum text. Twenty-four of them are the same verbs already presented in Chapter 4 according to their conjugations in the Babylonian Talmud, while the additional eight are common verbs in Targum Onkelos that are not so common in the Talmud. (Note: An alphabetical index of the verbs appears on both inside covers of this book.)

1. זבן	9. אזל	17. תוב	25. אתי
2. דבר	10. אמר	18. קום	26. הוי
3. קרב	11. אכל	19. נוח	27. שתי
4. עבד	12. אלף (ילף)	20. מות	28. שאל
5. נפק	13. ילד	21. עלל	29. הימן
6. נחת	14. ידע	22. גלי	30. סובר (סבר)
7. סלק	15. נתן/יהב	23. חזי	31. שיצי
8. הלך	16. יתב	24. עדי	32. שיזב

As with the Babylonian Aramaic verbs in Chapter 4, the thirty-two verbs that are common in Targum Onkelos have been classified according to their various types and arranged in the following order: The first four verbs are *strong* verbs whose three root-letters

---

1   For the conventions that apply to this chapter as well, see paragraphs 1, 2, 3, 6, 8 and 9 on pp. 48-49 (and substitute "Targum Onkelos" for "the Talmud").

are retained throughout their conjugations. Verbs 5 through 28, however, contain *weak* root-letters that are sometimes deleted: the initial נ in verbs 5 and 6, נפק and נחת; the problematic ל in verbs 7 and 8, סלק and הלך;[2] the initial א root-letter in verbs 9 to 12, אזל, אמר, אכל and אלף; the initial י root-letter in verbs 13 to 16, ידע, ילד, יתב and יהב; the middle root-letter of the ("hollow") verbs 17 to 20, מות and נוח, קום, תוב; one ל in verb 21, the ("geminate") עלל; the final י in verbs 22 to 27, הוי, אתי, עדי, חזי, גלי, שתי; and the middle root-letter א is sometimes deleted from verb 28, שאל. The last four verbs, 29 to 32, שיזב and שיצי סובר, הימן, are treated as having quadriliteral roots, which have their own particular problems.

◇ The following index shows which Aramaic *binyanim* are presented in the paradigms of these thirty-two Targum Onkelos verbs.

קַל: All of the triliteral roots.

אִתְפְּעֵל: (4) עבד, (11) אכל, (13) ילד, (15) יהב, (22) גלי

פַּעֵל: (1) זבן, (2) דבר, (3) קרב, (8) הלך, (12) אלף, (18) קום, (22) גלי, (24) עדי, (28) שאל

אִתְפַּעַל: (1) זבן, (3) קרב, (7) סלק, (18) קום

אַפְעֵל (or **הַפְעֵל**): (5) נפק, (6) נחת, (7) סלק, (11) אכל, (12) ילף, (13) ילד, (14) ידע, (16) יתב, (17) תוב, (18) קום, (19) נוח, (20) מות, (21) עלל, (22) גלי, (23) חזי, (24) עדי, (25) אתי

אִתַּפְעַל: (16) יתב, (17) תוב, (21) עלל, (23) חזי

שַׁפְעֵל and **אִשְׁתַּפְעַל**: (4) עבד

◇ The verbal forms that appear in this chapter are taken from the version of Targum Onkelos found in the traditional *ḥumash* of Yemenite Jews, which they call *Taj* (an Arabic word similar to the Aramaic תָּגָא, *crown*). For many generations the Jews of Yemen dedicated themselves to the Targum with remarkable devotion and preserved it with great care, so that their Targum texts are much more reliable than those printed in ordinary *ḥumashim*.

2   These two verbs both have a problematic middle ל, but their conjugations are quite different. The verb סלק sometimes behaves like an initial נ verb (i.e., נסק), while הלך, in *binyan* קל, behaves like a "hollow" root (i.e., הוך). For details, see the paradigms of the two verbs on pp. 169-173.

In spite of this superiority, the Yemenite superlinear[3] vocalization system has one major problem that defies a perfect solution: the absence of a *segol* vowel. In Yemenite manuscripts, the *segol* vowel that occurs in other traditions is always marked by the same sign that is used to indicate *pathaḥ*, and indeed it is always pronounced as *pathaḥ* in their ancient tradition. Thus when Yemenite vowels are to be converted to the Tiberian vowels in use today, it is not always clear whether that particular vowel sign should be represented by our *pathaḥ* or by our *segol*. Unfortunately, the various modern editions of the *Taj* that have been printed with Tiberian vocalization contain some flagrant errors and inconsistencies in this regard. We have made a serious effort to arrive at an accurate determination, but in some instances our decisions to vocalize with a *segol* rather than a *pathaḥ*, or vice versa, are debatable.[4]

◇   The publication of paradigms of Targum Onkelos verbs — in addition to the paradigms of Babylonian Talmud verbs in the previous chapter — was undertaken because the two Aramaic dialects are significantly different. Even a superficial comparison of the two chapters reveals one general distinction: In the conjugations of the verbs of the Talmud, a slot designated for a particular tense, person, gender, and number may contain several alternate forms[5] — but in the conjugation of the verbs of the Targum only one form is listed.[6]

The five pages that follow present three tables: (1) a two-page synopsis of the conjugation of the verb in the Talmud; (2) a two-page synopsis of the conjugation of the verb in the Targum; (3) a list of fourteen differences in verbal conjugations between the two Aramaic dialects — with each difference illustrated by at least one example introduced by a colon.

---

3   In our system of vocalization, the Tiberian system, most vowels are positioned under the consonant, but in the system that was used by Babylonian and Yemenite Jews for centuries, all vowel signs are placed above the line, i.e., above the consonant, hence the term *superlinear*.

4   For example, see the paradigm of the future of *binyan* קל of the verb עבד (p. 160).

5   For example, see the third-person feminine singular of the past tense conjugation of most verbs.

6   The only exception is the second-person masculine singular of the past tense.

A SYNOPSIS OF THE REGULAR VERBAL CONJUGATION IN THE BABYLONIAN TALMUD

	Prefix	1st root-letter	2nd root-letter	Form
Binyan קַל				
Past	—	Vocal *sheva*: *לְ	No *dagesh*: קַ	לְקַט (לְקֵיט)
Participle	—	*Kametz*: *לָ	No *dagesh*: קֵ	לָקֵיט
Future	לִי-	Silent *sheva*: לְ	No *dagesh*: *קוֹ	לִילְקוֹט (-קַט)
Imperative	—	Vocal *sheva*: *לְ	No *dagesh*: קוֹ	לְקוֹט (-קַט)
Gerund/Infin.	מִי-	Silent *sheva*: לְ	No *dagesh*: *קַ	(לְ)מִילְקַט

	Affix	1st root-letter	2nd root-letter	Form
Binyan פַּעֵל				
Past (and imp.)	—	*Pathaḥ*: *לַ	*Dagesh*: קֵּ	לַקֵּיט
Participle	מְ-	*Pathaḥ*: לַ	*Dagesh*: קֵּ	מְלַקֵּיט
Future	לְ-	*Pathaḥ*: לַ	*Dagesh*: קֵּ	לְלַקֵּיט
Gerund/Infin.	-וֹ-ֵי	*Pathaḥ*: לַ	*Dagesh*: קוֹ	(לְ)לַקּוֹטֵי

	Affix	1st root-letter	2nd root-letter	Form
Binyan אַפְעֵל				
Past (and imp.)	אַ-	Silent *sheva*: לְ	No *dagesh*: *קֵ	אַלְקֵיט
Participle	מַ-	Silent *sheva*: לְ	No *dagesh*: *קֵ	מַלְקֵיט
Future	לַ-	Silent *sheva*: לְ	No *dagesh*: *קֵ	לַלְקֵיט
Gerund/Infin.	אַ-וֹ-ֵי	Silent *sheva*: לְ	No *dagesh*: *קוֹ	(לְ)אַלְקוֹטֵי

* If, however, this consonant is one of the בג"ד כפ"ת letters, it takes a "light" *dagesh* (as in מַכְתֵּיב, לְמֶכְתַּב and כְּתַב).

Binyan אִתְפְּעֵל

	Affix	1st root-letter	2nd root-letter	Form
Past (and imp.)	אִיתְ־ אִי־	Vocal sh^{e}va: *לְ לִ	No dagesh: קַ קַ	אִיתְלְקִיט אִילְקִיט
Participle	מִיתְ־ מִי־	Vocal sh^{e}va: *לְ לִ	No dagesh: קַ קַ	מִיתְלְקִיט מִילְקִיט
Future	לִיתְ־ לִי־	Vocal sh^{e}va: *לְ לִ	No dagesh: קַ קַ	לִיתְלְקִיט לִילְקִיט
Gerund/Infin.	אִיתְ־־וֹ־ֵי אִי־־וֹ־ֵי	Vocal sh^{e}va: *לְ לִ	No dagesh: קוֹ קוֹ	(לְ)אִיתְלְקוֹטֵי (לְ)אִילְקוֹטֵי

Binyan אִתְפַּעַל

	Affix	1st root-letter	2nd root-letter	Form
Past (and imp.)	אִיתְ־ אִי־	Pathaḥ: *לַ לַ	Dagesh: קַ קַ	אִיתְלַקַט אִילַקַט
Participle	מִיתְ־ מִי־	Pathaḥ: *לַ לַ	Dagesh: קַ קַ	מִיתְלַקַט מִילַקַט
Future	לִיתְ־ לִי־	Pathaḥ: *לַ לַ	Dagesh: קַ קַ	לִיתְלַקַט לִילַקַט
Gerund/Infin.	אִיתְ־־וֹ־ֵי אִי־־וֹ־ֵי	Pathaḥ: *לַ לַ	Dagesh: קוֹ קוֹ	(לְ)אִיתְלַקוֹטֵי (לְ)אִילַקוֹטֵי

Binyan אִתַּפְעַל

	Affix	1st root-letter	2nd root-letter	Form
Past (and imp.)	אִיתַּ־	Silent sh^{e}va: לְ	No dagesh: *קַ	אִיתַּלְקַט
Participle	מִיתַּ־	Silent sh^{e}va: לְ	No dagesh: *קַ	מִיתַּלְקַט
Future	לִיתַּ־	Silent sh^{e}va: לְ	No dagesh: *קַ	לִיתַּלְקַט
Gerund/Infin.	אִיתַּ־־וֹ־ֵי	Silent sh^{e}va: לְ	No dagesh: *קוֹ	(לְ)אִיתַּלְקוֹטֵי

* If, however, this consonant is one of the בג"ד כפ"ת letters, it takes a "light" dagesh (as in אִתְכְּתִיב, אִתְכַּתַב and אִתַּכְתַב).

147

A SYNOPSIS OF THE REGULAR VERBAL CONJUGATION IN TARGUM ONKELOS

Binyan קַל				
	Prefix	**1ˢᵗ root-letter**	**2ⁿᵈ root-letter**	**Form**
Past	—	Vocal *shᵉva*: לְ*	No *dagesh*: קַ	לְקַט (לְקֵיט)
Participle	—	*Kametz*: לָ*	No *dagesh*: קֵ	לָקֵיט
Future	יִ-	Silent *shᵉva*: לְ	No *dagesh*: קוֹ*	יִלְקוֹט (-קַט)
Imperative	—	Vocal *shᵉva*: לְ*	No *dagesh*: קוֹ	לְקוֹט (-קַט)
Gerund/Infin.	מִ-	Silent *shᵉva*: לְ	No *dagesh*: קַ*	(לְ)מִלְקַט

Binyan פַּעֵל				
	Affix	**1ˢᵗ root-letter**	**2ⁿᵈ root-letter**	**Form**
Past (and imp.)	—	*Pathaḥ*: לַ*	*Dagesh*: קֵּ	לַקֵּיט
Participle	מְ-	*Pathaḥ*: לַ	*Dagesh*: קֵּ	מְלַקֵּיט
Future	יְ-	*Pathaḥ*: לַ	*Dagesh*: קֵּ	יְלַקֵּיט
Gerund/Infin.	אָ-	*Pathaḥ*: לַ	*Dagesh*: קָּ	(לְ)לַקָּטָא

Binyan אַפְעֵל				
	Affix	**1ˢᵗ root-letter**	**2ⁿᵈ root-letter**	**Form**
Past (and imp.)	אַ-	Silent *shᵉva*: לְ	No *dagesh*: קֵ*	אַלְקֵיט
Participle	מַ-	Silent *shᵉva*: לְ	No *dagesh*: קֵ*	מַלְקֵיט
Future	יַ-	Silent *shᵉva*: לְ	No *dagesh*: קֵ*	יַלְקֵיט
Gerund/Infin.	אַ- - -ָא	Silent *shᵉva*: לְ	No *dagesh*: קָ*	(לְ)אַלְקָטָא

* If, however, this consonant is one of the בג"ד כפ"ת letters, it takes a "light" *dagesh* (as in כְּתַב, יִכְתּוֹב and מַכְתֵּיב).

אִתְפְּעֵל *Binyan*				
	Affix	1st root-letter	2nd root-letter	Form
Past (and imp.)	אִתְ־	Vocal *shᵉva*: לְ*	No *dagesh*: ק	אִתְלְקֵיט
Participle	מִתְ־	Vocal *shᵉva*: לְ*	No *dagesh*: ק	מִתְלְקֵיט
Future	יִתְ־	Vocal *shᵉva*: לְ*	No *dagesh*: ק	יִתְלְקֵיט
Gerund/Infin.	אִתְ־ ־־ָא	Vocal *shᵉva*: לְ*	No *dagesh*: קָ	(לְ)אִתְלְקָטָא

אִתְפַּעַל *Binyan*				
	Affix	1st root-letter	2nd root-letter	Form
Past (and imp.)	אִתְ־	*Pathaḥ*: לַ*	*Dagesh*: קַּ	אִתְלַקַּט
Participle	מִתְ־	*Pathaḥ*: לַ*	*Dagesh*: קַּ	מִתְלַקַּט
Future	יִתְ־	*Pathaḥ*: לַ*	*Dagesh*: קַּ	יִתְלַקַּט
Gerund/Infin.	אִתְ־ ־־ָא	*Pathaḥ*: לַ*	*Dagesh*: קָּ	(לְ)אִתְלַקָּטָא

אִתַּפְעַל *Binyan*				
	Affix	1st root-letter	2nd root-letter	Form
Past (and imp.)	אִתַּ־	Silent *shᵉva*: ל	No *dagesh*: קַ*	אִתַּלְקַט
Participle	מִתַּ־	Silent *shᵉva*: ל	No *dagesh*: קַ*	מִתַּלְקַט
Future	יִתַּ־	Silent *shᵉva*: ל	No *dagesh*: קַ*	יִתַּלְקַט
Gerund/Infin.	אִתַּ־ ־־ָא	Silent *shᵉva*: ל	No *dagesh*: קָ*	(לְ)אִתַּלְקָטָא

* If, however, this consonant is one of the בג"ד כפ"ת letters, it takes a "light" *dagesh* (as in אִתַּכְתַּב, אִתְבְּתִיב and אִתַּכְתַּב).

149

DIFFERENCES BETWEEN VERBS IN THE TWO DIALECTS

	BABYLONIAN TALMUD	TARGUM ONKELOS
1. Past tense, 1st person singular (regular verbs)	Generally final ת is deleted: אֲמַרִי	With final ת: אֲמַרִית
2. Past tense, 2nd person masculine singular	Suffix ־תְּ: אֲמַרְתְּ	Suffix ־תְּ or ־תָּא: אֲמַרְתְּ, אֲמַרְתָּא
3. Past tense, 1st person plural	Suffix נָ־, ־ַן or ־נָא: כְּתַבְנָא, אֲמַרַן, יְהֵיבְנַן	Suffix ־נָא: כְּתַבְנָא
4. Verbs with 3rd root-letter י, past tense, 1st person singular	Suffix usually ־אִי: חֲזַאי	Suffix ־תִי or ־ת: חֲזֵיתִי, חֲזֵית
5. Verbs with 3rd root-letter י, past, 3rd person feminine singular	Suffix ־אִי or ־ת: חֲזַאי, חֲזָת	Suffix ־ת: חֲזָת
6. Verbs with 3rd root-letter י, past & future, 2nd & 3rd masculine plural	Suffix ־ו, ־תון: לֵיחֱזוּ, חֲזוֹ, חֲזֵיתוּן	Suffix ־וֹן, ־ו, ־תון: יִחְזוֹן, חֲזוֹ, חֲזֵיתוּן
7. Masculine-plural participle	Generally, final ן deleted: אָמְרִי	Final ן retained: אָמְרִין
8. Verbs with 3rd root-letter י, masculine-plural participle	Suffix usually ־וּ: חָזוּ	Suffix ־ַן: חָזַן
9. Combinations of participle with pronoun subject, 1st or 2nd persons	Very common: אָמְרִינַן	Quite rare: יָדַעְנָא
10. Future tense, 3rd person masculine singular and plural	Generally ־נִי or לִי־ (rarely ־יִ): נִיכְתּוֹב, לִיכְתּוֹב	Prefix ־יִ: יִכְתּוֹב
11. Future tense, 1st person plural	Usually ־נִי, sometimes ־לִי: לִיפְלוֹג, נִיכְתּוֹב	Prefix always ־נִ: נִכְתּוֹב
12. Infinitive/gerund of all binyanim except for binyan קַל	Ending ־וֹיֵ־: (לְ)קַבּוֹלֵי	Ending ־ָ־א: (לְ)קַבָּלָא
13. Binyanim אִתְפַּעֵל and אִתְפְּעֵל	Often ת deleted: אִיכַּפַּל, מִימַּלְכִי	Usually ת intact: מִתְמַלְכִין
14. Binyan אַפְעֵל, "hollow" verbs	Prefix sometimes as if 1st root-letter י: מוֹתִיב, אוֹקִים	Prefix with shᵉva or hataf: אָקֵים, מְקִים

(1) זבן (initial root-letter sibilant)

Both the meaning of this verb and its conjugated forms in Targum Onkelos are similar to those that appear in the Babylonian Talmud, which were explained above on p. 53. As in the Talmud, three *binyanim* are used by Onkelos: זְבַן in *binyan* קָל, *he bought*; זַבֵּין in *binyan* פַּעֵל, *he sold*; and אִזְדַּבַּן in *binyan* אִתְפַּעַל, *it was sold*.

קָל	פַּעֵל	אִתְפַּעַל

		PAST	
	bought קְנָה	sold מָכַר...	was sold נִמְכַּר
he/it m.	זְבַן	זַבֵּין	אִזְדַּבַּן
you m. pl.	—	זַבֵּינְתּוּן	—
they m.	—	זַבִּינוּ	—

		PARTICIPLE	
	buying קוֹנִים	selling מוֹכֵר	being sold נִמְכָּר
m.s.	—	מְזַבֵּין	מִזְדַּבַּן
m.pl.	זָבְנִין	—	—

קַל	פַּעֵל	אִתְפְּעַל
FUTURE		
will buy תִּקְנֶה	*will sell* תִּמְכֹּר...	*will be sold* יִמָּכֵר...

	קַל	פַּעֵל	אִתְפְּעַל
you m.s.	תִּזְבּוּן	תְּזַבֵּין	—
he/it m.	—	יְזַבֵּין	יִזְדַּבַּן
she/it f.	—	—	תִּזְדַּבַּן
we	—	נְזַבְּנֵּיהּ	—
you m. pl.	—	תְּזַבְּנוּן	תִּזְדַּבְּנוּן
they m.	—	יְזַבְּנוּן	יִזְדַּבְּנוּן

IMPERATIVE		
buy! קְנֵה!	*sell!* מְכֹר!	

	קַל	פַּעֵל	
m.s.	—	זַבֵּין	—
m.pl.	זְבוּנוּ	—	—

GERUND/INFINITIVE		
to buy לִקְנוֹת	*(to) sell* לִמְכֹּר, מָכֹר	
לְמִזְבַּן	לְזַבּוֹנַהּ, זַבָּנָא	

(2) דבר (final guttural)

In *binyan* קַל this verb is used to translate the Hebrew verb לקח, *take*, in the sense of *lead* — rather than in the sense of *pick up and/or move*, which is translated by the verb נסב.[7] *Binyan* פַּעֵל translates the Hebrew verbs נחה and נהג in the sense of *lead* or *bring*.[8] As in the previous verb סבר, the guttural consonant ר sometimes causes the preceding vowel to be *pathaḥ* — rather than the usual *tzerei*, e.g., דַּבַּר instead of דַּבֵּר.

In addition to these two *binyanim*, which are presented in the paradigm below, two forms from other *binyanim* occur in Targum Onkelos: one from *binyan* אִתְפְּעֵל (the reflexive/passive of the קַל): **אִדְּבַרַת**, *she was taken*, the feminine singular of the past tense, and the other from *binyan* אִתְפַּעַל (the reflexive/passive of the פַּעֵל): the masculine-plural participle, **מִדַּבְּרִין**, *being led*. In both of these forms, the consonant ת from the אִתְ- and מִתְ- prefixes is assimilated with the first root-letter ד — i.e., it is in effect deleted and represented by the strong *dagesh* in that consonant.

---

7 This distinction is clarified by Rashi in his commentary on בראשית מג:טו.

8 The standard Aramaic translation of the Hebrew verb דִּבֵּר, *speak*, is the verb מַלֵּל — which occasionally appears in Biblical Hebrew, e.g., מִי מִלֵּל לְאַבְרָהָם (בראשית כא:ז).

קַל	פַּעֵל

PAST	
took לָקַחְתִּי...	*led* הוֹלַכְתִּי / נָהַגְתִּי...
I דְּבָרִית	דַּבָּרִית
you m.s. דְּבַרְתָּא	דַּבָּרְתְּ
you f.s. דְּבַרְתְּ	——
he/it m. דְּבַר	דַּבַּר
she/it f. דְּבָרַת	——
they m. דְּבָרוּ	——

ACTIVE PARTICIPLE	
	leading מוֹלִיךְ, נוֹהֲגִין
m.s. ——	מְדַבַּר
m.pl. ——	מְדַבְּרִין

154

פְּעַל	קַל

FUTURE	
will lead אֲנָהֵג, יִנְהַג	*will take* אֶקַּח...

	פְּעַל	קַל	
I	אֲדַבֵּר	אֶדְבְּרִנּוּ	I
	—	תִּדְבַּר	you m.s.
he/it m.	יְדַבֵּר	יִדְבַּר	he/it m.
	—	נִדְבַּר	we
	—	תִּדְבְּרוּן	you m.pl.
	—	יִדְבְּרוּן	they m.

IMPERATIVE	
lead! נְחֵה!	*take!* קַח!, קְחוּ!

	פְּעַל	קַל	
m.s.	דַּבֵּר	דְּבַר	m.s.
	—	דְּבַרוּ	m.pl.

GERUND / INFINITIVE	
to lead לִנְהֹג	*to take* לְקַחַת
לְדַבָּרוּתְהוֹן	לְמִדְבַּר

155

(3) קרב (middle root-letter ר)

The basic meaning of this verbal root is the same in Hebrew and Aramaic. In *binyan* קַל the Aramaic verb functions like its Hebrew counterpart in the sense of *come near, approach*. Onkelos uses it to translate not only this verbal root in Biblical Hebrew but also the roots נגש and even נגע (which is usually translated into English as *touch*). The conjugation of the past tense of *binyan* קַל follows the פְּעֵיל pattern with a *tzerei* or *ḥirik* vowel instead of the more usual *pathaḥ*, as in the Talmudic verb סלק on p. 74 above. The active participle, e.g., קָרֵיב, usually functions as an adjective (like קָרוֹב in Hebrew).

In the Targum, the Aramaic פַּעֵל, קָרֵיב, translates the Hebrew הִפְעִיל form הִקְרִיב,[9] *he brought near* (especially: an offering to the altar).[10] The *binyan* אִתְפַּעַל form אִתְקָרַב is generally used reflexively like the Hebrew הִתְקָרֵב (*binyan* הִתְפַּעֵל) in the sense of *he brought himself near* (= *he came near*).

9   This is somewhat surprising, since the אַפְעֵל is the *binyan* that is generally used to express causality. Compare the Hebrew verb לִמֵּד, *he taught*, where the intensive *binyan* (פִּעֵל) is used in a causative sense, *causing to learn*.

10 Thus the form קָרֵיב is a homonym (cf. Chapter 6): it may be either a participle from *binyan* קַל — or the past tense, third-person, masculine singular of *binyan* פַּעֵל. In the latter case, there is a long vowel under the ק — a *kametz* instead of the usual *pathaḥ* — because the consonant ר cannot take a *dagesh*. The same compensation for the *dagesh* also occurs in *binyan* אִתְפַּעַל, e.g., אִתְקָרַב.

קַל	פַּעֵל	אִתְפַּעַל

	PAST	
came near/ approached ...קָרֵבְתָּ / נְגַשְׁתָּ	*brought near/ brought (an offering)* ...הַקְרֵבְתָּ / לַקַחְתָּ	*was brought/ came near* הָקְרַב, קָרְבוּ

	קַל	פַּעֵל	אִתְפַּעַל
I	——	קָרֵיבִית	——
you m.s.	קָרֵיבְתָּא	——	——
he/it m.	קָרֵיב	קָרֵיב	אִתְקָרַב
she/it f.	קָרֵיבַת	קָרֵיבַת	——
we	——	קָרֵיבְנָא	——
you m. pl.	קָרֵיבְתּוּן	——	——
they m.	קָרֵיבוּ	קָרֵיבוּ	אִתְקָרַבוּ
they f.	קָרֵיבָא	——	——

	PARTICIPLE	
near/coming near ...קָרוֹב / נְגָשׁ	*bringing near* מַקְרֵיב, מַקְרִיבִים	*coming near* קְרֵבִים

	קַל	פַּעֵל	אִתְפַּעַל
m.s.	קָרֵיב	מְקָרֵיב	——
f.s.	קָרֵיבָא	——	——
m.pl.	קָרֵיבִין	מְקָרְבִין	מִתְקָרְבִין

קַל	פַּעֵל	אִתְפְּעַל
FUTURE		
will come near תִּקְרַב / תִּגַּשׁ...	*will bring near* אַקְרִיב / אֶקַּח...	*will bring -self near* תִּתְקָרֵב / תִּגַּשׁ...
I —	אַקְרֵיב	—
you m.s. תִּקְרַב	תְּקָרֵיב	תִּתְקָרַב
he/it m. יִקְרַב	יְקָרֵיב	יִתְקָרַב
she/it f. תִּקְרַב	—	תִּתְקָרַב
you m. pl. תִּקְרְבוּן	תְּקָרְבוּן	תִּתְקָרְבוּן
they m. יִקְרְבוּן	יְקָרְבוּן	יִתְקָרְבוּן

	IMPERATIVE	
	come near! קְרַב!, גְּשׁוּ!	*bring near!* הַקְרֵב! / קַח!
m.s.	קְרַב	קָרֵיב	—
m.pl.	קְרוּבוּ	—	—

GERUND / INFINITIVE		
(to) come near לְקְרַב, קְרַב	*(to) bring near* לְהַקְרֵיב, בְּהַקְרֵיב	*to bring oneself near* לְהִתְקָרֵב
לְמִקְרַב, מִקְרַב	לְקָרָבָא, בְּקָרוֹבֵיהוֹן	לְאִתְקָרָבָא

(4) עבד (initial guttural)

Both the meaning of this verb and its conjugated forms in Targum Onkelos are similar to what has been described in the survey of the verb in the Talmud above on p. 59. Besides the *binyanim* that are presented in the paradigm, one form from *binyan* פַּעֵל occurs in Targum Onkelos, i.e., the feminine-singular participle, **מְעַבְּדָא**, *producing*.

	קַל	אִתְפְּעֵל	שַׁפְעֵל	אִשְׁתַּפְעַל
	PAST			
	made/did עָשִׂיתִי...	*was made/ was done* נַעֲשָׂה...	*subjugated* שֶׁעְבְּדוּ	*were subjugated* נִשְׁתַּעְבְּדוּ
I	עֲבַדִית	—	—	—
you m.s.	עֲבַדְתְּ, עֲבַדְתָּא	—	—	—
he/it m.	עֲבַד	אִתְעֲבִיד	—	—
she/it f.	עֲבַדַת	אִתְעֲבִידַת	—	—
we	עֲבַדְנָא	—	—	—
you m.pl.	עֲבַדְתּוּן	—	—	—
you f.pl.	עֲבַדְתִּין	—	—	—
they m.	עֲבַדוּ	—	שַׁעְבִּידוּ	אִשְׁתַּעְבְּדוּ
they f.	עֲבַדָא	—	—	—

קַל	אִתְפְּעֵל	שַׁפְעֵל	אִשְׁתַּפְעַל

	PARTICIPLE				
	ACTIVE *making/ doing* עוֹשֶׂה...	PASSIVE *made* עֲשׂוּיָה	REFL./PASS. *being done/ being made* נַעֲשֶׂה		
m.s.	עָבֵיד	——	מִתְעֲבֵיד	——	——
f.s.	עָבְדָא	עֲבִידָא	——	——	——
m.pl.	עָבְדִין	——	——	——	——

	FUTURE			
	will do/ make אֶעֱשֶׂה...	*will be done* יֵעָשֶׂה...	*will subjugate* יִשְׁעַבְדוּ	*will be subjugated* יִשְׁתַּעְבֵּד...
I	אֶעֱבֵיד	—	—	—
you m.s.	תַּעֲבֵיד	—	—	—
you f.s.	תַּעְבְּדִין	—	—	—
he/it m.	יַעֲבֵיד	יִתְעֲבֵיד	—	יִשְׁתַּעְבַּד
she/it f.	תַּעֲבֵיד	תִּתְעֲבֵיד	—	—
we	נַעֲבֵיד	—	—	—
you pl.	תַּעְבְּדוּן	—	—	—
they m.	יַעְבְּדוּן	—	יִשְׁעַבְּדוּן	—
they f.	יַעְבְּדָן	יִתְעַבְּדָן	—	יִשְׁתַּעְבְּדָן

קַל	אִתְפְּעֵל	שַׁפְעֵל	אִשְׁתַּפְעַל

	IMPERATIVE		
	do!/ *make!* עֲשֵׂה!...			*subjugate* *yourself!* הִשְׁתַּעְבְּדִי!
m.s.	עֲבֵיד	—	—	—
f.s.	עֲבִידִי	—	—	אִשְׁתַּעֲבַּדִי
m.pl.	עֲבִידוּ	—	—	—

	GERUND / INFINITIVE		
to do/ to make לַעֲשׂוֹת	*to be done* לְהֵעָשׂוֹת		
לְמֶעְבַּד	לְאִתְעֲבָדָא	—	—

161

(5) נפק (initial נ)

Both the meaning of this verb and its conjugated forms in Targum Onkelos are similar to what has been described in the survey of the verb in the Talmud above on p. 68. Besides the *binyanim* that are presented in the paradigm, Onkelos uses three forms from *binyan* אִתְפְּעַל (the reflexive/passive of *binyan* אַפְעֵל): the feminine-singular participle מִתַּפְּקָא, *is being taken out*, and two future forms יִתְּפַק, *it will be taken out*, and יִתַּפְּקוּן, *they will be taken out*.

	קָל	אַפְעֵל

	PAST	
	went out יָצָאתִי...	*took out* הוֹצֵאתִי...
I	נְפַקִית	אַפֵּיקִית
you m.s.	נְפַקְתָּא	אַפֵּיקְתָּא
he/it m.	נְפַק	אַפֵּיק
she/it f.	נְפַקַת	אַפֵּיקַת
we	נְפַקְנָא	——
you pl.	נְפַקְתּוּן	אַפֵּיקְתּוּן
they m.	נְפַקוּ	אַפֵּיקוּ
they f.	נְפַקָא	——

קַל	אַפְעֵל

	ACTIVE PARTICIPLE	
	going out יוֹצֵא...	
m.s.	נָפֵיק	——
f.s.	נָפְקַת-[11]	——
m.pl.	נָפְקִין	——
f.pl.	נָפְקָן	——

	FUTURE	
	will go out אֶצֵא...	*will take out* אוֹצִיא...
I	אֶפּוֹק	אַפֵּיק
you m.s.	תִּפּוֹק	תַּפֵּיק
he/it m.	יִפּוֹק	יַפֵּיק
she/it f.	תִּפּוֹק	תַּפֵּיק
we	תִּפְּקוּן	נַפֵּיק
you m. pl.	——	תַּפְּקוּן
they m.	יִפְּקוּן	יַפְּקוּן

11   This form is in the *construct* state. See above, p. 2, and below, p. 231.

קַל	אַפְעֵל

IMPERATIVE	
go out! צֵא!, צְאוּ!	take out! הוֹצֵא!, הוֹצִיאוּ!

you m.s.	פּוֹק	אַפֵּיק
you m. pl.	פּוֹקוּ	אַפֵּיקוּ

GERUND / INFINITIVE	
(to) go out לָצֵאת, יָצֹא	(to) take out לְהוֹצִיא, מוֹצָא־
לְמִיפַּק, מִיפַּק	לְאַפָּקָא, אַפָּקוּת־[12]

---

12   This form is in the *construct* state. See above, p. 2, and below, p. 231.

(6) נחת (initial נ and middle root-letter guttural)

Both the meaning of this verb and its conjugated forms in Targum Onkelos are similar to what has been described in the survey of the verb in the Talmud above, on p. 71. Besides the *binyanim* that are presented in the paradigm, Onkelos uses one form from *binyan* אִתַּפְעַל (the reflexive/passive of the אַפְעֵל): אִתָּחַת, *he was lowered*.

	קַל	אַפְעֵל
	PAST	
	went down ...יָרַדְתִּי	*brought down* ...הוֹרִידָה
I	נְחַתִית	—
he/it m.	נְחַת	—
she/it f.	נְחַתַת	אַחֵיתַת
we	נְחַתְנָא	אַחֵיתְנָא
they	נְחַתוּ	אַחֵיתוּ

	PARTICIPLE		
	ACTIVE *going down* ...יוֹרֵד	ACTIVE *bringing down* מוֹרִיד	PASSIVE *brought down* מוּרָד
m.s.	נָחֵית	מַחֵית	מַחַת
f.s.	נָחֲתָא	—	—
m.pl.	נָחֲתִין	—	—

אַפְעֵל	קַל

FUTURE	
will bring down תּוֹרִיד...	*will go down* אֵרֵד...

	אַפְעֵל	קַל
I	——	אֵיחוֹת
you m.s.	תַּחְתִּנֵּיהּ	תֵּיחוֹת
he/it m.	יַחֵית	יֵיחוֹת
we	——	נֵיחוֹת
you m. pl.	תַּחֲתוּן	——
they m.	יַחֲתוּן	יֵיחֲתוּן

IMPERATIVE	
bring down! הוֹרִידוּ!	*go down!* רֵד!, רְדוּ!

	אַפְעֵל	קַל
m.s.	——	חוֹת
m.pl.	אַחִיתוּ	חוּתוּ

GERUND / INFINITIVE	
to bring down לְהוֹרִיד	*(to) go down* לָרֶדֶת, יָרֹד

אַפְעֵל	קַל
לְאַחָתָא	לְמֵיחַת, מֵיחַת

(7) סלק (middle root-letter ל)

Both the meaning of this verb and its conjugated forms in Targum Onkelos are similar to what has been described in the survey of the verb in the Talmud above on p. 74. Besides the *binyanim* presented in the paradigm, two additional *binyanim* are used by Onkelos: *binyan* פַּעֵל, only in the expression **אַסַלֵּק (סַלָּקָא)** שְׁכִינְתִּי, *I will certainly remove My Shekhina*; and *binyan* אִתְפַּעַל (the reflexive/passive of the אַפְעֵל), from which two future forms occur, **תִּתַּסַּק**, *it will be brought up*, and **יִתַּסְקוּן**, *they will be brought up*.

	קַל	אַפְעֵל	אִתְפַּעַל
		PAST	
	went up עָלִיתִי...	*brought up* הֶעֱלֵיתִי...	*departed* נִסְתַּלַּק / נַעֲלָה...
I	סְלֵיקִית	אַסֵּיקִית	—
you m.s.	סְלֵיקְתָּא	אַסֵּיקְתָּא	—
he/it m.	סְלֵיק	אַסֵּיק	אִסְתַּלַּק
she/it f.	סְלֵיקַת	—	—
we	סְלֵיקְנָא	—	—
you m. pl.	סְלֵיקְתּוּן	אַסֵּיקְתּוּנָא	—
they m.	סְלֵיקוּ	אַסֵּיקוּ	אִסְתַּלַּקוּ
they f.	סְלֵיקָא	—	—

167

אִתְפְּעַל	אַפְעֵל	קַל

	PARTICIPLE	
departing מִסְתַּלֵק	bringing up מַעֲלֶה...	going up עוֹלֶה...

	אִתְפְּעַל	אַפְעֵל	קַל
m.s.	מִסְתַּלַק	מַסֵיק	סָלֵיק
f.s.	——	מַסְקָא	סָלְקָא
m.pl.	——	מַסְקֵי-[13]	סָלְקִין
f.pl.	——	מַסְקָן	סָלְקָן

	FUTURE	
	will bring up אַעֲלֶה...	will go up אֶעֱלֶה...

		אַפְעֵל	קַל
I	——	אַסֵיק	אֶסַק
you m.s.	——	תַּסֵיק	תִּסַק
he/it m.	——	יַסֵיק	יִסַק
she/it f.	——	——	תִּסַק
we	——	——	נִסַק
you m. pl.	——	תַּסְקוּן	תִּסְקוּן
they m.	——	יַסְקוּן	יִסְקוּן

13　This participle is in the *construct* state. See above, p. 2, and below, p. 231.

קַל	אַפְעֵל	אִתְפְּעַל

IMPERATIVE		
go up! ...!עֲלֵה	*bring up!/ raise!* !הַעֲלֵה	*depart!* !הֵעָלוּ/הִסְתַּלְקוּ
m.s.	סַק	אַסֵּיק	——
f.s.	סַקִי	——	——
m.pl.	סַקוּ	——	אִסְתַּלְקוּ

GERUND / INFINITIVE		
(to) go up לַעֲלוֹת, עֲלֹה	*(to) bring up* לְהַעֲלוֹת, הַעֲלֵה	*departing* ־הִסְתַּלְקוּת
לְמִסַּק, מִסַּק	לְאַסָּקָא, אַסָּקָא	־אִסְתַּלָקוּת[14]

---

14   This form is in the *construct* state. See above, p. 2, and below, p. 231.

169

(8) הלך (initial ה and middle root-letter ל)

This verbal root appears frequently in Biblical Hebrew, and its meaning (*walk*) is similar in Aramaic. In *binyan* קַל the past tense and the participle do not occur at all in Targum Onkelos, while the future, the imperative, and the infinitive are conjugated as if the root were הוך (somewhat like verb 18, קום) without any vestige of a ל as the middle root-letter.[15] In *binyan* פַּעֵל, however, the three root-letters of הלך remain intact, and its conjugation is regular.

	קַל	פַּעֵל
	PAST	
		walked ...הָלַךְ / הִתְהַלֵּךְ
he/it m.	——	הַלֵּיךְ
we	——	הַלֵּיכְנָא
you m. pl.	——	הַלֵּיכְתּוּן
they m.	——	הַלֵּיכוּ
	ACTIVE PARTICIPLE	
		walking ...הוֹלֵךְ / מְהַלֵּךְ
m.s.	——	מְהַלֵּיךְ
f.s.	——	מְהַלְּכָא
f.pl.	——	מְהַלְּכָן

15 In Biblical Hebrew, on the other hand, it is the initial root-letter ה that does not appear in the future, the imperative, and (usually) the infinitive, where the verb is conjugated as if the root were ילך. Compare such forms as אֵלֵךְ and לָלֶכֶת with אֵשֵׁב and לָשֶׁבֶת from the root ישׁב.

קַל	פְּעַל
FUTURE	
will go/walk ...אֵלֵךְ	*will walk* יִתְהַלֵּךְ

	קַל	פְּעַל
I	אֵיהָךְ	—
you m.s.	תְּהָךְ	—
he/it m.	יְהָךְ	יְהַלֵּיךְ
she/it f.	תְּהָךְ	—
we	נְהָךְ	—
you m. pl.	תְּהָכוּן	—
they m.	יְהָכוּן	—

IMPERATIVE	
	walk! !הִתְהַלֵּךְ
m.s.	—	הַלֵּיךְ

GERUND / INFINITIVE	
to walk/go לָלֶכֶת	*to walk* לָלֶכֶת
לִמְהָךְ	לְהַלָּכָא

(9) אֲזַל (initial א)

This verb, like its Talmudic counterpart, is used only in *binyan* קַל. Both the meaning of this verb and its conjugated forms in Targum Onkelos are similar to what has been described in the survey of the verb in the Babylonian Talmud above on p. 96. The exception is the conjugation of the imperative: in the Targum the first root-letter א is always retained, as in אִיזֵיל; while in the Babylonian Talmud it is deleted, as in זִיל.

קַל

	PAST
	went הָלַכְתִּי...
I	אֲזַלִית
you m.s.	אֲזַלְתָּא
he/it m.	אֲזַל
she/it f.	אֲזַלַת
they m.	אֲזַלוּ
they f.	אֲזַלָא

	going הוֹלֵךְ...
m.s.	אָזֵיל
f.s.	אָזְלָא
m.pl.	אָזְלִין

קַל

FUTURE
will go   ...אֵלֵךְ

I		אִיזֵיל
you m.s.		תֵּיזֵיל
you f.s.		תֵּיזְלִין
he/it m.		יֵיזֵיל
she/it f.		תֵּיזֵיל
we		נֵיזֵיל
you m. pl.		תֵּיזְלוּן
they m.		יֵיזְלוּן

IMPERATIVE
go!   ...לֵךְ!

m.s.		אִיזֵיל
f.s.		אִיזִילִי
m.pl.		אִיזִילוּ

GERUND / INFINITIVE
(to) go   לָלֶכֶת, הָלֹךְ

לְמֵיזַל, מֵיזַל

173

(10) אמר (initial א and final ר)

The verb אמר, *say*, appears frequently in *binyan* קַל, which is presented in the following paradigm. As in Babylonian Aramaic (see p. 102), the first root-letter א is deleted in the future tense and in the infinitive; however, the third-root letter ר, which is sometimes deleted in Babylonian Aramaic, always remains intact in Targum Onkelos. In the reflexive/passive *binyan* אִתְפְּעֵל (which is not uncommon in the Talmud) only two forms are attested in Targum Onkelos: אִתְאֲמַר, *it was said*, and יִתְאֲמַר, *it will be said*.

קַל

	PAST
	said
	אֲמָרִתִּי...
I	אֲמָרִית
you m.s.	אֲמָרְתְּ
he/it m.	אֲמַר
she/it f.	אֲמַרַת
we	אֲמַרְנָא
you m. pl.	אֲמַרְתּוּן
they m.	אֲמַרוּ
they f.	אֲמָרָא

קַל

	PARTICIPLE	
	ACTIVE *saying* אוֹמֵר...	**PASSIVE** *said* אָמוּר, אֲמוּרָה
m.s.	אֲמַר	אֲמִיר
f.s.	אָמְרָא	אֲמִירָא
m.pl.	אָמְרִין	——

	FUTURE
	will say אֹמַר...
I	אֵימַר
you m.s.	תֵּימַר
he/it m.	יֵימַר
she/it f.	תֵּימַר
we	נֵימַר
you m. pl.	תֵּימְרוּן
they m.	יֵימְרוּן

קַל

IMPERATIVE
say!
אֱמֹר!, אִמְרִי!

	IMPERATIVE
m.s.	אֵימַר
f.s.	אֵימַרִי

GERUND / INFINITIVE
(to) say
לוֹמַר, אָמֹר

	GERUND / INFINITIVE
לְמֵימַר, מֵימָר

(11) אכל (initial א)

Both the meaning of this verb and its conjugated forms in Targum Onkelos are similar to what has been described in the survey of the verb in the Talmud above on p. 99.

	קַל	אִתְפְּעֵל	אַפְעֵל
	PAST		
	ate אֲכַלְתִּי...		*fed* הֶאֱכַלְתִּי, הֶאֱכִיל
I	אֲכַלִית	—	אוֹכֵלִית
you m.s.	אֲכַלְתָּא, אֲכַלְתְּ	—	—
he/it m.	אֲכַל	—	אוֹכְלָךְ
she/it f.	אֲכַלַת	—	—
you m. pl.	אֲכַלְתּוּן	—	—
they m.	אֲכַלוּ	—	—
they f.	אֲכַלָא	—	—

	PARTICIPLE			
	ACTIVE *eating* אוֹכֵל...	PASSIVE *eaten* אֲכוּלֵי-	REFL./PASS. *is eaten* נֶאֱכָל...	
m.s.	אָכֵיל	—	מִתְאֲכֵיל	—
f.s.	אָכְלָא	—	מִתְאַכְלָא	—
m.pl.	אָכְלִין	אֲכִילֵי-[16]	—	—

16 This participle is in the *construct* state. See above, p. 2, and below, p. 231.

אַפְעֵל	אִתְפְּעֵל	קַל

		FUTURE		
	will feed יַאֲכִיל	*will be eaten* יֵאָכֵל...	*will eat* אֹכַל...
I	—	—	אֵיכוֹל
you m.s.	—	—	תֵּיכוֹל
he/it m.	יוֹכֵיל	יִתְאֲכֵיל	יֵיכוֹל
she/it f.	—	תִּתְאֲכֵיל	תֵּיכוֹל
we	—	—	נֵיכוֹל
you m. pl.	—	—	תֵּיכְלוּן
they m.	—	יִתְאַכְלוּן	יֵיכְלוּן

		IMPERATIVE	
			eat! אֱכֹל!, אִכְלוּ!
m.s.	—	—	אֱכוֹל
m.pl.	—	—	אִכְלוּהִי

	GERUND / INFINITIVE	
		"be eaten" הֵאָכֵל	*(to) eat* לְאֶכֹל, אֱכֹל
—	אִתְאֲכָלָא	לְמֵיכַל, מֵיכַל

(12) אלף (initial א)

Both the meaning of this verb and its conjugated forms in Targum Onkelos are similar to what has been described in the survey of the verb ילף in the Talmud on p. 83. As noted in that chapter, it is uncertain as to whether אלף or ילף should be regarded as the root of some verbal forms. In Targum Onkelos all the forms attested can be explained as deriving from אלף — including the passive participle with a suffix (indicating the subject), אֲלֵיפְנָא, *I am accustomed*, a form which cannot be explained as a derivative of the root ילף.

קַל	פַּעֵל (אַפְעֵל)[17]
PAST	
	taught לְמַדְתִּי, לְמֵד
I ——	אַלֵיפִית
he/it m. ——	אַלְפֵיה
ACTIVE PARTICIPLE	
	teaching מְלַמֵד, מְלַמְּדִים
m.s. ——	מַלֵיף
m.pl. ——	מַלְפִין
PASSIVE PARTICIPLE WITH SUFFIX	
am accustomed לָמוּד אֲנִי / רָגִיל אֲנִי	
I אֲלֵיפְנָא	——

17 *Binyan* פַּעֵל from אלף (or perhaps *binyan* אַפְעֵל from ילף).

פַּעֵל (אַפְעֵל) [18]	קַל

FUTURE		
	will learn תִּלְמַד...	*will teach* אֲלַמֵּד / אוֹרֶה...
I	—	אַלֵּיף
you m.s.	תֵּילַף	תַּלֵּיפֻנּוּן
he/it m.	יֵילַף	—
you m. pl.	תֵּילְפוּן	תַּלְּפוּן
they m.	יֵילְפוּן	יַלְּפוּן

IMPERATIVE		
		teach! לַמֵּד!
m.s.	—	אַלֵּפַה

GERUND/INFINITIVE		
	(to) learn לָמֹד	*to teach* לְלַמֵּד / לְהוֹרוֹת
	מֵילַף	לְאַלָּפָא, לְאַלּוֹפֵיהוֹן

---

18 *Binyan* פַּעֵל from אלף (or perhaps *binyan* אַפְעֵל from ילף).

(13) ילד (initial root-letter י)

As in Hebrew, this verb appears in *binyan* קַל in the sense of *give birth*; its passive, *binyan* אִתְפְּעֵל in the sense of *be born*; and in the causative אַפְעֵל *binyan* meaning *father, beget*. In the last *binyan* the initial root-letter י becomes ו, e.g.,אוֹלִיד, as in its Hebrew counterpart הוֹלִיד.

Besides the *binyanim* presented in the paradigm, one form from *binyan* פַּעֵל occurs — the feminine-plural participle **מְיַלְּדָן**, *delivering a baby*. In addition, two forms are attested from *binyan* אִתְפַּעַל, with an intensified, reflexive meaning: one, **אִתְיַלַּדוּ**, appears both in the past tense, *they reproduced*, and in the imperative, *reproduce!* — and the other in the future, **יִתְיַלְּדוּן**, *they will be reproduced*.

	קַל	אִתְפְּעֵל	אַפְעֵל
	PAST		
	gave birth יְלַדְתִּי...	*was born* אִתְיְלִיד...	*he fathered; she gave birth* אוֹלִיד
I	יְלִידִית	—	—
he/it m.	—	אִתְיְלִיד	אוֹלִיד
she/it f.	יְלִידַת	אִתְיְלִידַת	אוֹלִידָה; אוֹלִידָא
they m.	—	אִתְיְלִידוּ	—
they f.	יְלִידָא	אִתְיְלִידָא	—

קַל	אִתְפְּעֵל	אַפְעֵל
PARTICIPLE		

	ACTIVE *giving birth* יוֹלְדוּת	PASSIVE *born* יְלוּד...		
m.s.	—	יְלִיד	—	—
f.s.	—	יְלִידָא	—	—
m.pl.	—	יְלִידֵי-[19]	—	—
f.pl.	יַלְדָן	—	—	—

	FUTURE		

	will give birth תֵּלְדִי...	*will be born* יְוָלֵד	*will father* תּוֹלִיד...
you m.s.	—	—	תּוֹלֵיד
you f.s.	תְּלִידִין	—	—
he/it m.	—	יִתְיְלִיד	יוֹלֵיד
she/it f.	תְּלִיד	—	—
you m. pl.	—	—	תּוֹלְדוּן
they f.	יְלִידָן	—	—

	GERUND/INFINITIVE		
	to give birth לְלֶדֶת		
	לְמֵילַד	—	—

19 This participle is in the construct state. See above, p. 2, and below, p. 231.

(14) יד״ע (initial י and final guttural)

Both the meaning of this verb and its conjugated forms in Targum Onkelos are similar to what has been described in the survey of the verb in the Talmud above on p. 81 — with one significant exception: in Targum Onkelos the causative *binyan* of this verb, e.g., הוֹדַע, is formed by the addition of a ה prefix, as in all Hebrew verbs and as in some verbs in Biblical Aramaic — but unlike the Babylonian Aramaic form אוֹדַע. Besides that *binyan* and *binyan* קל, which are presented in the paradigms, three passive forms occur in *binyan* אתְפְּעֵל: אתְיְדַע, *it was known*, in the past tense, and the two future forms יִתְיְדַע and תִּתְיְדַע, *it will be known*. In addition, a secondary Aramaic root מוֹדַע, derived from יד״ע, has generated such forms as אשְׁתְּמוֹדַע, *he recognized*, in *binyan* אשְׁתַּפְעַל, the reflexive of שַׁפְעֵל — in effect, forming the five-letter root שמוד״ע.

קַל		הַפְעֵל
PAST		
knew יְדַעְתִּי...		*made known* הוֹדַעְתִּי...
I	יְדַעִית	הוֹדַעִית
you m.s.	יְדַעְתְּ, יְדַעְתָּא	הוֹדַעְתַּנִי
he/it m.	יְדַע	הוֹדַע
she/it f.	יְדַעַת	——
we	יְדַעְנָא	——
you m.pl.	יְדַעְתּוּן	——
you f.pl.	יְדַעְתִּין	——
they m.	יְדַעוּ	——
they f.	יְדַעָא	——

הַפְעֵל	קַל

	PARTICIPLE	
	ACTIVE *knowing* יוֹדֵעַ, יוֹדְעִים	PASSIVE *known* יָדוּעַ	
m.s.	יָדַע	יְדִיעַ	——
m.pl.	יָדְעִין	——	——

	ACTIVE PARTICIPLE WITH SUFFIX	
	know ...יוֹדֵעַ אֲנִי	*make known/announce* מוֹדִיעַ אֲנִי
I	יָדַעְנָא	מְהוֹדַעְנָא
you m.s.	יָדַעְתְּ	——
you m. pl.	יָדְעִיתּוּן	——

	FUTURE	
	will know ...אֶדַע	*will make known* תּוֹדִיעַ, יוֹדִיעַ
I	אֶדַע	——
you m.s.	תֵּדַע	תְּהוֹדַע
he/it m.	——	יְהוֹדַע
we	נֵדַע	——
you m. pl.	תֵּדְעוּן	——
they m.	יֵדְעוּן	——

184

קַל	הַפְעֵל
IMPERATIVE	

	know! דַע!, דְעוּ!	make known! הוֹדַע!
m.s.	דַּע	הוֹדַעְנִי
m.pl.	דְּעוּ	——

GERUND / INFINITIVE	
(to) know לְדַעַת, יָדוֹעַ	to make known לְהוֹדִיעַ
לְמִידַּע, מִידָּע	לְהוֹדָעוּתָךְ

(15) יהב (initial י)/נתן (initial נ)

As in Babylonian Aramaic, the verbal root יהב, *give*, is parallel to the Hebrew root נתן in the past tense, the participle, and the imperative of *binyan* קַל and in the reflexive/passive *binyan*, אִתְפְּעֵל. As for the future tense and the infinitive, no forms of this verb have been attested in Targum Onkelos, but forms from the root נתן are used instead. Compare the survey of the Babylonian Aramaic root that is presented above on p. 86.

קַל	אִתְפְּעֵל
PAST	
gave נָתַתִּי...	*was given* נִיתַּן...
I	יְהָבִית	—
you m.s.	יְהַבְתְּ	—
he/it m.	יְהַב	אִתְיְהִיב
she/it f.	יְהַבַת	אִתְיְהִיבַת
we	יְהַבְנָה	—
they m.	יְהַבוּ	אִתְיְהִיבוּ

PARTICIPLE		
ACTIVE *giving* נוֹתֵן...	PASSIVE *given* נִיתָּן...	REFLEXIVE/PASSIVE *being given* נִיתָּן
m.s.	יָהֵיב	יְהִיב	מִתְיְהִיב
m.pl.	יָהֲבִין	יְהִיבִין	—

קַל	אִתְפְּעֵל

FUTURE	
will give אֶתֵּן...	*will be given* יִנָּתֵן...

	קַל	אִתְפְּעֵל
I	אֶתֵּין	—
you m.s.	תִּתֵּין	—
he/it m.	יִתֵּין	יִתְיְהִיב
she/it f.	תִּתֵּין	תִּתְיְהִיב
we	נִתֵּין	—
you m. pl.	תִּתְּנוּן	—
they m.	יִתְּנוּן	יִתְיַהֲבוּן

IMPERATIVE	
give! be prepared! (let's!) תֵּן!... הָבָה!...	

	קַל	אִתְפְּעֵל
m.s.	הַב	—
f.s.	הַבִי	—
m.pl.	הַבוּ	—

GERUND / INFINITIVE	
(to) give לָתֵת, נָתוֹן	

קַל	אִתְפְּעֵל
לְמִתַּן, מִתָּן	—

(16) יתב (initial י)

As noted in the survey of the Babylonian Aramaic root above on page 89, the root יתב is parallel to the Hebrew root ישב, because of the correspondence ("the consonantal shift") between the Hebrew שׁ and the Aramaic ת. In the past tense of *binyan* קל, all the forms are conjugated in the פְּעֵיל pattern, e.g., יְתֵיב, *he sat*, like סְלֵיק (in verb 7 in this chapter). In the אַפְעֵל and אִתְפְּעַל *binyanim*, the initial root-letter becomes ו as in the Talmud.

	קַל	אַפְעֵל	אִתְפְּעַל
	PAST		
	sat יָשַׁבְתִּי...	caused to dwell הוֹשַׁבְתִּי...	lived הִתְיַשַּׁבְתָּ / גַּרְתָּ...
I	יְתֵיבִית	אוֹתֵיבִית	——
you m.s.	——	——	אִתּוֹתַבְתְּ
he/it m.	יְתֵיב	אוֹתֵיב	אִתּוֹתַב
she/it f.	יְתֵיבַת		——
we	יְתֵיבְנָא	——	——
you m. pl.	יְתֵיבְתּוּן	——	——
they m.	יְתִיבוּ	——	אִתּוֹתַבוּ
	ACTIVE PARTICIPLE		
	sitting/living יוֹשֵׁב...		
m.s.	יָתֵיב	——	——
f.s.	יָתְבָא	——	——
m.pl.	יָתְבִין	——	——

קַל	אַפְעֵל	אִתְּפְּעֵל

FUTURE		
will sit תֵּשֵׁב...		*will live* יִתְיַשֵּׁב/יִחְיֶה

	קַל	אַפְעֵל	אִתְּפְּעֵל
you m.s.	תִּתֵּיב	—	—
he/it m.	יִתֵּיב	—	יִתּוֹתַב
she/it f.	תִּתֵּיב	—	—
we	נִתֵּיב	—	—
you m. pl.	תִּתְּבוּן	—	—
they m.	יִתְּבוּן ; לִיתְּבוּן	—	—

IMPERATIVE		
sit!/live! שֵׁב!...	*settle!* הוֹשֵׁב!	

	קַל	אַפְעֵל	
m.s.	תִּיב	אוֹתֵיב	—
f.s.	תִּיבִי	—	—
m.pl.	תִּיבוּ	—	—

GERUND / INFINITIVE		
to sit / to live לָשֶׁבֶת		*to live* לְהִתְיַשֵּׁב / לָגוּר

קַל	אַפְעֵל	אִתְּפְּעֵל
לְמִיתַּב	—	לְאִתּוֹתָבָא

189

(17) תוב ("hollow" root)

Verbal forms from the Aramaic root תוב, *return*, regularly translate Biblical forms from the Hebrew root שוב, based upon the correspondence ("the consonantal shift") between the Aramaic ת and the Hebrew שׁ. Thus, the Aramaic קַל form, תָּב, *he returned* (in an intransitive sense, i.e., *he came back*), serves to translate the Biblical שָׁב or וַיָּשָׁב from the corresponding Hebrew *binyan*.[20]

Onkelos uses the causative *binyan* אַפְעֵל, e.g., אֲתֵיב, *he returned* (in a transitive sense, i.e., *he brought back*), *he replied*, to translate both the cognate Hebrew verb, e.g., הֵשִׁיב and וַיָּשֶׁב, as well as the verb ענה. In like manner, the reflexive/passive אִתְּפְעַל form, אִתָּתַב, *he was returned*, is used to translate the Hebrew הוּשַׁב. The conjugation of the last two *binyanim* in the paradigms below differs markedly from that of its Babylonian Aramaic counterpart recorded in the paradigms in Chapter 4 on pages 93-95 above.

קַל	אַפְעֵל	אִתְּפְעַל
PAST		
came back שַׁבְתִּי...	*brought back* הֵשִׁיב...	*was returned* הוּשַׁב
I	תַּבִית	—	—
he/it m.	תָּב	אֲתֵיב	אִתָּתַב
she/it f.	תַּבַת	אֲתֵיבַת	—
we	תַּבְנָא	אֲתֵיבְנָא	—
you m. pl.	תַּבְתּוּן	אֲתֵיבְתּוּן	—
they m.	תָּבוּ	אֲתֵיבוּ	—

20 The Aramaic verb הדר is frequently used in this sense in the Babylonian Talmud (see Chapter 4, Verb 5, p. 64), but it does not function this way in Targum Onkelos.

קַל	אַפְעֵל	אִתְּפְעַל

	PARTICIPLE		
	ACTIVE *coming back* שָׁב, שָׁבִים	**ACTIVE** *returning* מֵשִׁיב...	**PASSIVE** *returned* מוּשָׁב	
m.s.	תָּאֵיב	מְתִיב	מְתִיב	—
m.pl.	תָּיְבִין	מְתִיבִין	—	

	FUTURE		
	will come back/ *return* אָשׁוּב...	*will bring back/* *return* אָשִׁיב...	*will be restored/* *will be answered* תּוּשַׁב, יוּשַׁב
I	אֲתוּב	אָתִיב/אַתִיב[21]	—
you m.s.	תְּתוּב	תָּתִיב	תִּתָּתַב
he/it m.	יְתוּב	יָתִיב	יִתָּתַב
she/it f.	תְּתוּב	תָּתִיב	—
we	נְתוּב	—	—
you m. pl.	תְּתוּבוּן	תָּתִיבוּן/תְּתִיבוּן[21]	—
they m.	יְתוּבוּן	יָתִיבוּן	—
they f.	—	יָתִיבוּן/יָתִיבָן[21]	—

21   Versions within the Yemenite tradition differ with regard to the vocalization of this form.

קַל	אַפְעֵל	אִתְפְּעַל

IMPERATIVE		
come back!/return! שׁוּב!...	restore!/return! הָשֵׁב!	
m.s. תּוּב	אַתֵּיב	—
f.s. תּוּבִי	—	—
m.pl. תּוּבוּ	—	—

GERUND / INFINITIVE		
(to) come back לָשׁוּב, שׁוֹב	to bring back / to reply לְהָשִׁיב	
לְאָתָבָא, לְאָתָבוּתֵיהּ לְמִתַּב, מְתַב		—

(18) קוּם ("hollow" root)

Onkelos uses the Aramaic verb קוּם in *binyan* קַל to translate the Hebrew verbs: קוּם, *rise*, and עמד, *stand*. The Aramaic קַיֵּים in *binyan* פַּעֵל is mostly used with the meanings: *swear* (= take an oath) or *promise*, but occasionally *set up*, *establish* and *fulfill*; its reflexive/passive אִתְקַיַּים, from *binyan* אִתְפַּעַל, means *survive*.

The causative form אֲקֵים in *binyan* אַפְעֵל — whose conjugation is significantly different from its Babylonian Aramaic counterpart presented in Chapter 4 (pp. 132-135) — is used in the senses of *set up*, *establish*, *raise* and *cause to stand*. *Binyan* אִתַּפְעַל (the reflexive/passive of אַפְעֵל) has generated only two forms: **אִתָּקַם**, *it was set up*, and **יִתָּקַם**, *it will be stood up*, and hence it is not presented in the paradigms below.

	קַל	פַּעֵל	אִתְפַּעַל	אַפְעֵל
		PAST		
	stood קַמְתָ...	*swore* קַיֵּמְתִי...	*survived* נִתְקַיֵּם / חַי...	*set up* הֶעֱמַדְתִי...
I	——	קַיֵּימִית	——	אֲקֵימִית
you m.s.	קַמְתָּא	קַיֵּימְתָּא	——	אֲקֵימְתָּא
he/it m.	קָם	קַיֵּים	אִתְקַיַּים	אֲקֵים
she/it f.	קָמַת	——	——	——
you m.pl.	קַמְתּוּן	קַיֵּימְתּוּן	——	——
you f.pl.	——	קַיֵּימְתִּין	——	——
they m.	קָמוּ	קַיֵּימוּ	אִתְקַיַּימוּ	——
they f.	קָמָא	קַיֵּימָא	——	——

	קַל	פַּעֵל	אִתְפַּעַל	אַפְעֵל

	PARTICIPLE			
	standing עוֹמֵד, עוֹמְדִים	*fulfilling* מְקַיֵּם	*surviving* מִתְקַיֵּם / חַי	*setting up* מֵקִים, מְקִימִים
m.s.	**קָאֵים**	**מְקַיֵּים**	**מִתְקַיַּים**	**מְקִים**
m.pl.	**קָיְמִין**	—	—	**מְקִימִין**

	FUTURE			
	will stand/ rise תַּעֲמֹד / תָּקוּם...	*will establish/ swear* אֲקַיֵּם...	*will survive* יִתְקַיֵּם / יִחְיֶה...	*will set up/ establish* אָקִים...
I	—	**אֲקַיֵּים**	—	**אֲקִים**
you m.s.	**תְּקוּם**	**תְּקַיֵּים**	—	**תְּקִים**
he/it m.	**יְקוּם**	**יְקַיֵּים**	**יִתְקַיַּים**	**יְקִים**
she/it f.	**תְּקוּם**	—	**תִּתְקַיַּים**	—
we	**נְקוּם**	**נְקַיֵּים**	—	—
you m.pl.	—	**תְּקַיְּימוּן**	—	**תְּקִימוּן**
you f.pl.	—	תְּקַיְּמַנַּה	—	—
they m.	**יְקוּמוּן**	**יְקַיְּימוּן**	—	**יְקִימוּן**
they f.	**יְקוּמָן**	—	—	—

קַל	פַּעֵל	אִתְפַּעַל	אַפְעֵל
IMPERATIVE			
rise!/stand!	*swear!*	*survive!*	*establish!*
...קוּם! / עֲמֹד!	קַיֵּם!, קַיְּמוּ!	חֲיִי!	הָקֵם!
m.s. קוּם	קַיֵּים	—	אֲקֵים
f.s. קוּמִי	—	—	—
m.pl. קוּמוּ	קַיְּימוּ	אִתְקַיְּימוּ	—

GERUND / INFINITIVE			
to stand/ *to rise*	*(to) fulfill/* *keep alive*		*(to) raise up/* *establish*
לַעֲמֹד / לָקוּם	(לְ)קַיֵּם		לְהָקִים, הָקֵם
לְמִקָם	(לְ)קַיָּימָא, לְקַיָּימוּתָנָא	—	לְאָקָמָא, אָקָמָא

(19) נוח ("hollow" root with initial נ)

Both the meaning of this verb and its conjugated forms in Targum Onkelos are similar to what has been described in the survey of this verb in the Talmud above on p. 136 — except for the fact that *binyan* אִתְפְּעֵל is not used in the Targum at all.

	קַל	אַפְעֵל
	PAST	
	rested נָח, נָחָה, נָחוּ	*kept* הִנִּיחָה
he/it m.	נָח	—
she/it f.	נַחַת	אֲחַתְּתֵיהּ
they	נָחוּ	—
	ACTIVE PARTICIPLE	
		giving rest מֵנִיחַ
m.s.	—	מַנַּח
	FUTURE	
	will rest תָּנוּחַ...	*will calm / will give rest* אָנִיחַ, יָנִיחַ
I	—	אָנִיחַ
you m.s.	תְּנוּחַ	—
he/it m.	יְנוּחַ	יְנִיחַ
you m. pl.	תְּנוּחוּן	—
they m.	יְנוּחוּן	—

אַפְעֵל	קַל

IMPERATIVE	
leave aside! הַנַּח!	
אַנַּח	——

m.s.

GERUND / INFINITIVE	
to place לְהַנִּיחַ	
לְאַנָחוּתֵהּ	——

(20) מות ("hollow" verb)

Both the meaning of this verb and its conjugated forms in Targum Onkelos are similar to what has been described in the survey of this verb in the Talmud on p. 139 — with the addition of the causative *binyan*, אַפְעֵל, in the Targum.

קַל	אַפְעֵל

	PAST	
	died מֵת...	*put to death* הֵמִית
he/it m.	מִית	אֲמִית
she/it f.	מִיתַת	——
we	מִיתְנָא	——
they m.	מִיתוּ	——

	ACTIVE PARTICIPLE	
	dying מֵת...	*putting to death* מֵמִית
m.s.	מָאִית	מְמִית
f.s.	מָיְתָא	——
m.pl.	מָיְתִין	——

קַל	אַפְעֵל

	FUTURE	
	will die אָמוּת...	*will put to death* תְּמִית
I	אֲמוּת	——
you m.s.	תְּמוּת	תְּמִית
he/it m.	יְמוּת	——
she/it f.	תְּמוּת	——
we	נְמוּת	——
you m. pl.	תְּמוּתוּן	——
they m.	יְמוּתוּן	——
they f.	יְמוּתָן	——

GERUND / INFINITIVE	
(to) die לָמוּת, מוֹת	
לִמְמָת, מְמָת	——

199

(21) עלל ("geminate" root)

The meaning of this verb and its conjugated forms in *binyan* קל and in the causative *binyan* אַפְעֵל in Targum Onkelos are similar to those described in the survey of this verb in the Talmud above on p. 129 above — with the addition of *binyan* אִתַּפְעַל, the reflexive/passive of *binyan* אַפְעֵל.

Besides the *binyanim* presented in the paradigms below, the form תְּעֹלֵיל, from the rare פָּעֵל *binyan*, appears twice in Targum Onkelos, in his translation of (ויקרא יט:י; דברים כד:כא) לֹא תְעוֹלֵל, *you may not pick immature grapes ("oleloth")*.

	קל	אַפְעֵל	אִתַּפְעַל
	PAST		
	entered בָּאתִי...	*brought in* הֵבֵאתָ...	*was brought in...* הוּבָא...
I	עַלִית	—	—
you m.s.	—	אַעֵילְתָּנָא	—
he/it m.	עַל	אַעֵיל	אִתָּעַל
she/it f.	עַלַת	—	—
they m.	עַלוּ	אַעֵילוּ	אִתָּעַלוּ
they f.	עַלָא	—	—
	PARTICIPLE		
	entering בָּא, בָּאִים	*bringing in* מֵעֵיל	*being brought in* מוּבָא, מוּבָאִים
m.s.	עָלֵיל	מַעֵיל	מִתָּעַל
m.pl.	עָלִין	—	מִתָּעַלִין

200

קַל	אַפְעֵל	אִתְּפְעַל

	FUTURE		
	will enter אָבוֹא...	*will bring in* אָבִיא...	*will be brought in* יוּבָא
I	אֵיעוֹל	אַעֵיל	——
you m.s.	תֵּיעוֹל	תַּעֵיל	——
he/it m.	יֵיעוֹל	יַעֵיל	יִתָּעַל
she/it f.	תֵּיעוֹל	——	——
we	נֵיעוֹל	נַעֵילִנּוּן	——
you m. pl.	תֵּיעֲלוּן	תַּעֵילוּן	——
they m.	יֵיעֲלוּן	יַעֵילוּן	——

	IMPERATIVE		
	come! בֹּא!...	*bring in!* הָבֵא!	
m.s.	עוֹל	אַעֵיל	——
f.s.	עוֹלִי	——	——
m.pl.	עוֹלוּ	——	——

	GERUND / INFINITIVE		
	(to) enter לָבוֹא, בּוֹא	*(to) bring in* לְהָבִיא, הָבֵא	
	לְמֵיעַל, מֵיעַל	לְאַעָלָא, אַעוֹלֵי, לְאַעָלוּתָךְ	——

201

(22) גְּלִי (final root-letter י)

The Aramaic root גלי, like its Hebrew cognate גלה, is used in two entirely different senses: (1) *exile* and (2) *reveal*. The active participle and the future of *binyan* קַל as well as all of *binyan* אַפְעֵל, appear in the former sense; while the past, the passive participle and the infinitive of *binyan* קַל, in addition to the entire *binyan* פַּעֵל and *binyan* אִתְפְּעֵל, appear in the latter sense. In addition to these *binyanim* — all of which are presented in the paradigms below — just two forms are attested from *binyan* אִתְפַּעַל: **אִתְגַּלִּי**, *he became exposed*, and **תִּתְגְּלֵי**, *it will become exposed*.

	קַל	אִתְפְּעֵל	פַּעֵל	אַפְעֵל
	PAST			
	went into exile גְּלָה	revealed myself... נִגְלֵיתִי...	revealed גִּלָּה	exiled הֶגְלָה
I	—	אִתְגְּלִיתִי	—	—
he	גְּלָא	אִתְגְּלִי	גַּלִּי	אַגְלִינּוּן

		PARTICIPLE			
	ACTIVE going into exile גּוֹלֶה	PASSIVE revealed גָּלוּי...	REFL./PASS. revealing oneself נִגְלֶה		ACTIVE driving into exile מַגְלֶה
m.s.	גָּלֵי	גְּלִי	מִתְגְּלֵי	—	מַגְלֵי
m.pl.	—	גְּלַן	—	—	—
f.pl.	—	גַּלְיָן	—	—	—

קַל	אִתְפְּעֵל	פַּעֵל	אַפְעֵל
FUTURE			
will go into exile יְגְלוּ	*will reveal myself...* אֲגַלֵה...	*will reveal* תְּגַלֵה...	*will drive into exile* יַגְלֵה

	קַל	אִתְפְּעֵל	פַּעֵל	אַפְעֵל
I	—	אֶתְגְּלֵי	—	—
you m.s.	—	—	תְּגַלֵי	—
he/it m.	—	יִתְגְּלֵי	יְגַלֵי	יַגְלֵי
she/it f.	—	תִּתְגְּלֵי	תְּגַלֵי	—
we	—	נִתְגְּלֵי	—	—
they m.	יִגְלוֹן	—	—	—
they f.	—	יִתְגַּלְיָן	—	—

IMPERATIVE	
	reveal yourself! הִגְּלֵה!
m.s.	אִתְגְּלִי

GERUND/INFINITIVE			
"go into exile" גְּלֹה	*to reveal oneself* לְהִגְּלוֹת	*to reveal* לְגַלוֹת	
מִגְלָא	לְאִתְגְּלָאָה	לְגַלָּאָה	—

(23) חזי (initial guttural and final י)

Both the meaning of this verb and its conjugated forms in Targum Onkelos are similar to what has been described in the survey of the verb in the Talmud above on p. 108 — with *binyan* קַל (e.g., חֲזָא, *he saw*) translating the Biblical Hebrew in the same *binyan* (e.g., רָאָה), and the causative *binyan* אַפְעֵל (e.g., אַחְזִי, *he showed*) translating the parallel Hebrew הִפְעִיל (e.g., הֶרְאָה).

In addition, in the Yemenite editions of the Targum, *binyan* אִתַּפְעַל (the reflexive/passive of the causative אַפְעֵל *binyan*, e.g., אִתַּחְזִי) occurs, even as a translation of נִרְאָה or וַיֵּרָא, where there is no hint at a causative meaning! According to other traditions, however, in such cases the *binyan* אִתְפְּעֵל (e.g., **אִתְחֲזִי**) is used, as mentioned in the footnotes.

קַל	אַפְעֵל	אִתַּפְעַל
	PAST	
saw רָאִיתִי...	*showed* הֶרְאֵיתָ, הֶרְאָה	*were shown/appeared* הָרְאֵיתָ, נִרְאָה, נִרְאוּ
I חֲזֵיתִי, חֲזֵית	——	——
you m.s. חֲזֵיתָא	אַחְזִיתָךְ	אִתַּחְזֵיתָא
he/it m. חֲזָא	אַחְזִי	אִתַּחְזִי[22]
she/it f. חֲזָת	——	——
we חֲזֵינָא	——	——
you m. pl. חֲזֵיתוֹן	——	——
they m. חֲזוֹ	——	אִתַּחְזִיאוּ[22]
they f. חֲזָאָה	——	——

22 In many versions of Targum Onkelos, -אִתְחֲ from *binyan* אִתְפְּעֵל is used instead.

קַל	אַפְעֵל	אִתְפְּעֵל

		PARTICIPLE	
	ACTIVE *seeing* רוֹאֶה...	PASSIVE *worthy* רָאוּי...	ACTIVE *showing* מַרְאֶה	REFLEXIVE/PASSIVE *shown* מָרְאֶה
m.s.	חָזֵי חֲזֵי [23], חָזֵי		מַחְזֵי	מִתַּחְזֵי
f.s.	חָזְיָא	חַזְיָא	—	—
m.pl.	חָזַן	—	—	—
f.pl.	חָזְיָן	—	—	—

		FUTURE	
	will see אֶרְאֶה...	*will show* אַרְאֶה, יַרְאֶה	*will be seen/shown* יֵרָאֶה...
I	אֶחֱזֵי	אַחְזִינָךְ	—
you m.s.	תֶּחֱזֵי	—	—
he/it m.	יֶחֱזֵי	יַחְזֵינַנִי	יִתַּחְזֵי[24]
she/it f.	תֶּחֱזֵי	—	תִּתַּחְזֵי[24]
we	נֶחֱזֵי	—	—
you m.pl.	תֶּחְזוֹן	—	תִּתַּחְזוֹן[24]
you f.pl.	תֶּחְזְיָן	—	—
they m.	יֶחְזוֹן	—	יִתַּחְזוֹן[24]

23 This form, which is identical with the active participle, regularly appears in Yemenite editions as a *passive* participle as well.

24 In many versions of Targum Onkelos: ־יִתְחֲ and ־תִּתְחֲ from *binyan* אִתְפְּעֵל.

קָל	אַפְעֵל	אִתְפְּעֵל

	IMPERATIVE		
	see!	*show!*	
	רְאֵה!, רְאוּ!	הַרְאֵה!	
m.s.	חֲזִי	אַחְזִינִי	—
m.pl.	חֲזוֹ	—	—

	GERUND / INFINITIVE		
	(to) see	*to show*	*to be seen*
	לִרְאוֹת, רָאֹה	לְהַרְאוֹת	לְהֵרָאוֹת
	לְמִחְזֵי, מִחְזָא	לְאַחְזָאָה	לְאִתַּחֲזָאָה[25]

---

25 In many versions of Targum Onkelos, לְאִתְחֲזָ- from *binyan* אִתְפְּעֵל is used instead.

(24) עדי (initial guttural and final י)

This Aramaic verb is used most frequently by Onkelos in the sense of *move away* in *binyan* קַל (e.g., עֲדָא = Biblical Hebrew סָר or עָבַר) and *remove* (e.g., אַעְדִי = הֵסִיר) in the causative *binyan* אַפְעֵל, as presented in the paradigm below. In addition two forms from the אִתַּפְעַל *binyan* (the reflexive/passive of the אַפְעֵל) are attested: **אִתַּעְדָא**, *it (f.) was removed*, and the participle **מִתַּעְדָא**, *being removed*.

The פַּעֵל *binyan* of this verb has an entirely different meaning, *become pregnant* (e.g., עַדִּיאַת, *she conceived*).

קַל	פַּעֵל	אַפְעֵל
PAST		
passed/ moved away	conceived/ became pregnant	removed
עֲבַר / סָר...	הָרְתָה, הָרוּ	הֵסִיר / בִּטֵּל...
he/it m. עֲדָא	—	אַעְדִי
she/it f. —	עַדִּיאַת	אַעְדִיאַת
they m. עֲדוֹ	—	אַעְדִיאוּ
they f. —	עַדִּיאָה	—

PARTICIPLE		
ACTIVE moving away	PASSIVE becoming pregnant	ACTIVE removing
עוֹבֵר / סָר	מְעֻבֶּרֶת	מַעֲבִיר / מֵסִיר
m.s. עֲדֵי	—	מַעְדֵי
f.s. —	מְעַדְיָא	—

קַל	פְּעֵל	אַפְעֵל
FUTURE		
will move away	*will become pregnant*	*will remove*
יָסוּר, יָסוּרוּ	תִּתְעַבַּר	אַעֲבִיר / אָסִיר...

	קַל	פְּעֵל	אַפְעֵל
I	—	—	אַעְדֵּי
you m.s.	—	—	תַּעְדֵּי
he/it m.	יְעְדֵּי	—	יַעְדֵּי
she/it f.	—	תְּעַדֵּי	תַּעְדֵּי
you m. pl.	—	—	תַּעְדּוֹן
they m.	יְעִידוּן	—	—

			IMPERATIVE
			remove!
			הָסֵר!, הָסִירוּ!
m.s.	—	—	אַעְדִּי
m.pl.	—	—	אַעְדוּ

			GERUND / INFINITIVE
			to remove
			לְהָסִיר
	—	—	לְאַעְדָּאָה

(25) אֲתֵי (initial א and final י)

Both the meaning of this verb and its conjugated forms in Targum Onkelos are similar to what has been described in the survey of the verb in the Talmud on p. 123 — with *binyan* קַל (e.g., אֲתָא, *he came*) translating the Biblical Hebrew in the same *binyan* (e.g., בָּא), and the causative *binyan* אַפְעֵל (e.g., אַיְתִי, *he brought*) translating the parallel Hebrew הִפְעִיל (e.g., הֵבִיא). In addition to these common *binyanim*, which are presented in the paradigms below, Onkelos uses three forms from *binyan* אִתַּפְעַל (the reflexive/passive of the אַפְעֵל): **אִתֲּתִיאַת**, *it (f.) was brought*, **יִתֲּתֵי**, *it will be brought*, and **יִתֲּתוֹן**, *they will be brought*.

	קַל	אַפְעֵל
	PAST	
	came בָּאתִי...	*brought* הֵבֵאתִי...
I	אֲתֵיתִי, אֲתֵית	אַיְתֵיתִי[26]
you m.s.	אֲתֵיתָא	אַיְתֵיתָא[26]
he/it m.	אֲתָא	אַיְתִי[26]
she/it f.	אֲתָת	אַיְתֵיתֵיה[26]
we	אֲתֵינָא	—
you m. pl.	אֲתֵיתוֹן	אַיְתֵיתוֹן[26]
they m.	אֲתוֹ	אַיְתִיאוּ, אַיְתוֹ[26]
they f.	אֲתָאָה	—

---

26 In some editions of Targum Onkelos: -אֲיִ — rather than -אֲיֵ.

אַפְעֵל	קַל

ACTIVE PARTICIPLE		
coming ...בָּא	*bringing* ...מֵבִיא
m.s.	אָתֵי	מֵיתֵי[27]
f.s.	אָתְיָא	—
m.pl.	אָתַן	מֵיתַן[27]
f.pl.	אָתְיָן	מֵיתְיָן[27]

FUTURE		
will come ...אֵבָא	*will bring* ...אֵבִיא
I	אֵיתֵי	אַיְתֵי
you m.s.	תֵּיתֵי	תַּיְתֵי
he/it m.	יֵיתֵי	יַיְתֵי
she/it f.	תֵּיתֵי	תַּיְתֵי
we	נֵיתֵי	—
you m. pl.	תֵּיתוֹן	תַּיְתוֹן
they m.	יֵיתוֹן	יַיְתוֹן
they f.	יֵיתְיָן	יַיְתְיָן

27 In some editions of Targum Onkelos: ־מַיְ — rather than ־מֵי.

קַל	אַפְעֵל

	IMPERATIVE	
	come! ...!בּוֹא	*bring!* ...!הָבֵא
m.s.	אִיתָא	אִיתָא[28]
f.s.	אִיתָא	——
m.pl.	אִיתוֹ	אִיתוֹ[28]

	GERUND / INFINITIVE	
	(to) come לְבוֹא, בּוֹא	*to bring* לְהָבִיא
	לְמֵיתֵי, מֵיתָא	לְאֵיתָאָה[28]

28   In some editions of Targum Onkelos: -אֵי — rather than -אֵי.

(26) הוי (initial guttural and final י)

In Targum Onkelos this Aramaic verb הוי, *be*, like its Biblical Hebrew counterpart היה, is used only in *binyan* קַל. Most of the future forms (e.g., תְּהֵי) do not have a consonantal *vav*.

קַל	
PAST	
was ...הֲוֵיתִי	
I	הֲוֵיתִי
you m.s.	הֲוֵיתָא
he/it m.	הֲוָה
she/it f.	הֲוָת
we	הֲוֵינָא
you m. pl.	הֲוֵיתוֹן
they m.	הֲווֹ
they f.	הֲוָאָה

ACTIVE PARTICIPLE	
being ...הֲוֶה	
m.s.	הָוֵי
f.s.	הָוְיָה
m.pl.	הָוַן

212

x

קַל

FUTURE

will be
אֶהְיֶה...

I		אֱהֱוֵי, אֵיהֵי
you m.s.		תְּהֵי
he/it m.		יְהֵי
she/it f.		תְּהֵי
we		נְהֵי
you m.pl.		תְּהוֹן
you f.pl.		תְּהְוְיָן
they m.		יְהוֹן
they f.		יְהְוְיָן

IMPERATIVE

be!
הֱיֵה!...

m.s.		הֱוִי
f.s.		הֱוַאי
m.pl.		הֱווּ

GERUND/INFINITIVE

(to) be
לִהְיוֹת, הָיָה

	לְמִהְוֵי, מִהְוָה

213

(27) שְׁתִי (initial sibilant and final י)

As in the conjugation in the Babylonian Talmud described above on p. 120, this verb appears only in *binyan* קַל in Targum Onkelos — except for only one form in the אִתְפְּעֵל *binyan*, **יִשְׁתֵּתִי**, *it will be drunk*. Like its counterpart in the Talmud, the third-person masculine singular form in the past tense שְׁתִי ends in יָ-, rather than in the final אָ- that appears in most final semi-vowel verbs (e.g., חֲזָא). The prosthetic א, however, which is fairly common in the conjugation of the Talmudic verb, appears in Onkelos only in the imperative form אֲשֶׁתְּ (*drink!*). The suffix of the first-person singular of the past tense is תִי- in Targum Onkelos, e.g., in the form שְׁתֵיתִי — rather than the suffix אִי- in the Aramaic of the Talmud (e.g., שְׁתַאי).

קַל	
PAST	
drank שְׁתֵיתִי...	
I	שְׁתֵיתִי
he/it m.	שְׁתִי
she/it f.	שְׁתִיאַת
you m. pl.	שְׁתֵיתוֹן
they m.	שְׁתִיאוּ
ACTIVE PARTICIPLE	
drinking שָׁותֶה...	
m.s.	שָׁתֵי
f.s.	שָׁתְיָא
m.pl.	שָׁתַן

קַל

FUTURE
will drink
אֶשְׁתֶּה...

I	אֶשְׁתֵּי
you m.s.	תִּשְׁתֵּי
he/it m.	יִשְׁתֵּי
we	נִשְׁתֵּי
you m. pl.	תִּשְׁתּוֹן

IMPERATIVE
drink!
שְׁתֵה!

m.s.	אֵשְׁתְּ

GERUND / INFINITIVE
to drink
לִשְׁתּוֹת

	לְמִשְׁתֵּי

(28) שׁאל (middle root-letter א)

Both the meaning of this verb and its conjugated forms in Targum Onkelos are similar to what has been described in the survey of the verb in the Talmud on p. 78. Only one form is attested from the causative אַפְעֵל *binyan*, אַשְׁאֵילוּנוּ, *they granted them their requests*, and that *binyan* has been omitted from the paradigm.

	קַל	פַּעֵל
	PAST	
	asked שָׁאַלְתִּי...	*asked, longed* שָׁאַל, הִתְאַוּוּ
I	שְׁאֵילִית	—
you m.s.	שְׁאֵילְתָּא	—
he/it m.	שְׁאֵיל	שָׁאֵיל
they m.	שְׁאֵילוּ	שָׁאֵילוּ

	ACTIVE PARTICIPLE	
	asking שׁוֹאֵל	*longing/lusting* מְשָׁאֲלִים / מִתְאַוִּים
m.s.	שָׁאֵיל	—
m.pl.	—	מְשָׁאֲלֵי

קַל	פַּעֵל

	FUTURE	
	will ask תִּשְׁאַל...	
you m.s.	תִּשְׁאַל	—
he/it m.	יִשְׁאַל	—
she/it f.	תִּשְׁאַל	—
they m.	יִשְׁאֲלוּן	—

	IMPERATIVE	
	ask! שְׁאַל!	
m.s.	שְׁאַל	—

	GERUND / INFINITIVE	
	to ask לִשְׁאַל	*"ask"* שְׁאוֹל
	לְמִשְׁאַל	שָׁאֲלָא

(29) הימן (quadriliteral)

Both the meaning of this verb and its conjugated forms in Targum Onkelos are similar to what has been described in the survey of the verb in the Talmud on p. 141. All the forms have an active meaning (like *binyan* פַּעֵל) — except for the passive participles, e.g., מְהֵימַן, *believed, trustworthy*, and the unique passive future form **יִתְהֵימְנוּן**, *they will be verified*, which is omitted from the paradigm below.

PAST	
believed/trusted הֶאֱמִין...	
he/it m.	הֵימִין
you m. pl.	הֵימִינְתּוּן
they m.	הֵימִינוּ

PARTICIPLE		
ACTIVE *believing* מַאֲמִינִים		**PASSIVE** *believed/trustworthy* נֶאֱמָן...
m.s.	—	מְהֵימַן
m.pl.	מְהֵימְנִין	מְהֵימְנִין
f.pl.	—	מְהֵימְנָן

FUTURE	
will believe תַּאֲמִין, יַאֲמִינוּ	
you m.s.	תְּהֵימִין
they m.	יְהֵימְנוּן

(30) **סובר** (quadriliteral with initial sibliant and final *resh*)

The verb סבר (*think, hold an opinion,* or *consider*), which appears frequently in *binyan* קַל in the Babylonian Talmud, is also used occasionally by Onkelos in the active participle **סָבַר**, *understanding* (*i.e., learned*), and the passive participles **סְבִיר** (s.) and **סְבִירִין** (pl.), *contemplating*; as well as in *binyan* פַּעֵל, **סַבָּרִית**, *I hoped*, and **סַבָּרוּ**, *they understood.*

In the paradigm below, the same consonants (ס, ב, ר) are also prominent in the conjugated forms of the rare *binyan* פּוֹעֵל²⁹ — most of which are used in Targum Onkelos to translate forms of the Biblical Hebrew verb נשׂא, *bear.* According to modern scholars, however, the *quadriliteral* סובר is the root of the forms presented in the paradigm below, and the forms conjugated from the triliteral root סבר that appear in Targum Onkelos (which we enumerated in the previous paragraph) are not related to them.³⁰

The third root-letter of this verb, the ר, which functions like a guttural consonant, sometimes causes the preceding vowel to be *pathaḥ* rather than the usual *tzerei* or *ḥirik*: e.g., מְסוֹבַר, *bearing*, and סַבַּרוּ, *they understood.*

פּוֹעֵל
PAST
bore   נָשָׂא, נָשְׂאָה

he/it m.	**סוֹבְרֵךְ**
she/it f.	**סוֹבַרַת**

---

29 Another example of this Aramaic *binyan* פּוֹעֵל in Targum Onkelos (Yemenite editions) is the form סוֹפֵיק, *he supplied* (דברים ב:ז; לב:י). For a discussion of the parallel Hebrew *binyan*, see Rav Y. Mecklenburg, *HaKetav VeHaKabbala*, on אֲרַמִּי אֹבֵד אָבִי (דברים כו:ה).

30 See, for instance, Michael Sokoloff, *Dictionary of Jewish Palestinan Aramaic*, 2nd ed. (Ramat Gan, Israel: Bar Ilan University Press, 2002), p. 369. Cf. R. Avraham Bakrat, ספר זכרון על פירוש רש"י (ed. M. Phillip, Petaḥ Tikva, 5738), p. 236 on שמות טו:יג.

פּוֹעֵל

ACTIVE PARTICIPLE
bearing
נוֹשֵׂא

m.s.		מְסוֹבַר

FUTURE
will bear
אֶשָּׂא, תִּשָּׂא, יִשְׂאוּ

I		אֲסוֹבַר
you m.s.		תְּסוֹבַר
they		יְסוֹבְרוּן

IMPERATIVE
bear!
שָׂא!

m.s.		סוֹבַרְהִי

GERUND / INFINITIVE
to bear
לָשֵׂאת

		לְסוֹבָרָא

(31) **שֵׁיצֵי** (quadriliteral with initial sibilant and final י)

This four-letter root is probably derived from the שַׁפְעֵל *binyan* of the root יצי or יצא, and it has two different meanings: (1) *cast out (of the world)* or *destroy* and (2) *complete*, as in *Ezra* 6:15. The paradigm below includes active forms (derived from *binyan* שַׁפְעֵל) and passive forms (from *binyan* אִשְׁתַּפְעַל).

	ACTIVE	PASSIVE
	PAST	
	completed/destroyed כְּלִיתִי / הִשְׁמַדְתִּי...	would have been cast out הוּשְׁמַדְתָּ
I	שֵׁיצִיתִי	——
you m.s.	——	אִשְׁתֵּיצִיתָא
he/it m.	שֵׁיצִי	——
she/it f.	שֵׁיצִיאַת	——
they m.	שֵׁיצִיאוּנוּן	——

ACTIVE	PASSIVE

FUTURE	
will destroy אֲכַלֶּה / אַשְׁמִיד...	*will be cast out* אֶשָׁמֵד / אֶכָּרֵת...

	ACTIVE	PASSIVE
I	אֲשֵׁיצֵי	אִשְׁתֵּיצֵי
you m.s.	תְּשֵׁיצֵי	תִּשְׁתֵּיצֵי
he/it m.	יְשֵׁיצֵי	יִשְׁתֵּיצֵי
she/it f.	תְּשֵׁיצֵי	———
you m. pl.	תְּשֵׁיצוֹן	תִּשְׁתֵּיצוּן
they m.	יְשֵׁיצוּן	יִשְׁתֵּיצוּן
they f.	———	יִשְׁתֵּיצְיָן

IMPERATIVE	
destroy! כַּלֵּה! / הַשְׁמֵד!	

	ACTIVE	PASSIVE
m.s.	שֵׁיצִי	———

GERUND / INFINITIVE	
to destroy לְכַלּוֹת / לְהַשְׁמִיד	*"be destroyed"* הִשָׁמֵד
לְשֵׁיצָאָה, לְשֵׁיצָיוּתֵיהּ	אִשְׁתֵּיצָאָה

(32) שֵׁיזֵב (quadriliteral with initial sibilant)

This four-letter root probably developed from the שַׁפְעֵל *binyan* of the root עזב, with the *tzerei* vowel representing an original ע consonant.[31] The Biblical Hebrew root עזב is sometimes used in the sense of *help* or *save*, as in עָזֹב תַּעֲזֹב עִמּוֹ (שמות כג:ה), which is the meaning of this Aramaic verb. The paradigm below includes both active forms (derived from *binyan* שַׁפְעֵל) and reflexive/passive forms (mostly from *binyan* אִשְׁתַּפְעַל).

	ACTIVE	REFLEXIVE/PASSIVE
	PAST	
	saved הַצַּלְתִּי, הִצִּיל	*was saved* נִצְּלָה
you	שֵׁיזֵבְתָּא	—
he/it m.	שֵׁיזֵיב	—
she/it f.	—	אִשְׁתֵּיזַבַת
	PARTICIPLE	
	saving מַצִּיל	*saved* מֻצָּל
m.s.	מְשֵׁיזֵיב	מְשֵׁיזֵיב, מְשֵׁיזְבָא (def.)

---

31   See Morag (above, p. 15 note 8), p. 284.

ACTIVE	REFLEXIVE/PASSIVE

FUTURE	
will save אַצֵּיל, יַצִּילוּ	*will escape* אֶמָּלֵט, יִמָּלֵט

	ACTIVE	REFLEXIVE/PASSIVE
I	אֲשֵׁיזֵיב	אֶשְׁתֵּיזַב
he/it m.	——	יִשְׁתֵּיזַב
they m.	יְשֵׁיזְבוּן	——

IMPERATIVE	
save! הַצֵּל!	*escape!* הִמָּלֵט!

	ACTIVE	REFLEXIVE/PASSIVE
m.s.	שֵׁיזֵיבְנִי	אִשְׁתֵּיזַב

GERUND/INFINITIVE	
(to) save (לְ)הַצִּיל, הַצֵּל	*to be saved/to escape* לְהִנָּצֵל/לְהִמָּלֵט
לְשֵׁיזָבָא, שֵׁיזָבָא, לְשֵׁיזָבוּתָךְ	לְאִשְׁתֵּיזָבָא

6

HOMOGRAPHS AND HOMONYMS

IN THE BABYLONIAN TALMUD

The paradigms of the thirty verbs presented in Chapter 4 are designed to help students determine the exact meaning of Aramaic verbal forms — according to the *binyan*, tense, person, number, and gender. However, some verbal forms are ambiguous. For example, the very common verbal form אמרי may either be אֲמַרִי, *I said*, or אָמְרִי, *they say*. In fact, the same ambiguity — between the first person singular of the past tense and the masculine plural form of the active participle — regularly occurs in *binyan* קַל. Or consider אַפֵּיק, a form in *binyan* אַפְעֵל from the root נפק that has three different meanings: (1) *he took out* (third-person masculine singular of the past tense); (2) *I will take out* (first-person singular of the future tense); and (3) *take out!* (the masculine singular of the imperative). The same ambiguity occurs in the אַפְעֵל *binyan* of many other Aramaic verbs.

◊   A word *spelled* just like another word but representing a different grammatical form and having a different meaning is called a *homograph*. There may be a difference in pronunciation, for example, אֲמַרִי as opposed to אָמְרִי. (Bear in mind that most editions of the Talmud are not vocalized.) If the pronunciation is also the same (as in אַפֵּיק), it is a *homonym* as well. When the student confronts a homograph, he can use the grammatical knowledge he has gleaned from our verbal paradigms to reduce to a minimum the number of possible explanations. Then he must be guided by the Talmudic context in which the particular verbal forms appear in order to determine which meaning is most appropriate. In some cases, this determination will be easy; in other cases, it will be more difficult.

אמרי 6.1

For example, consider the uses of the homograph אמרי in the following two quotations where the meanings are quite clear from the contexts:

*I also **said** [it] from this pasuk*	**אֲנָא נַמִּי מֵהָדֵין קְרָא אֲמַרִי**
	(כתובות כה, ב)

*the ḥakhamim **say***	**אָמְרִי רַבָּנָן** (בבא מציעא ג, א)

In the first example, it is obvious that the pronoun אֲנָא, *I*, is the subject of the verb אֲמַרִי, *I said*. In the second example, on the other hand, the plural noun רַבָּנָן is clearly the subject of אָמְרִי, which therefore has a plural meaning, *[they] say*.

אפיק 6.2

In like manner, consider the uses of אַפֵּיק in the following three quotations:

*Rava applied pressure on him... **and took** 400 zuz **away** from him for tzedaka*	**רָבָא כַּפְיֵיהּ...וְאַפֵּיק מִינֵּיהּ ד' מְאָה** זוּזֵי לִצְדָקָה (כתובות מט, ב)

*He (= King Aḥashverosh) thought: Now they certainly will not be redeemed again; **I will take out** the vessels of the Beth HaMikdash and use them*	אֲמַר: הַשְׁתָּא וַדַּאי תּוּ לָא מִיפָּרְקִי; **אַפֵּיק** מָאנֵי דְבֵי מַקְדְּשָׁא וְאִשְׁתַּמַּשׁ בְּהוּ (מגילה יא, ב)

*He said to him: Go, **remove** [them]!*	אֲמַר לֵיהּ: זִיל, **אַפֵּיק!** (חולין קלב, ב)

In the first example, the third-person singular of the past tense fits the context best since רָבָא appears to be the subject. In the last example, the use of the adjacent imperative זִיל indicates that אַפֵּיק, too, is imperative. The middle example is not so clear, but it probably refers to the king's plan to use the holy vessels in the future.

◊   The following ten homographs are taken from our verbal paradigms. For each homograph, we have presented two (or more) different explanations of its grammatical form, which are then illustrated by an example from the Talmud.

6.3 פלוג

On the one hand, פְּלוֹג, *they distinguished*, is the third-person masculine plural of the past tense from the verb פלג. On the other hand, פְּלוֹג (*divide!*) is the masculine-singular imperative.

the ḥakhamim **did** not **distinguish**	לָא פְּלוֹג רַבָּנַן (יבמות קז, א)
Divide in this way!	פְּלוֹג הָכִי! (בבא מציעא ז, א)

6.4 זבין

The masculine singular of the active participle from the קַל of זבן is זָבֵין, *buying*, whereas זַבֵּין from *binyan* פַּעֵל is a masculine-singular form — either from the third person of the past, *he sold*, or the imperative (*sell!*).

a merchant who **buys** *or sells*	תַּגְרָא דְזָבֵין וּמְזַבֵּין (בבא קמא פח, ב)
a certain man who **sold** *his property with the intention of "going up" to Eretz Yisrael*	הַהוּא גַבְרָא דְזַבֵּין לְנִכְסֵיה אַדַּעְתָּא לְמִיסַק לְאַרְעָא דְיִשְׂרָאֵל (קידושין נ, א)

6.5 עביד

The masculine-singular participle is usually spelled the same way whether it is active or passive, but the vocalization differs. עָבֵיד, *doing*, is active, while עֲבִיד — *made, done*, or *used (to)* — is passive.[1]

How **does he do** *so?*	הֵיכִי עָבֵיד הָכִי? (ברכות יד, ב)
Shall I say [that a non-Jew] may also **be made** *an agent?*	אֵימָא שְׁלִיחַ נַמֵי עֲבִיד?[2] (קידושין מא, ב)
a man who **is used** *to renting*	גַּבְרָא דַעֲבִיד לְמֵיגַר (בבא קמא כ, א)

1 Besides these two participial forms, עֲבֵיד serves as the imperative (*do!*), and occasionally it means the same as עֲבַד in the past tense, *he did*.
2 In recent vocalized editions of the Talmud, this word has been confused with its homograph, עָבֵיד, *making*.

6.6 חזי

This form is another common homograph. חָזֵי, *seeing,* is the active participle, while חֲזֵי, *seen* or *fit,* is the passive participle. In addition, חֲזִי is the masculine singular imperative (*see!*).

perhaps **he will see**[3] an argument and reverse the judgment	דִּילְמָא חָזֵי טַעְמָא וְסָתַר דִּינָא (שבת ט, ב)
fit for kindling	חֲזֵי לְהַסָּקָה (בבא בתרא יט, ב)
Go out [and] **see** what people do!	פּוּק חֲזִי מַאי עַמָּא דָבַר! (ברכות מה, רע"א)

6.7 מהדרינן

This homograph is an active participle from the root הדר with a pronoun suffix (מהדרי+אֲנַן). It represents two different *binyanim,* and it has two separate meanings: מַהְדְּרִינַן in the אַפְעֵל *binyan* means *we bring back* or *we return (something),* while מְהַדְּרִינַן in the פַּעֵל *binyan* is generally used with the preposition אַ־ and means *we seek (after)* or *we pursue (zealously).*

we return a lost article	מַהְדְּרִינַן אֲבִידְתָא (חולין צה, ב)
we seek [to be consistent with] R. Méir	מְהַדְּרִינַן אַרַבִּי מֵאִיר (גיטין ד, א)

6.8 הואי

In the past tense of the *binyan* קַל of הוי, the form הֲוַאי is a homonym. It may be either the first-person singular, *I was,* or the third-person feminine singular, *she was.*[4]

If **I had been** there, I would have said something better than all of them.	אִי הֲוַאי הָתָם, הֲוָה אֲמִינָא מִילְתָא דַעֲדִיפָא מִכּוּלְּהוּ. (מגילה ז, א)
That **was** an error.	הַהִיא טָעוּתָא הֲוַאי. (ברכות כז, ב)

---

3 The Aramaic participle sometimes has a future meaning. See p. 27 above.
4 This homonym also occurs in the conjugations of other verbs that have י as their final root-letter: חֲזַאי, *I* or *she saw,* and אֲתַאי, *I* or *she came.*

228

6.9 מייתי

This homograph serves as an active participle of two *different verbs.*
The form מַיְיתֵי, *bringing,* is the אַפְעֵל (causative) masculine-singular
participle from the root אתי, whereas מָיְיתֵי, *dying,* is the קַל
masculine-plural participle from the root מות.

What proof **does he bring?**	מַאי רְאָיָה **מַיְיתֵי?** (כתובות עו, א)
they eat, but **they do** *not* **die**	קָא אָכְלֵי, וְלָא **מָיְיתֵי** (עירובין כט, א)

6.10 ליתיב

This form may be the third-person masculine singular of the future,
binyan קַל, from one of two roots: either ישב, *sit,* or נתב, which is
related to יהב, *give* (see verb 12 in Chapter 4).

Let *the master* ***sit*** *on bolsters or cushions!*	**לֵיתֵיב** מָר אַבָּרִים וּכְסָתוֹת! (מועד קטן טז, ב)
Whatever he gives (= *pays*) *him —* ***he must give*** *him from the best quality.*	כָּל דְּיָהֵיב לֵיהּ — מִ"מֵּיטַב" **לֵיתֵיב** לֵיהּ. (בבא קמא ז, ב ע"פ שמות כב:ד)

6.11 מותיב

This אַפְעֵל participle may be derived either from the root תוב, in
which case it would mean *retorting* or *objecting,* or from יתב, meaning
seating.

He **raises** *it* (= *the objection*)*, and he* [*himself*] *answers it.*	הוּא **מוֹתִיב** לַהּ, וְהוּא מְפָרֵק לַהּ. (שבת קמה, רע"א)
In the summer Rav Shesheth **seats** *the students where the sun reaches.*	רַב שֵׁשֶׁת בְּקֵיטָא **מוֹתִיב** לְהוּ לְרַבָּנָן הֵיכָא דְּמָטְיָא שִׁימְשָׁא. (שבת קי"ט, סע"א)

6.12 זבנה

Besides the personal-pronoun suffixes attached to Aramaic (and Hebrew) verbs that indicate the *subject*, pronoun suffixes are sometimes attached to verbs to express a *direct object*. The table of direct-object suffixes presented at the end of Chapter 8 of this work reveals that a few of those suffixes are spelled the same as *subject* suffixes. For instance, as in Hebrew a ה- suffix serves two different functions: As a vowel letter, it is used in forming the third-person feminine singular of the past tense; but as a consonantal ה (with a dot in it called *mappik*), it expresses the feminine-singular direct-object suffix, *her* or *it*. Thus in the past tense of the פָּעַל *binyan* — זבנה may be either זַבְּנָה, *she sold*, or זַבְּנָהּ, *he sold it*. Here, too, the student must rely upon the Talmudic context to help him determine which interpretation is correct:

[if] **she sold** to him	זַבְּנָה אִיהִי לְדִידֵיהּ (בבא בתרא נ, א)
[if] **he sold it** [or] bequeathed it [or] gave it away as a gift	זַבְּנָהּ, אוֹרְתַהּ, יַהֲבַהּ בְּמַתָּנָה (בבא מציעא לה, א)

Furthermore, the same direct-object suffix is sometimes attached to the imperative, as in the following Talmudic passage, which contains two instances of this usage from two different *binyanim*. In the first form, זַבְּנָהּ, (*buy it!*) the suffix is attached to the imperative of *binyan* קַל; in the second form, זַבְּנָהּ, (*sell it!*), the suffix is attached to the imperative of *binyan* פָּעַל.

Go [and] **buy it** from him without a guarantee, and then **sell it** to her with a guarantee!	זִיל זַבְּנָהּ מִינֵּיהּ שֶׁלֹּא בַּאֲחָרָיוּת, וַהֲדַר זַבְּנָהּ נִיהֲלָהּ בַּאֲחָרָיוּת! (בבא בתרא קסט, ב)

◊ In conclusion, the occurrence of homographs in the Talmud certainly makes the student's task more difficult. Nevertheless, if the student is aware of the phenomenon, and if he is familiar with the paradigms of the Aramaic verb, he should be able to cope with the difficulty successfully.

7

THE ARAMAIC NOUN AND ADJECTIVE

7.1 THE NOUN

The noun appears in one of three *states* in Aramaic:

The *absolute state* — the simple form of the noun. Example: מֶלֶךְ, a *king*

The *construct state*[1] — in which one noun is closely connected with the following word (usually another noun). A hyphen is sometimes placed after the noun in the construct state to emphasize the connection. Example: מֶלֶךְ־יִשְׂרָאֵל, *king of Israel*

The *emphatic* (or *definite*) *state* — in which the definite article suffix אָ-
is added to the noun. Example: מַלְכָּא, *the king*

The following tables present Aramaic nouns, singular and plural, in all three states, with their Hebrew parallels.

◇ **THE MASCULINE NOUN**[2]

	ABSOLUTE		CONSTRUCT		EMPHATIC	
	ARAMAIC	HEBREW	ARAMAIC	HEBREW	ARAMAIC	HEBREW
Singular	מֶלֶךְ	מֶלֶךְ	מֶלֶךְ־	מֶלֶךְ־	מַלְכָּא	הַמֶּלֶךְ
Singular	עָלַם	עוֹלָם	עָלַם־	עוֹלָם־	עָלְמָא	הָעוֹלָם
Plural	מַלְכִין	מְלָכִים	מַלְכֵי־	מַלְכֵי־	מַלְכַיָּא	הַמְּלָכִים
Plural	עָלְמִין	עוֹלָמִים	עָלְמֵי־	עוֹלְמֵי־	עָלְמַיָּא	הָעוֹלָמִים

1 For a fuller discussion of the *construct state*, see p. 2 above.
2 In both Hebrew and Aramaic, the sign of plurality of masculine nouns is really the י. Both the final ם- in the Hebrew plural and the final ן- in the Aramaic absolute plural are of minor importance, as is evident from their absence from the plural of the construct state. The י, however, is always retained.

◊ THE FEMININE NOUN[3]

	ABSOLUTE		CONSTRUCT		EMPHATIC	
	ARAMAIC	HEBREW	ARAMAIC	HEBREW	ARAMAIC	HEBREW
Singular	מְדִינָא/ה	מְדִינָה	מְדִינַת־	מְדִינַת־	מְדִינְתָּא	הַמְּדִינָה
Singular	מַלְכוּ	מַלְכוּת	מַלְכוּת־	מַלְכוּת־	מַלְכוּתָא	הַמַּלְכוּת
Plural	מְדִינָן	מְדִינוֹת	מְדִינָת־	מְדִינוֹת־	מְדִינָתָא	הַמְּדִינוֹת
Plural	מַלְכְוָן	מַלְכִיּוֹת	מַלְכְוָת־	מַלְכִיּוֹת־	מַלְכְוָתָא	הַמַּלְכִיּוֹת

The tables that have been presented are correct in theory and reflect the actual usage in Biblical Aramaic. In practice, however, the situation is somewhat different in the Aramaic of the Babylonian Talmud.

In the first place, the distinction in meaning between the absolute state and the emphatic state (i.e., with the definite-article suffix אָ־) is not so consistent. In the singular of nouns of both genders and in the plural of feminine nouns, the emphatic state is often used instead of the absolute — even where the definite article is not logically required.

Example: חַד גַּבְרָא, *one man*; מְדִינָתָא, *cities*

3　　In both Hebrew and Aramaic, a ת־ suffix is usually an indicator of femininity, while plurality is expressed in Hebrew by a change of the preceding vowel to a *ḥolam* (with a ו, but often without a ו in Biblical Hebrew). In Aramaic, the sign of plurality is really the *kametz* vowel, which corresponds to the Hebrew *ḥolam*. The ת־ in the construct and emphatic states expresses femininity, and the final ן־ in the absolute state is of no semantic significance.

Sometimes, however, the form without the definite-article suffix אָ־
is used, especially as a predicate noun.

Example: הֲוִי גְבַר!, *be a man!*

Secondly, in the plural of masculine nouns (and adjectives), forms
such as מַלְכֵי are often used not only in the construct state but even
in the absolute and emphatic states. Thus, in Babylonian Aramaic —
but not in the Targumim — מַלְכֵי may mean either *the kings of* or *kings*
or *the kings*.

In Aramaic, as in Hebrew, personal-pronoun suffixes are sometimes
added to the construct form of nouns, e.g., to מְדִינַת־, מַלְכֵי־, and
מְדִינָת־, respectively. See the paradigms in Chapter 8, pp. 237-238.

7.2 THE ADJECTIVE

Aramaic adjectives are similar in form to nouns. The following table
presents the adjective חַכִּים, *wise*.

◇ **THE MASCULINE ADJECTIVE**

	ABSOLUTE		EMPHATIC	
	ARAMAIC	HEBREW	ARAMAIC	HEBREW
Singular	חַכִּים	חָכָם	חַכִּימָא	הֶחָכָם
Plural	חַכִּימִין, חַכִּימֵי	חֲכָמִים	חַכִּימַיָּא	הַחֲכָמִים

◇ **THE FEMININE ADJECTIVE**

	ABSOLUTE		EMPHATIC	
	ARAMAIC	HEBREW	ARAMAIC	HEBREW
Singular	חַכִּימָא	חֲכָמָה	חַכִּימְתָּא	הַחֲכָמָה
Plural	חַכִּימָן	חֲכָמוֹת	חַכִּימָתָא	הַחֲכָמוֹת

These tables of adjectives too are correct in theory, but the practice in Babylonian Aramaic is somewhat different, as explained above (pp. 232-233) with regard to the nouns.

The adjective usually follows the noun it modifies. Here are some examples:

גַּבְרָא חַכִּימָא, a/the wise man   גַּבְרֵי חַכִּימֵי, (the) wise men

מְדִינָה רַבָּה, a great city   מְדִינְתָא רַבְּתָא, the great city

מְדִינָתָא רַבְרְבָתָא, (the) great cities

7.3 DETERMINING GENDER

The tables in this chapter present *only*[4] the *common* plural forms for masculine and feminine nouns (and adjectives), respectively. As in Hebrew, however, some masculine nouns use plural suffixes that are generally attached to feminine nouns – and some feminine nouns use plural suffixes that are generally attached to masculine nouns.

Examples: The plural form of the masculine Aramaic noun אַרְיָא (Hebrew: אֲרִי), *lion*, is אַרְיָוָתָא (Hebrew: אֲרָיוֹת), while the plural of the feminine noun מִילְתָא (Hebrew: מִלָּה), *thing* or *word*, is מִילֵי (Hebrew [usually]: מִלִּים).

Consequently, the only reliable guide for knowing the gender of an Aramaic (or Hebrew) noun is the gender of the adjective or verb that agrees with it grammatically.

Examples: From the passage: (ע"ז ע, א) הַהוּא אַרְיָא דַּהֲוָה נָהֵים, *that (m.) lion which was roaring (m.)*, it is clear that the gender of the noun אַרְיָא is masculine. Similarly, the passage: (פסחים קו, א) חֲדָא מִילְתָא הִיא, *it (f.) is one (f.) matter*, proves that מִילְתָא is feminine.

---

4   For a comprehensive presentation of Babylonian Aramaic nouns in all their diversity, see Epstein (above, p. 15 note 10), pp. 105-124, and the work of S. Morag and Y. Kara, ארמית במסורת תימן, לשון התלמוד הבבלי: שם העצם (Jerusalem: Magnes, 2002), pp. 235, 236.

8

THE ARAMAIC PRONOUN (including suffixes)

8.1 DEMONSTRATIVES

There is a variety of *demonstrative* pronouns and adjectives in Aramaic — some pointing to objects that are nearby and others to those that are far away (or previously mentioned).

◇ **NEAR**

TALMUD BAVLI ARAMAIC	ONKELOS ARAMAIC	HEBREW PARALLEL	ENGLISH TRANSLATION
הַאי, דֵּין, הָדֵין, דְּנָא, דְּנָן, עֲדֵי	דֵּין, הָדֵין, דְּנָן	זֶה, הַזֶּה	*this (m.s.)*
הָא, דָּא, הָדָא, עֲדָא	דָּא, הָדָא	זֹאת, הַזֹּאת	*this (f.s.)*
הָנֵי, אִילֵין, הָלֵין, עֲדֵי	אִלֵין, הָאִלֵין	אֵלּוּ, הָאֵלּוּ	*these*

◇ **DISTANT**

TALMUD BAVLI ARAMAIC	ONKELOS ARAMAIC	HEBREW PARALLEL	ENGLISH TRANSLATION
הַאִיךְ, הַהוּא, אִידָךְ, דֵּיכִי	הַהוּא, דֵּיכִי	הַהוּא	*that (m.s.)*
הָךְ, הַהִיא, אִידֵךְ	הַהִיא	הַהִיא	*that (f.s.)*
הָנַךְ, הַנְהוּ, אִינָךְ	הָאִנּוּן	הָהֵם	*those*

8.2 INDEPENDENT PERSONAL PRONOUNS

TALMUD BAVLI ARAMAIC	ONKELOS ARAMAIC	HEBREW PARALLEL	ENGLISH TRANSLATION
אֲנָא	אֲנָא	אֲנִי, אָנֹכִי	*I*
אַתְּ, אַנְתְּ	אַתְּ	אַתָּה	*you (m.s.)*
אַתְּ	אַתְּ	אַתְּ	*you (f.s.)*
הוּא, אִיהוּ, נִיהוּ[1]	הוּא	הוּא	*he/it (m.)*
הִיא, אִיהִי, נִיהִי[1]	הִיא	הִיא	*she/it (f.)*
אֲנַן, אֲנַחְנָא	אֲנַחְנָא, נַחְנָא	אָנוּ, אֲנַחְנוּ	*we*
אַתּוּן, אַנְתּוּ	אַתּוּן	אַתֶּם	*you (m.pl.)*
——	אַתִּין	אַתֶּן	*you (f.pl.)*
אִינְהוּ, אִינוּן, נִינְהוּ[1]	אִנּוּן	הֵם	*they (m.)*
אִינְהִי, נִינְהִי[1]	אִנִּין	הֵן	*they (f.)*

8.3 POSSESSIVE PERSONAL-PRONOUN SUFFIXES AFTER NOUNS

Personal-pronoun suffixes are used frequently in Aramaic. They are often added to nouns, prepositions, the relative pronoun ־דְּ and verbs.

The following table presents *personal-pronoun suffixes* that are added to the *construct* forms of Aramaic nouns and the forms that are created by their combination with the masculine noun, יוֹם. We have presented an *artificially* complete paradigm — in other words, not every suffix is actually found in the Talmud or in Targum Onkelos in combination with this particular noun.

---

1   The forms נִיהוּ, נִיהִי, נִינְהוּ and נִינְהִי are used only at the end of clauses and in questions.

◇ **AFTER THE SINGULAR (MASCULINE) NOUN (⁻יוֹמ)**

ARAMAIC SUFFIX	TALMUD BAVLI ARAMAIC	ONKELOS ARAMAIC	HEBREW PARALLEL	ENGLISH TRANSLATION
⁻י, ⁻אִי, ⁻	יוֹמִי, יוֹמַאי, יוֹם²	יוֹמִי, יוֹם²	יוֹמִי	*my day*
⁻ךְ, ⁻ךָ	יוֹמָךְ, יוֹמָיךְ	יוֹמָךְ	יוֹמְךָ	*your (m.s.) day*
⁻יךְ, ⁻כִי	יוֹמִיךְ	יוֹמִיךְ, יוֹמַכִי	יוֹמֵךְ	*your (f.s.) day*
⁻יה	יוֹמֵיה³	יוֹמֵה	יוֹמוֹ	*his/its (m.) day*
⁻ה	יוֹמַה³	יוֹמַה	יוֹמָה	*her/its (f.) day*
⁻ן, ⁻ין, ⁻נָא	יוֹמַן, יוֹמִין	יוֹמָנָא	יוֹמֵנוּ	*our day*
⁻כוֹן, ⁻כוּ, ⁻ייכוּ	יוֹמְכוֹן, יוֹמְכוּ, יוֹמַייכוּ	יוֹמְכוֹן	יוֹמְכֶם	*your (m.pl.) day*
⁻ייכִי, ⁻כֵין	יוֹמַייכִי	יוֹמְכֵין	יוֹמְכֶן	*your (f.pl.) day*
⁻הוֹן, ⁻הוּ, ⁻ייהוּ	יוֹמְהוֹן, יוֹמְהוּ, יוֹמַייהוּ	יוֹמְהוֹן	יוֹמָם	*their (m.) day*
⁻הִי, ⁻הֵין	יוֹמְהִי	יוֹמְהֵין	יוֹמָן	*their (f.) day*

◇ The same suffixes may be added to the *construct* state of singular feminine nouns: מְדִינְתִּי, *my city*; מְדִינְתָּךְ, *your (m.) city*; מְדִינְתִּיךְ, *your (f.) city*; מְדִינְתֵּיה, *his city*; מְדִינְתַּה, *her city*; מְדִינְתַּן, *our city*; מְדִינְתְּכוֹן, *your (m.pl.) city*; מְדִינְתְּכִי, *your (f.pl.) city*; מְדִינְתְּהוֹן, *their (m.) city*; מְדִינְתְּהִי, *their (f.) city*.

2   Occasionally, the first-person singular (*my*) has no suffix at all, e.g., אָמְרָה לִי אֵם (ברכות לט, רע"ב ועוד), *my mother told me* (Epstein [above p. 15 note 10], p. 122. See Yemenite versions of Targum Onkelos, e.g., (ת"א בראשית יב:יג) אֲחָת *my sister.*

3   With certain (biliteral) nouns, the third-person singular suffix is ⁻הִי in Targum Onkelos (often ⁻ה in the Babylonian Talmud) for the masculine and ⁻הָא in Targum Onkelos (sometimes ⁻הָ in the Babylonian Talmud) for the feminine. Examples: אֲבוּהַ, אֲבוּהָא, *his father;* אֲבוּהַ, אֲבוּהִי, *her father.*

◊ AFTER THE PLURAL (MASCULINE) NOUN (יוֹמֵי־)

ARAMAIC SUFFIX	TALMUD BAVLI ARAMAIC	ONKELOS ARAMAIC	HEBREW PARALLEL	ENGLISH TRANSLATION
־ַאי, ־ַי, ־ִי	יוֹמַאי, יוֹמִי	יוֹמַי, יוֹמֵי	יָמַי	*my days*
־ָיךְ, ־ָךְ	יוֹמָיךְ	יוֹמָךְ	יָמֶיךְ	*your (m.s.) days*
־ַיִךְ, ־ַךְ, ־ִיךְ	יוֹמֵיךְ	יוֹמַךְ, יוֹמִיךְ	יָמַיִךְ	*your (f.s.) days*
־וֹהִי, ־ֵיה	יוֹמוֹהִי, יוֹמֵיה	יוֹמוֹהִי	יָמָיו	*his/its (m.) days*
־ָהָא	יוֹמַהָא	יוֹמַהָא	יָמֶיהָ	*her/its (f.) days*
־ִין, ־ָנָא [4]	יוֹמִין[4]	יוֹמַנָא	יָמֵינוּ	*our days*
־ַייכוּ, ־ְיכוֹן	יוֹמַייכוּ	יוֹמֵיכוֹן	יְמֵיכֶם	*your (m.pl.) days*
־ַייכִי, ־ְיכֵין	יוֹמַייכִי	יוֹמֵיכֵין	יְמֵיכֶן	*your (f.pl.) days*
־ְיהוֹן, ־ַייהוּ	יוֹמֵייהוֹן, יוֹמַייהוּ	יוֹמֵיהוֹן	יְמֵיהֶם	*their (m.) days*
־ַייהִי, ־ְיהֵין	יוֹמַייהִי	יוֹמֵיהֵין	יְמֵיהֶן	*their (f.) days*

◊   Suffixes may be added to the *construct* state of plural feminine nouns: מְדִינָתַי or מְדִינָתָאי, *my cities*; מְדִינָתָךְ, *your (m.) cities*; מְדִינָתָהָא, *your (f.) cities*; מְדִינָתֵיה or מְדִינָתוֹהִי, *his cities*; מְדִינָתָהָא, *her cities*; מְדִינָתַנָא or מְדִינָתִין, *our cities*; מְדִינָתֵיכוֹן or מְדִינָתַייכוּ, *your (m. pl.) cities*; מְדִינָתֵיכֵן or מְדִינָתַייכִי, *your (f. pl.) cities*; מְדִינָתֵיהוּ or מְדִינָתֵיהוֹן, *their (m.) cities*; מְדִינָתֵיהֵין or מְדִינָתַייהִי, *their (f.) cities*.

---

4   ין־ is the common pronunciation of this suffix, but יִן־ may be more correct.

◇ AFTER אִית and לֵית

The same personal-pronoun suffixes that are sometimes added to nouns may also be appended to אִית, which, like its Hebrew counterpart יֵשׁ, expresses the idea of *being*. When the combination is rendered into English, the suffix serves as a subject pronoun. For example: (תרגום אונקלוס לדברים א:י) אִיתֵיכוֹן יוֹמָא דֵין כְּכוֹכְבֵי שְׁמַיָּא, *you are today like stars in the sky.*

Suffixes may also be attached to the negative form, לֵית (= לָא + אִית), *is not*, which functions like its Hebrew counterpart אֵין.

TALMUD BAVLI ARAMAIC	ONKELOS ARAMAIC	HEBREW PARALLEL	ENGLISH TRANSLATION
——	אִיתַנִי	הֱיוֹתִי	*my being*
——	אִיתָךְ	יֶשְׁךָ	*you (s.) are*
אִיתֵיהּ	אִתוֹהִי	יֶשְׁנוֹ	*he/it (m.) is*
אִיתָא, אִיתַהּ	——	יֶשְׁנָהּ	*she/it (f.) is*
אִיתֵינַן⁵	——	יֶשְׁנֶנּוּ	*we are*
אִיתַנְכוּ, אִיתִינְכוּ	אִיתֵיכוֹן	יֶשְׁכֶם	*you (pl.) are*
אִיתַנְהוּ, אִיתַנְהוֹן, אִיתִינוּן	——	יֶשְׁנָם	*they are*
——	לֵיתָךְ⁶	אֵינְךָ	*you (s.) are not*
לֵיתֵיהּ, לֵיתוֹהִי	לֵיתוֹהִי⁶	אֵינוֹ	*he/it (m.) is not*
לֵיתָא, לֵיתַהּ	לֵיתַהָא⁶	אֵינָהּ	*she/it (f.) is not*
——	לֵיתֵיכוֹן	אֵינְכֶם	*you (pl.) are not*
לֵיתַנְהוּ, לֵיתִנְיְהוּ⁷	לֵיתְנוּן	אֵינָם	*they are not*

5   According to the Munich Ms.: אִיתְנַן.
6   Non-Yemenites vocalize the first syllable of these forms as well: לֵי-.
7   According to Munich Ms. (Strack): לֵיתְנוּ.

8.4 PERSONAL-PRONOUN SUFFIXES AFTER PREPOSITIONS

Personal-pronoun suffixes are often appended to *prepositions*. The following six tables present the forms created by combining the suffixes with six common Aramaic prepositions.

◇ **AFTER ־לְ: PREPOSITION; DIRECT-OBJECT INDICATOR**

The prefix ־לְ has two distinct functions in Aramaic: Sometimes it serves as a preposition, meaning *to* or *for* (or *by*),[8] and sometimes it is an indicator of the direct object that follows.[9] In the latter case, the ־לְ prefix functions like אֶת in Hebrew and is not translated in English. Both alternatives are presented in the English and Hebrew translations below.

TALMUD BAVLI ARAMAIC	ONKELOS ARAMAIC	HEBREW PARALLEL	ENGLISH TRANSLATION
לִי	לִי	לִי; אוֹתִי	*to/for me; me*
לָךְ	לָךְ	לְךָ; אוֹתְךָ	*to/for you (m.s.); you*
לִיךְ, לִיכִי	לִיךְ, לִיכִי	לָךְ; אוֹתָךְ	*to/for you (f.s.); you*
לֵיה	לֵיה	לוֹ; אוֹתוֹ	*to/for him/it (m.); him/it*
לַה	לַה	לָה; אוֹתָה	*to/for her/it (f.); her/it*
לַן, לַנָא	לַנָא	לָנוּ; אוֹתָנוּ	*to/for us; us*
לְכוֹן, לְכוּ	לְכוֹן	לָכֶם; אֶתְכֶם	*to/for you (pl.); you*
לְהוֹן, לְהוּ	לְהוֹן	לָהֶם; אוֹתָם	*to/for them; them*

---

8   See the discussion of *the passive voice* on p. 256 below.
9   See the discussion of *the direct-object indicator* on pp. 251-253 below.

◇ AFTER THE PREPOSITION נִיהֲל־

In the Babylonian Talmud, the preposition נִיהֲל־, *to* or *for*, is used — *always* with a personal-pronoun suffix — to express the *indirect* object in sentences in which the *direct* object has already been expressed, either by ־ל with a suffix or by a pronoun suffix added to the verb.

Example 1:

*and he may give it **to her***   וְיָהֵיב לֵיהּ **נִיהֲלַהּ** (גיטין כא, סע״ב)

Example 2:

*I told it **to him***   אֲנָא אֲמַרִיתָא **נִיהֲלֵיהּ** (עירובין כט, א)

TALMUD BAVLI ARAMAIC	HEBREW PARALLEL	ENGLISH TRANSLATION
נִיהֲלִי	לִי	to/for me
נִיהֲלָךְ	לְךָ	to/for you (m.s.)
נִיהֲלִיךְ	לָךְ	to/for you (f.s.)
נִיהֲלֵיהּ	לוֹ	to/for him/it (m.)
נִיהֲלַהּ	לָהּ	to/for her/it (f.)
נִיהֲלַן	לָנוּ	to/for us
נִיהֲלַיְיכוּ	לָכֶם	to/for you (pl.)
נִיהֲלַיְיהוּ	לָהֶם	to/for them

◊ AFTER THE PREPOSITIONS עַל and עִילָוֵי

TALMUD BAVLI ARAMAIC	ONKELOS ARAMAIC	HEBREW PARALLEL	ENGLISH TRANSLATION
עֲלַי, עִילָוַאי, עִילָוַי	עֲלַי, עִלָוַי	עָלַי	*on me*
עֲלָךְ, עֲלָיךְ, עִילָוָוךְ, עִילָוָךְ, עִילָוָיךְ	עֲלָךְ, עִלָוָךְ	עָלֶיךָ	*on you (m.s.)*
עֲלָךְ, עֲלִיךְ, עִילָוִיךְ	—	עָלַיִךְ	*on you (f.s.)*
עֲלֵיה, עֲלוֹהִי, עִילָוֵיה	עֲלוֹהִי, עִלָווֹהִי	עָלָיו	*on him/it (m.)*
עֲלַה, עִילָוַה, עִילָוַוה	עֲלַה	עָלֶיהָ	*on her/it (f.)*
עֲלַן, עִילָוַון	עֲלַנָא	עָלֵינוּ	*on us*
עֲלַייכו	עֲלֵיכוֹן, עִלָוֵויכוֹן	עֲלֵיכֶם	*on you (pl.)*
עֲלֵייהוֹן, עֲלַייהוּ, עִילָוַייהוּ	עֲלֵיהוֹן, עִלָוֵויהוֹן	עֲלֵיהֶם	*on them*

◊ AFTER THE PREPOSITION כְּוָת־ (or ־כְּוָת)

TALMUD BAVLI ARAMAIC	ONKELOS ARAMAIC	HEBREW PARALLEL	ENGLISH TRANSLATION
כְּוָותִי, כְּוָתִי	כְּוָתִי	כְּמוֹתִי, כָּמוֹנִי	*like me*
כְּוָותָךְ	כְּוָתָךְ	כְּמוֹתְךָ, כָּמוֹךָ	*like you (m.s.)*
כְּוָותֵיה, כְּוָתֵיה	כְּוָתֵיה	כְּמוֹתוֹ, כָּמוֹהוּ	*like him/it (m.)*
כְּוָותַה, כְּוָתַה	כְּוָתַה	כְּמוֹתָה, כָּמוֹהָ	*like her/it (f.)*
כְּוָותַן, כְּוָותִין[10]	כְּוָתָנָא	כְּמוֹתֵנוּ, כָּמוֹנוּ	*like us*
כְּוָותַייכוּ	כְּוָתְכוֹן	כְּמוֹתְכֶם, כָּמוֹכֶם	*like you (pl.)*
כְּוָותַייהוּ	כְּוָתְהוֹן	כְּמוֹתָם, כָּמוֹהֶם	*like them*

---

10   ־ִין is the common pronunciation of this suffix, but ־ִַן may be more correct.

◊ AFTER THE PREPOSITION (מִן) ־מִינֵ [11]

TALMUD BAVLI ARAMAIC	ONKELOS ARAMAIC	HEBREW PARALLEL	ENGLISH TRANSLATION
מִינַאי, מִינִּי	מִנִּי	מִמֶּנִּי	*from me; than I*
מִינָךְ	מִנָּךְ	מִמְּךָ	*from you (m.s.); than you*
מִינֵךְ	מִנִּיךְ	מִמֵּךְ	*from you (f.s.); than you*
מִינֵיה	מִנֵּיה	מִמֶּנּוּ	*from him/it (m.); than he/it*
מִינַּה	מִנַּה	מִמֶּנָּה	*from her/it (f.); than she/it*
מִינַּן	מִנַּנָא	מִמֶּנּוּ	*from us; than we*
מִינַּייכוּ, מִינְּכוֹן	מִנְּכוֹן	מִכֶּם	*from you (pl.); than you*
מִינַּייהוּ, מִינְהוֹן	מִנְּהוֹן	מֵהֶם	*from them; than them*

◊ AFTER THE PREPOSITION בַּהֲדֵי

TALMUD BAVLI ARAMAIC	HEBREW PARALLEL	ENGLISH TRANSLATION
בַּהֲדַאי, בַּהֲדִי	עִמִּי	*with me*
בַּהֲדָךְ	עִמְּךָ	*with you (m.s.)*
בַּהֲדֵיה	עִמּוֹ	*with him/it (m.)*
בַּהֲדַה	עִמַּה	*with her/it (f.)*
בַּהֲדַן	עִמָּנוּ	*with us*
בַּהֲדַייכוּ	עִמָּכֶם	*with you (pl.)*
בַּהֲדַייהוּ	עִמָּהֶם	*with them*

11 When suffixes are added, the preposition מִן, *from* or *than*, is spelled ־מִינֵ in the Babylonian Talmud but without a י in Onkelos.

Other prepositions to which the same suffixes are added include (בְּ)אַפֵּי, *in the presence of*; בֵּינֵי, *between*; בָּתַר, *after*; (אַ)גַבֵּי, *with regard to*; (בְּ)גוֹ, *within*; קְדָם, *before*; קַמֵּי, *before*; and תְּחוֹת, *under*.

8.5 POSSESSIVE PRONOUNS AND ADJECTIVES:
FORMED BY PERSONAL-PRONOUN SUFFIXES ADDED TO THE RELATIVE PRONOUN דִי

The *relative pronoun* דִּי־, *that* or *which*, is often combined with לְ and a personal-pronoun suffix to produce a *possessive pronoun* or *adjective*, such as (דִּי+לִי=דִּילִי), *mine*. Even more common in the Babylonian Talmud are forms like דִּידִי, where the לְ has changed to a ד in imitation of the first ד (through the linguistic process called *assimilation*).

TALMUD BAVLI ARAMAIC	ONKELOS ARAMAIC	HEBREW PARALLEL	ENGLISH TRANSLATION
דִּידִי, דִּילִי	דִּילִי	שֶׁלִּי	*mine*
דִּידָךְ, דִּילָךְ	דִּילָךְ	שֶׁלְּךָ	*yours (m.s.)*
דִּידִיךְ, דִּילִיךְ	דִּילִיךְ	שֶׁלָּךְ	*yours (f.s)*
דִּידֵיה, דִּילֵיה	דִּילֵיה	שֶׁלּוֹ	*his/its (m.)*
דִּידַה, דִּילַה	דִּילַה	שֶׁלָּה	*hers/its (f.)*
דִּידַן, דִּילַן	דִּילַנָא	שֶׁלָּנוּ	*ours*
דִּידְכוּ, דִּילְכוּ	דִּילְכוֹן	שֶׁלָּכֶם	*yours (pl.)*
דִּידְהוּ, דִּילְהוּ	דִּילְהוֹן	שֶׁלָּהֶם	*theirs (m.)*
דִּידְהִי	דִּילְהֵין	שֶׁלָּהֶן	*theirs (f.)*

8.6 REFLEXIVE PRONOUNS: FORMED BY ADDING POSSESSIVE SUFFIXES TO THE NOUN ־נַפְשׁ

Personal-pronoun suffixes are appended to the noun ־נַפְשׁ (lit. *soul*) to form *reflexive pronouns*, e.g., נַפְשֵׁיה, *himself*, and occasionally to the noun ־גְּרַמ (lit. *bone*), producing the form לְגַרְמֵיה, *for himself*, (like לְעַצְמוֹ in Hebrew).

TALMUD BAVLI ARAMAIC	ONKELOS ARAMAIC	HEBREW PARALLEL	ENGLISH TRANSLATION
נַפְשַׁאי	נַפְשִׁי	עַצְמִי	*myself*
נַפְשָׁךְ	נַפְשָׁךְ	עַצְמְךָ	*yourself (m.s.)*
נַפְשִׁיךְ	——	עַצְמֵךְ	*yourself (f.s.)*
נַפְשֵׁיה, גַּרְמֵיה	נַפְשֵׁיה	עַצְמוֹ	*himself/itself (m.)*
נַפְשַׁה	נַפְשַׁה	עַצְמָה	*herself/itself (f.)*
נַפְשִׁין[12]	נַפְשַׁנָא	עַצְמֵנוּ	*ourselves*
נַפְשַׁייכוּ	נַפְשְׁכוֹן	עַצְמְכֶם	*yourselves (m.pl.)*
נַפְשַׁייהוּ	נַפְשְׁהוֹן	עַצְמָם	*themselves (m.pl.)*

8.7 PERSONAL-PRONOUN OBJECT SUFFIXES AFTER VERBS

As in Hebrew, *personal-pronoun suffixes* are sometimes added to verbs to indicate *direct objects*. Here is a list of the suffixes that are usually employed in this manner and the forms created when they are combined with the third-person masculine singular (שָׁקַל) and plural (שָׁקְלוּ) of the past tense of the Aramaic verb שקל, *take*. These suffixes should not be confused with those that indicate the subject in the conjugation of the Aramaic verb in Chapters 3, 4 and 5.

In a similar fashion, the same suffixes are added to the rest of the conjugation of the past tense and to the future, to the imperative, and to the infinitive.

Examples: לִיתְבְּעֵינֵיה, *let him sue him*; שָׁקְלִינְהוּ, *take them*!

12   ־ין is the common pronunciation of this suffix, but ־ין may be more correct.

AFTER 3RD-PERSON MASCULINE SINGULAR (PAST TENSE)

ARAMAIC SUFFIXES	TALMUD BAVLI ARAMAIC	ONKELOS ARAMAIC	ENGLISH TRANSLATION
——	שְׁקַל	שְׁקַל	*he took*
נַ־, נִי־	שַׁקְלַן, שַׁקְלַנִי	שַׁקְלַנִי	*he took me*
ךְ־	שַׁקְלָךְ	שַׁקְלָךְ	*he took you (m.s.)*
יךְ־	שַׁקְלִיךְ	שַׁקְלִיךְ	*he took you (f.s.)*
יה־	שַׁקְלֵיה	שַׁקְלֵיה	*he took him/it (m.)*
א־, ה־	שַׁקְלָא, שַׁקְלַה	שַׁקְלַה	*he took her/it (f.)*
נַ־, ינַן־, נָא־	שַׁקְלַן, שַׁקְלִינַן	שַׁקְלָנָא	*he took us*
כוֹן־	שַׁקְלְכוֹן	שַׁקְלְכוֹן	*he took you (m.pl.)*
נְהוּ־, ינוּן־	שַׁקְלִינְהוּ, שַׁקְלִינּוּן	שְׁקַלִינוּן	*he took them (m.)*
ינְהִי־, יּנִין־	שַׁקְלִינְהִי	שְׁקַלִינִין	*he took them (f.)*

AFTER 3RD-PERSON MASCULINE PLURAL (PAST TENSE)

ARAMAIC SUFFIXES	TALMUD BAVLI ARAMAIC	ONKELOS ARAMAIC	ENGLISH TRANSLATION
——	שְׁקַלוּ	שְׁקַלוּ	*they took*
נַ־, נִי־	שַׁקְלוּן	שַׁקְלוּנִי	*they took me*
ךְ־	שַׁקְלוּךְ	שַׁקְלוּךְ	*they took you (s.)*
ה־, הוּ־, הִי־	שַׁקְלוּה, שַׁקְלוּהוּ	שַׁקְלוּהִי	*they took him/it (m.)*
ה־, הָא־	שַׁקְלוּהָ, שַׁקְלוּהָא	שַׁקְלוּהָא	*they took her/it (f.pl.)*
ן־, נָא־	שַׁקְלוּן	שַׁקְלוּנָא	*they took us*
כוֹן־	שַׁקְלוּכוֹן	שַׁקְלוּכוֹן	*they took you (m.pl.)*
נְהוּ־, נּוּן־	שַׁקְלוּנְהוּ, שַׁקְלִינּוּן	שְׁקַלוּנּוּן	*they took them (m.)*
נְהִי־, נִין־	שַׁקְלוּנְהִי	שְׁקַלוּנִין	*they took them (f.)*

9

NUMBERS

In Aramaic, as in Hebrew, the distinction between masculine and feminine in numerals *three* to *ten* is the reverse of what would be expected. The numbers that modify masculine nouns (for example, the Aramaic חַמְשָׁא and the Hebrew חֲמִשָּׁה) end in א‑ or ה‑,[1] but the ones that are treated as feminine (for example, the Aramaic תְּלָת and the Hebrew שָׁלֹשׁ) do not.

9.1 CARDINAL NUMBERS

MASCULINE				FEMININE		
T. BAVLI	ONKELOS	HEBREW		T. BAVLI	ONKELOS	HEBREW
חַד	חַד	אֶחָד	1	חֲדָא	חֲדָא	אַחַת
תְּרֵי, תְּרֵין	תְּרֵין	שְׁנֵי, שְׁנַיִם	2	תַּרְתֵּי, תַּרְתֵּין	תַּרְתֵּין	שְׁתֵּי, שְׁתַּיִם
תְּלָתָא	תְּלָתָא	שְׁלֹשָׁה	3	תְּלָת	תְּלָת	שָׁלֹשׁ
אַרְבְּעָא, אַרְבְּעָה	אַרְבְּעָא	אַרְבָּעָה	4	אַרְבַּע, אַרְבְּעֵי	אַרְבַּע	אַרְבַּע
חַמְשָׁא, חַמְשָׁה	חַמְשָׁא	חֲמִשָּׁה	5	חֲמֵשׁ, חֲמֵישׁ	חֲמֵישׁ	חָמֵשׁ
שִׁיתָּא	שִׁיתָּא	שִׁשָּׁה	6	שִׁית	שִׁית	שֵׁשׁ
שַׁבְעָא, שַׁבְעָה, שַׁב	שַׁבְעָא	שִׁבְעָה	7	שַׁב, שְׁבַע	שְׁבַע	שֶׁבַע
תְּמָנְיָא	תְּמָנְיָא	שְׁמוֹנָה	8	תְּמָנֵי, תְּמָנְיָא	תַּמְנֵי	שְׁמוֹנֶה
תִּשְׁעָה	תִּשְׁעָא	תִּשְׁעָה	9	תְּשַׁע	תְּשַׁע	תֵּשַׁע

1   In some Aramaic texts the final א is more common, but in others the final ה predominates.

247

MASCULINE				FEMININE		
T. BAVLI ARAMAIC	ONKELOS ARAMAIC[2]	HEBREW PARALLEL		T. BAVLI ARAMAIC	ONKELOS ARAMAIC[2]	HEBREW PARALLEL
עֲשָׂרָה	עַסְרָא	עֲשָׂרָה	10	עֲסַר, עֲשַׂר	עֲסַר	עֶשֶׂר
חַד סַר, חַדְסַר, חֲדֵיסַר	חַד עֲסַר	אַחַד עָשָׂר	11	חַד סְרֵי	חֲדָא עַסְרֵי	אַחַת עֶשְׂרֵה
תְּרֵיסַר, תְּרֵי עֲשַׂר	תְּרֵי עֲסַר	שְׁנֵים עָשָׂר	12	תַּרְתֵּי סְרֵי	תַּרְתֵּא עַסְרֵי	שְׁתֵּים עֶשְׂרֵה
תְּלֵיסַר, תְּלָת עֲשַׂר	תְּלָתָא עֲסַר	שְׁלֹשָׁה עָשָׂר	13	תְּלֵיסְרֵי, תְּלָת סְרֵי, תְּלָת עֲשְׂרֵי, תְּלָת עֲשְׂרֵה	תְּלָת עַסְרֵי	שְׁלֹשׁ עֶשְׂרֵה
אַרְבֵּיסַר, אַרְבֵּסַר	אַרְבְּעַת עֲסַר[3]	אַרְבָּעָה עָשָׂר	14	אַרְבַּסְרֵי, אַרְבַּע סְרֵי	אַרְבַּע עַסְרֵי	אַרְבַּע עֶשְׂרֵה
חֲמֵיסַר	חֲמֵישַׁת עֲסַר[3]	חֲמִשָּׁה עָשָׂר	15	חֲמֵסְרֵי	חֲמֵישׁ עַסְרֵי	חֲמֵשׁ עֶשְׂרֵה
שִׁיתְּסַר	שִׁיתַּת עֲסַר	שִׁשָּׁה עָשָׂר	16	שִׁיתְּסְרֵי, שִׁית סְרֵי, שִׁית עַשְׂרֵה	שִׁית עַסְרֵי	שֵׁשׁ עֶשְׂרֵה
שֵׁיבְּסַר, שַׁבְסַר	שִׁבְעַת עֲסַר[3]	שִׁבְעָה עָשָׂר	17	שַׁבְסְרֵי, שֵׁיבְסְרֵי, שַׁב עֲשְׂרֵה, שְׁבַע עֲשְׂרֵה	שְׁבַע עַסְרֵי	שְׁבַע עֶשְׂרֵה
תְּמָנֵיסַר	תְּמָנַת עֲסַר	שְׁמוֹנָה עָשָׂר	18	תַּמְנֵי סְרֵי	[תַּמְנֵי עַסְרֵי][4]	שְׁמוֹנֶה עֶשְׂרֵה
תְּשַׁסַר	[תִּשְׁעַת עֲסַר][4]	תִּשְׁעָה עָשָׂר	19	תְּשַׁסְרֵי	תְּשַׁע עַסְרֵי	תְּשַׁע עֶשְׂרֵה

2   Some editions of Targum Onkelos have the readings עֲשַׂר, עֲשָׂרָה or (עַשְׂרָא) and עַשְׂרֵי instead of עֲסַר, עַסְרָא and עַסְרֵי, respectively.

3   Surprisingly, in some editions: עַסְרָא.

4   This number does not occur in Onkelos but in Targum Yonathan to the Prophets.

	COMMON GENDER		
	TALMUD BAVLI ARAMAIC	ONKELOS ARAMAIC	HEBREW PARALLEL
20	עֶשְׂרִין	עֶסְרִין	עֶשְׂרִים
30	תְּלָתִין	תְּלָתִין	שְׁלֹשִׁים
40	אַרְבְּעִין	אַרְבְּעִין	אַרְבָּעִים
50	חַמְשִׁין	חַמְשִׁין	חֲמִשִּׁים
60	שִׁיתִּין, שְׁתִּין	שִׁתִּין	שִׁשִּׁים
70	שַׁבְעִין	שַׁבְעִין	שִׁבְעִים
80	תְּמָנִין, תְּמָנָן	תְּמָנַן	שְׁמוֹנִים
90	תִּשְׁעִין	תִּשְׁעִין	תִּשְׁעִים
100	מְאָה	מְאָה	מֵאָה
200	מָאתָן	מָאתַן	מָאתַיִם
300	תְּלָת מְאָה	תְּלָת מְאָה	שְׁלֹשׁ מֵאוֹת
400	אַרְבַּע מְאָה	אַרְבַּע מְאָה	אַרְבַּע מֵאוֹת
1,000	אֲלַף, אַלְפָּא	אֲלַף, אַלְפָּא	אֶלֶף
2,000	תְּרֵי אַלְפֵי	תְּרֵין אַלְפִין	אַלְפַּיִם
3,000	—	תְּלָתָא אַלְפִין	שְׁלֹשֶׁת אֲלָפִים
4,000	אַרְבְּעָה אַלְפֵי, אַלְפִין	אַרְבְּעָה אַלְפִין	אַרְבַּעַת אֲלָפִים
10,000	רִבּוֹא, רִבְבְתָא	רִבּוֹתָא	רִבּוֹא, רְבָבָה
600,000	שִׁיתִּין רִיבְּוָותָא, שִׁיתִּין רִבְּוָן	שֵׁית מְאָה אַלְפִין	שִׁשִּׁים רִבּוֹא, שֵׁשׁ מֵאוֹת אֶלֶף

9.2 ORDINAL NUMBERS[5]

MASCULINE				FEMININE		
T. BAVLI	ONKELOS	HEBREW		T. BAVLI	ONKELOS	HEBREW
קַמָּא קַמָּא, קַדְמָאָה	קַדְמָאי קַדְמָאָה	רִאשׁוֹן הָרִאשׁוֹן	1st	קַמַיְיתָא, קַדְמַיְיתָא	קַדְמֵיתָא	הָרִאשׁוֹנָה
תִּנְיָין תִּנְיָינָא	תִּנְיָן תִּנְיָנָא	שֵׁנִי הַשֵּׁנִי	2nd	[תִּנְיֵיתָא]	תִּנְיֵיתָא	הַשְּׁנִיָּה
תְּלִיתַאי	תְּלִיתַי (-אי) תְּלִיתָאָה	שְׁלִישִׁי הַשְּׁלִישִׁי	3rd	—	תְּלִיתֵיתָא	הַשְּׁלִישִׁית
רְבִיעָאָה	רְבִיעַי (-אי) רְבִיעָאָה	רְבִיעִי הָרְבִיעִי	4th	—	רְבִיעֵיתָא	הָרְבִיעִית
—	חֲמִישַׁי (-אי) חֲמִישָׁאָה	חֲמִישִׁי הַחֲמִישִׁי	5th	—	חֲמִישֵׁיתָא	הַחֲמִישִׁית
—	שְׁתִיתַי (-אי) שְׁתִיתָאָה	שִׁשִּׁי הַשִּׁשִּׁי	6th	—	שְׁתִיתֵיתָא	הַשִּׁשִּׁית
שְׁבִיעָאָה	שְׁבִיעָאָה	הַשְּׁבִיעִי	7th	שְׁבִיעָתָא	שְׁבִיעֵיתָא	הַשְּׁבִיעִית
—	תְּמִינָאָה	הַשְּׁמִינִי	8th	—	תְּמִינֵיתָא	הַשְּׁמִינִית
—	תְּשִׁיעָאָה	הַתְּשִׁיעִי	9th	—	תְּשִׁיעֵיתָא	הַתְּשִׁיעִית
עֲשִׂירָאָה	עֲסִירָאָה	הָעֲשִׂירִי	10th	—	—	—

9.3 FRACTIONS[5]

ABSOLUTE				CONSTRUCT		
BAVLI	ONKELOS	HEBREW		BAVLI	ONKELOS	HEBREW
פַּלְגָּא	פַּלְגּוּת-	חֵצִי	1/2	פַּלְגּוּ-	פַּלְגּוּת-	חֲצִי-
תִּילְתָּא	—	שְׁלִישׁ	1/3	—	תַּלְתּוּת-	שְׁלִישׁ-
רְבִיעֵיתָא, רְבִיעֲתָא, רִיבְעָא	—	רֶבַע	1/4	—	רַבְעוּת-	רֶבַע-
חוּמְשָׁא	—	חֲמִישִׁית	1/5	—	חוּמְשׁ-	חֲמִישִׁית-
שְׁתוּתָא	—	שִׁשִּׁית	1/6	—	—	—
עִישׂוּרָא	—	עֲשִׂירִית	1/10	—	—	—

5   Plural forms — e.g., קַדְמָאֵי (m.) and קַדְמָיָיתָא (f.), *the first (ones)*, and תִּילְתֵּי, *thirds* — also occur, but they have not been included in this table.

10

FOUR ASPECTS OF TALMUDIC SYNTAX

Most of the material that has been presented in the previous chapters falls under the category of *morphology*, the study of the grammatical forms of individual words. This brief chapter deals with *syntax*, the branch of linguistics that studies sentence structure and the relationships between words within a sentence. A thorough investigation of the syntax of the Babylonian Talmud is beyond the scope of this work. Nevertheless, we will attempt to provide the student with an insight into several aspects of Talmudic syntax that may confuse the native English speaker. In the following para-graphs, we will explain four phenomena: *the direct-object indicator, the anticipatory pronoun suffix, the "hanging case"* and *the passive voice (which is sometimes equivalent to the active voice)*.

10.1 THE DIRECT-OBJECT INDICATOR

The native English speaker learns the crucial distinction between *subject* and *direct object* long before he can understand the terminology. The critical factor is *word order,* with the subject usually placed before the verb and the direct object following the verb. Thus the English-speaking child quickly grasps the difference between:

The dog bit the man.

and

The man bit the dog.

◊   The Hebrew language, especially Biblical Hebrew, often employs a different device to indicate the direct object: the word אֶת. This direct-object indicator, which is not to be translated into English, is placed directly before the noun that functions as the direct object. For example, in the clause הַכֶּלֶב נָשַׁךְ אֶת הָאָדָם, it is quite clear that the dog did the biting. The same is true even when,

251

for emphasis, the sentence begins with the direct object, as in the
sentence אֶת הָאָדָם נָשַׁךְ הַכֶּלֶב. Nevertheless, אֶת does not mark *every*
direct object in Hebrew.[1] When it is not used, the reader must rely
upon the context to recognize the direct object.

◊   In the Targumim, יָת corresponds to the Biblical Hebrew אֶת as
a direct-object indicator. For example, Onkelos translates אֶת הַשָּׁמַיִם
in the very first *pasuk* of the Torah as יָת שְׁמַיָּא. On the other hand, יָת
(without a suffix) does not occur at all in Biblical Aramaic,[2] and it is
seldom used in the Babylonian Talmud.[3] How, then, can the student
identify a direct object in a Talmudic text? He should pay special
attention to the consonant ־ל, which serves as a direct-object
indicator, as in the following two examples:[4]

| *when you strike a child* | כִּי מָחֵית לִינוּקָא (בבא בתרא כא, א) |
| *they cast his wine into vessels of gold and silver* | רְמוֹ לְחַמְרֵיהּ בְּמָאנֵי דַהֲבָא וְכַסְפָּא (תענית ז, סע"א) |

◊   A word of caution, however, must be borne in mind. Although
the prefix ־ל is often employed to indicate a direct object, this is not
its exclusive function. As in Hebrew, the Aramaic ־ל prefix
sometimes means *to* or *for* and introduces an *indirect object*, as in
the following Talmudic passage:

| *and she gives bread **to** poor people* | וְיָהֲבָא רִיפְתָּא לְעַנִיֵּי (תענית כג, ב) |

1   See the article by HaRav Ezra Zion Melamed, "אֶת" בְּשִׁירַת הַמִּקְרָא, which was
    originally published in the jubilee volume ע"ז לדוד (בן גוריון) (Jerusalem, 1964),
    pp. 568-584, and subsequently in his *Biblical Studies in Texts, Translations, and
    Commentators* (Jerusalem: Magnes, 1984), pp. 200-216.
2   The form יָתְהוֹן (= אוֹתָם) occurs only once, in דניאל ג:יב.
3   It is found with some frequency in the tractate נדרים. Otherwise, the Talmud
    uses it chiefly in proverbs, in official documents, and in quotations from the
    Targumim.
4   This direct-object indicator is occasionally found in Hebrew as well, for
    example, וְיוֹאָב וַאֲבִישַׁי אָחִיו הָרְגוּ לְאַבְנֵר (שמואל ב ג:ל), *and Yoav and Avishai his
    brother killed Avner*. The case of וְאָהַבְתָּ לְרֵעֲךָ כָּמוֹךָ (ויקרא יח:יח) is somewhat
    ambiguous. See the commentaries of R. Avraham Ibn Ezra and the Ramban on
    that pasuk. This usage is also familiar to us from its appearance in חַד גַּדְיָא, the
    popular Aramaic song at the end of the Passover Haggada, e.g., אֲכַל לְגַדְיָא, *he
    ate the kid*.

Consequently, when the student confronts a ־ל prefix in a Talmudic text, he must be aware of both alternatives, *direct object* versus *indirect object*, and be guided by the context of the particular passage.[5] In the last example, since the noun רִיפְתָּא, *bread*, is already the direct object, the word לְעַנְיֵי must be functioning as an indirect object, *to poor people*. On the other hand, in the first two examples, יְנוּקָא and חַמְרֵיה, respectively, are definitely direct objects — since the passage contains no other words that could serve in that capacity.

10.2 THE ANTICIPATORY PRONOUN SUFFIX

If the student comes across the expression (חולין קז, ב) אַשְׁכְּחֵיה לִשְׁמוּאֵל, he is faced with a dilemma. The form אַשְׁכְּחֵיה, a combination of the verb אַשְׁכַּח and the pronoun suffix ־ֵיה, means *he found him* (or *it*). But how should one interpret the ־ל prefix before the noun שְׁמוּאֵל? There are two possibilities:

a)   At first glance, it would seem that the pronoun suffix ־ֵיה (*him* or *it*) is a direct object and that לִשְׁמוּאֵל is an indirect object, meaning *to/for Shemuel*. The apparent translation would then be: *He found it for Shemuel.*

b)   If we study this quotation in context, however, we are able to see that our first interpretation has missed the mark. The complete sentence that appears in the text of the Babylonian Talmud is אֲבוּה דִּשְׁמוּאֵל אַשְׁכְּחֵיה לִשְׁמוּאֵל דְּקָא בָכֵי. It is very difficult to translate: *Shemuel's father found it* (or *him*) *for Shemuel who was crying.* What is *it*? (Or, alternatively, who is *him*?) There is no person or thing in the Talmudic context to which the direct-object pronoun suffix ־ֵיה can refer — other than שְׁמוּאֵל. Since the direct object ־ֵיה (*him*) does refer to *Shemuel,* it stands to reason that לִשְׁמוּאֵל is a *direct object* as well — with the ־ל prefix a direct-object indicator. Thus the correct translation is: *Shemuel's father found (him) Shemuel who was crying.* The pronoun suffix that has been added to the verb *anticipates*

---

5   We are referring exclusively to ־ל prefixed to a *noun* or to a *pronoun* suffix. See Chapter 3, *The Aramaic Verb*, pp. 34-35, regarding the ־ל prefix that is used in the future tense of the verb.

the subsequent direct object.[6] In English, however it is redundant to write both *him* and *Shemuel*; therefore *him* has been placed within parentheses.

◇   In the Babylonian Talmud, the use of this *anticipatory pronoun suffix* attached to a verb is quite common. Here are two more examples:

and he slammed (it) the gate in his face	וְטַרְקֵ**יה** לְבָבָא בְּאַנְפֵּיה (בבא מציעא פו, א)
the king sought to kill (them) all of them	בְּעָא מַלְכָּא לְמִקְטְלִ**ינְהוּ** לְכוּלְּהוּ (תענית כא, סע״א)

◇   Targum Onkelos occasionally uses the same pattern, as in the following translation:

and he pitched (it) his tent   וּפְרְסֵ**יה** לְמַשְׁכְּנֵיה (=וַיֵּט אָהֳלֹה, בראשית יב:ח)

◇   A personal-pronoun suffix may also be attached to a *noun* in anticipation of the noun that follows it. In such cases, the letter ־דְ is prefixed to the second noun, as in the following example:

*in (his) locality, **that of** Rav Huna*   בְּאַתְרֵ**יה דְּרַב** הוּנָא (פסחים ג, א)

This construction is the equivalent of the construct state, in this case, בְּאַתַר רַב הוּנָא, *in the locality of Rav Huna*.[7]

◇   A personal-pronoun suffix may also be attached to a *preposition* (such as ־קַמֵּ, *before*, and ־כְּוָת, *according to*) in anticipation of the noun that follows it. In such cases, the letter ־דְּ is prefixed to that noun but not translated in English.

Abbayei was sitting before (him) Rabba	אַבַּיֵּי הֲוָה יָתֵיב קַמֵּ**יה דְּרַבָּה** (בבא מציעא ל, ב)
It makes sense according to (him) Rav.	כְּוָתֵ**יה דְּרַב** מִסְתַּבְּרָא. (ברכות מ, ב)

6   This phenomenon does occur in Biblical Hebrew. See, for example, וַתִּרְאֵ**הוּ** אֶת הַיֶּלֶד (שמות ב:ו), *and she saw (him), the boy*, and the classical commentaries there. See also (שמות לה:ה) יְבִיאֶהָ אֶת תְּרוּמַת ה' and Ramban's commentary there.

7   For an explanation of the *construct state* and the use of this construction in Mishnaic Hebrew, see p. 2 above.

10.3 THE "HANGING" CASE

As we have mentioned above, the native English speaker expects the order of a sentence to be *subject, verb, object,* as in: *The dog bit the man.* Although many sentences in both Hebrew and Aramaic are arranged in the same order, there are also other alternatives. One particular pattern, which can be called *the hanging case*[8] *(casus pendens* in Latin), sometimes causes confusion. In this usage the noun that is being emphasized is placed at the beginning of the sentence — even when that noun is *not* the *grammatical* subject but an object. Later in the sentence, that noun is often reinforced by a pronoun that refers back to it.

◇   Consider the following illustration from the Torah:

(pron.)   (object)

וְהַלֵּוִי בִּשְׁעָרֶיךָ — לֹא תַעַזְבֶנּוּ (דברים יד:כז)

and the Levite in your gates — you shall not neglect (him)[9]

The Torah emphasizes הַלֵּוִי בִּשְׁעָרֶיךָ, *the Levite in your gates,* by placing it first in the *pasuk* and leaving it "hanging" there, even though הַלֵּוִי is clearly *not* the grammatical subject of the verb תַעַזְבֶנּוּ. (The grammatical subject of that verb is *you,* which is implied by the second-person singular prefix תַ-.) The force of וְהַלֵּוִי בִּשְׁעָרֶיךָ is subsequently re-emphasized by נּוּ-, the direct-object suffix *him,* of the verb תַעַזְבֶנּוּ. In English translation, it is sometimes smoother to add an expression like *as for* before the hanging case, as in the following Biblical example:

(pron.)   (object)

אַדְמַתְכֶם — לְנֶגְדְּכֶם זָרִים אֹכְלִים אֹתָהּ (ישעיה א:ז)

[as for] ***your land*** *— in front of you, foreigners are devouring* ***it***

◇   In the Babylonian Talmud, the hanging case appears fairly frequently. Consider the following two examples:

---

8   Some grammarians call it the *nominative absolute.*
9   Since the pronoun is redundant in English, we have placed it within parentheses in our translation.

        (pron.)   *(object)*

כּוּלְהוּ נִכְסָיךְ — יוֹסֵף מוֹקִיר שַׁבֵּי אָכֵיל **לְהוּ.** (שבת קיט, א)

All your possessions — Yosef, the honorer of Sabbaths, will consume **them.**

        (pron.)   *(object)*

ר' חִיָּיא בַּר יוֹסֵף — יְהַבוּ **לֵיה** זוּזֵי אַמִּלְחָא... (בבא מציעא מח, רע״ב)

R. Ḥiyya b. Yosef — [some people] gave **him** money towards [the purchase of] salt...

In the last example, an inexperienced student could mistake *R. Ḥiyya b. Yosef* for the grammatical subject and translate: *R. Ḥiyya b. Yosef gave him money...*, an error that would totally distort the Talmudic passage. In order to avoid that mistake, the student must be sensitive to the possible occurrence of the hanging case, and he must recognize that *R. Ḥiyya b. Yosef* cannot possibly be the subject, because the verb יְהַבוּ (*gave*) has a plural form that requires a plural grammatical subject.

10.4   THE PASSIVE VOICE (= THE ACTIVE VOICE)

Like Hebrew, the Aramaic verbal system contains certain *binyanim* (patterns) that are *active* and others that are *passive* (or *reflexive*).[10] In *binyan* קַל, moreover, both the *active* participle and the *passive* participle appear frequently.[11] When the prepositional prefix -ל is used with the *passive* voice, it is best translated *to* or *by* — depending on the particular verb. The construction thus formed can also be rendered smoothly in the active voice in English, with the person referred to by this prefix serving as the subject. Consider the following examples (which are all from the same tractate):

it became known to him=he knew אִיתְיְדַע לֵיה (שבת עא, ב)

it was heard by me explicitly=I heard explicitly (שבת מ, רע״א) בְּפֵירוּשׁ שְׁמִיעַ לִי

כְּר' יְהוּדָה סְבִירָא לֵיה (שבת לא ע״ב)

like R. Yehuda it is thought by him=he holds like R. Yehuda

it was asked by them=they asked אִיבַּעְיָא לְהוּ (שבת יא, רע״ב)

it is not wiped by you=you do not wipe (yourselves) (שבת פב, א) לָא מְקַנַּח לְכוּ

nor is a louse killed by you=nor do you kill a louse (שם) לָא קָטִיל לְכוּ כִּינָא

---

10   See pp. 18-21 above.   11   See pp. 27 and 29 above.

APPENDICES

A REGULAR ARAMAIC VERB IN THE BABYLONIAN TALMUD (SIMPLE)

	אתְפְּעֵל¹	פְּעֵל (קל)	פְּעַל (קל)
	PAST		
I	אי(ת)כְּתִיבִי(ת)	תְּקֵיפִי(ת)	כְּתַבִי(ת)
you (s.)	אי(ת)כְּתַבְתְּ	תְּקֵיפְתְּ	כְּתַבְתְּ
he/she	אי(ת)כְּתֵיב ‏, f. אי(ת)כְּתִיבָא ‏, f. אי(ת)כַּתְבָה/א	תְּקֵיף ‏, f. תְּקֵיפַת ‏, f. תְּקֵיפָה/א	כְּתַב ‏, f. כְּתַבַת ‏, f. כְּתַבָה/א
we	אי(ת)כַּתְבִינַן	תְּקֵיפְנַן, תְּקֵיפְנָא, תְּקֵיפִינַן, תְּקֵיפַן	כְּתַבְנַן, כְּתַבְנָא, כְּתַבִינַן, כְּתַבַן
you (pl.)	אי(ת)כַּתְבִיתוּ	תְּקֵיפְתּוּן, f. תְּקֵיפְתִּין תְּקֵיפִיתוּ	כְּתַבְתּוּן, f. כְּתַבְתִּין כְּתַבִיתוּ
they	אי(ת)כְּתִיבוּ ‏, f. אי(ת)כַּתְבָן ‏, אי(ת)כְּתוּב, אי(ת)כַּתְבוּ	תְּקֵיפוּ, f. תְּקֵיפָה, תְּקֵיף, f. תְּקֵיפָן	כְּתַבוּ, f. כְּתַבָה, כְּתוּב, f. כְּתַבָן
	ACTIVE PARTICIPLE		
s.		תָּקֵיף, f. תָּקְפָא/ה	כָּתֵיב, f. כָּתְבָא/ה
pl.		תָּקְפִי(ן), f. תָּקְפָן	כָּתְבִי(ן), f. כָּתְבָן, כָּתְבוּ
	PASSIVE/REFLEXIVE PARTICIPLE	**PASSIVE PARTICIPLE**	
s.	מִי(ת)כְּתֵיב, f. מִי(ת)כַּתְבָא	תְּקִיף, f. תְּקִיפָא/ה	כְּתִיב, f. כְּתִיבָא/ה
pl.	מִי(ת)כַּתְבִי(ן), f. מִי(ת)כַּתְבָן	תְּקִיפִי(ן), f. תְּקִיפָן	כְּתִיבִי(ן), f. כְּתִיבָן

---

1   For important details about the prefixes in *binyan* אתְפְּעֵל, see above p. 25 and
p. 36, note 27.

	אִתְפְּעֵל²	פְּעַל (קל)	פְּעַל (קל)
		(ACTIVE) PARTICIPLE WITH SUFFIXES	
I		תְּקֵיפְנָא	כָּתֵיבְנָא
you (s.)		תְּקְפַתְּ	כָּתְבַתְּ
we		תְּקֵפִינַן	כָּתְבִינַן
you (pl.)		תְּקְפִיתוּ	כָּתְבִיתוּ
	PARTICIPLE WITH SUFFIXES	**(PASSIVE) PARTICIPLE WITH SUFFIXES**	
I	מִי(תְ)כְּתֵיבְנָא	תְּקִיפְנָא	כְּתִיבְנָא
you (s.)	מִי(תְ)כְּתֵיבַתְּ	תְּקִיפַתְּ	כְּתִיבַתְּ
we	מִי(תְ)כַּתְבִינַן	תְּקִיפִינַן	כְּתִיבִינַן
you (pl.)	מִי(תְ)כַּתְבִיתוּ	תְּקִיפִיתוּ	כְּתִיבִיתוּ
		FUTURE	
I	אִי(תְ)כְּתֵיב	אִיתְּקַף	אֶיכְתּוֹב
you (s.)	f. תִּי(תְ)כַּתְבִי(ן) תִּי(תְ)כְּתֵיב	f. תִּיתְּקְפִי(ן) תִּיתְּקַף	f. תִּיכְתְּבִי(ן) תִּיכְתּוֹב
he/she	f. תִּי(תְ)כְּתֵיב לִי(תְ)כְּתֵיב, נִי(תְ)כְּתֵיב	f. תִּיתְּקַף לִיתְּקַף, נִיתְּקַף	f. תִּיכְתּוֹב לִיכְתּוֹב, נִיכְתּוֹב
we	נִי(תְ)כְּתֵיב, לִי(תְ)כְּתֵיב	נִיתְּקַף, לִיתְּקַף	נִיכְתּוֹב, לִיכְתּוֹב
you (pl.)	תִּי(תְ)כַּתְבוּ	תִּיתְּקְפוּ(ן)	תִּיכְתְּבוּ(ן)
they	לִי(תְ)כַּתְבוּ(ן), נִי(תְ)כַּתְבוּ	לִיתְּקְפוּ, נִיתְּקְפוּ, לִיתְּקוֹף, נִתְקוֹף	לִיכְתְּבוּ, נִיכְתְּבוּ, לִיכְתּוֹב, נְכְתּוֹב
		IMPERATIVE	
(you s.)	f. אִי(תְ)כְּתֵיבִי אִי(תְ)כְּתֵיב	f. תְּקֵפִי תְּקַף	f. כְּתוּבִי כְּתוֹב
(you pl.)		f. תְּקֵפִין תְּקֵפוּ	f. כְּתוּבִין כְּתוּבוּ
		GERUND / INFINITIVE	
	אִי(תְ)כְּתוֹבֵי	מִיתְּקַף, מִיתְּקְפָא	מִיכְתַּב, מִיכְתְּבָא

2 For important details about the prefixes in *binyan* אִתְפְּעֵל, see above p. 25 and p. 36, note 27.

A REGULAR ARAMAIC VERB IN THE BABYLONIAN TALMUD (INTENSIVE)

	אִתְפַּעַל³	פַּעֵל
	PAST	
I	אִי(תְ)קַדְּשִׁי	קַדִּישִׁי(ת)
you (s.)	אִי(תְ)קַדַּשְׁתְּ	קַדִּישְׁתְּ
he/she	אִי(תְ)קַדַּשׁ אִי(תְ)קַדַּשׁת f., אִי(תְ)קַדְּשָׁא/ה f.	קַדִּישׁ קַדִּישָׁה f., קַדִּישַׁת f.
we	אִי(תְ)קַדְּשִׁנַן	קַדִּישְׁנַן, קַדִּישְׁנָא
you (pl.)	אִי(תְ)קַדַּשִׁיתוּ	קַדִּישְׁתּוּ(ן)
they	אִי(תְ)קַדְּשׁוּ, אִי(תְ)קַדִּישׁ אִי(תְ)קַדְּשָׁן f.	קַדִּישׁוּ, קָדוּשׁ קַדִּישָׁא, קַדִּישָׁן f.
		ACTIVE PARTICIPLE
s.		מְקַדֵּישׁ מְקַדְּשָׁא/ה f.
pl.		מְקַדְּשִׁי(ן), מְקַדְּשׁוּ מְקַדְּשָׁן f.
	PASSIVE / REFLEXIVE PARTICIPLE	**PASSIVE PARTICIPLE**
s.	מִ(תְ)קַדַּשׁ מִ(תְ)קַדְּשָׁא f.	מְקַדַּשׁ מְקַדְּשָׁא f.
pl.	מִ(תְ)קַדְּשִׁי(ן) מִ(תְ)קַדְּשָׁן f.	מְקַדְּשִׁי(ן) מְקַדְּשָׁן f.

3   For important details about the prefixes in *binyan* אִתְפַּעַל, see above pp. 25-26 and p. 36, note 27.

	אִתְפַּעַל[4]	פַּעֵל
		ACTIVE PARTICIPLE WITH SUFFIXES
I		מְקַדֵּישְׁנָא
you (s.)		מְקַדְּשַׁתְּ
we		מְקַדְּשִׁינַן
you (pl.)		מְקַדְּשִׁיתוּ(ן)
	PARTICIPLE WITH SUFFIXES	**PASSIVE PARTICIPLE WITH SUFFIXES**
I	מִ(ת)קַדַּשְׁנָא	מְקַדַּשְׁנָא
you (s.)	מִ(ת)קַדְּשַׁתְּ	מְקַדְּשַׁתְּ
we	מִ(ת)קַדְּשִׁינַן	מְקַדְּשִׁינַן
you (pl.)	מִ(ת)קַדְּשִׁיתוּ(ן)	מְקַדְּשִׁיתוּ(ן)
	FUTURE	
I	אִי(ת)קַדַּשׁ	אֲקַדֵּישׁ
you (s.)	f. תִּי(ת)קַדְּשִׁי(ן) תִּי(ת)קַדַּשׁ	f. תְּקַדְּשִׁי(ן) תְּקַדֵּישׁ
he/she	f. תִּי(ת)קַדַּשׁ לִי(ת)קַדַּשׁ, נִי(ת)קַדַּשׁ	f. תְּקַדֵּישׁ לִיקַדֵּישׁ, לְקַדֵּישׁ, נְקַדֵּישׁ, נִיקַדֵּישׁ
we	נִי(ת)קַדַּשׁ, לִי(ת)קַדַּשׁ	נְקַדֵּישׁ, לְקַדֵּישׁ
you (pl.)	תִּי(ת)קַדְּשׁוּ	תְּקַדְּשׁוּ
they	f. לִי(ת)קַדְּשָׁן לִי(ת)קַדְּשׁוּ(ן), נִי(ת)קַדְּשׁוּ, לִיקַדּוּשׁ, נִקַדּוּשׁ	f. לְקַדְּשָׁן לְקַדְּשׁוּ, לִיקַדְּשׁוּ, נְקַדְּשׁוּ, נִיקַדְּשׁוּ
	IMPERATIVE	
(you s.)	f. אִי(ת)קַדַּשִׁי אִי(ת)קַדַּשׁ	f. קַדִּישִׁי קַדִּישׁ
you (pl.)	אִי(ת)קַדְּשׁוּ	קַדִּישׁוּ
	GERUND / INFINITIVE	
	אִי(ת)קַדּוּשֵׁי	קַדּוּשֵׁי

4   For important details about the prefixes in *binyan* אִתְפַּעַל, see above pp. 25-26 and p. 36, note 27.

A REGULAR ARAMAIC VERB IN THE BABYLONIAN TALMUD (EXTENSIVE)

	אַפְעֵל		
	FUTURE		**PAST**
I	אַפְקֵיד		אַפְקֵידִי(ת)
you (s.)	f. תַּפְקְדִי	תַּפְקֵיד	אַפְקֵידְתְּ
he/she	f. תַּפְקֵיד	לַפְקֵיד, לִיפְקֵיד, נַפְקֵיד	א/f. אַפְקִידָה, אַפְקְדָה, f. אַפְקְדָת אַפְקֵיד
we		נַפְקֵיד, לַפְקֵיד	אַפְקִידְנָן, אַפְקְדִינַן, אַפְקְדָן
you (pl.)		תַּפְקְדוּ	אַפְקֵידְתּוּן, אַפְקְדִיתוּ
they	f.לַפְקְדָן	לַפְקְדוּ, לִיפְקְדוּ, נַפְקְדוּ	f. אַפְקְדָן אַפְקִידוּ, אַפְקְדוּ, אַפְקוּד
	PASSIVE PARTICIPLE		**ACTIVE PARTICIPLE**
s.	f. מַפְקְדָא	מַפְקַד	f. מַפְקְדָא/ה מַפְקֵיד
pl.	f. מַפְקְדָן	מַפְקְדִי(ן), מַפְקְדוּ	f. מַפְקְדָן מַפְקְדִי(ן), מַפְקְדוּ
	PASSIVE PARTICPLE WITH SUFFIXES		**ACTIVE PARTICIPLE WITH SUFFIXES**
I	מַפְקַדְנָא		מַפְקֵידְנָא
you (s.)	מַפְקְדַתְּ		מַפְקְדַתְּ
we	מַפְקְדִינַן		מַפְקְדִינַן
you (pl.)	מַפְקְדִיתוּ		מַפְקְדִיתוּ
	IMPERATIVE		
s.	f. אַפְקִידִי		אַפְקֵיד
pl.	f. אַפְקִידִין		אַפְקִידוּ
	GERUND / INFINITIVE		
	אַפְקוֹדֵי		

Binyan אִתַּפְעַל serves as the reflexive or the passive of *binyan* אַפְעֵל, but since few forms from this *binyan* are found in the Babylonian Talmud — and almost none from regular verbs — a complete artificial paradigm would be pointless. For forms from the אִתַּפְעַל that do occur, see the paradigms of יתב on pp. 89-91, of תוב on pp. 93-95 and the introduction to the verb קום on p. 132.

EXERCISE 1: TRANSPOSITION OF TALMUDIC VERBAL FORMS (FROM BINYAN קַל TO OTHER BINYANIM)

The left-hand column contains a list of eighteen verbal forms in the קַל binyan with their English translations next to them. The third column contains a list of eighteen verbal forms that correspond to those in the first column in all respects except one: these forms are in other binyanim. The numbers placed in brackets next to them refer the reader back to the number of the verb in the paradigms in Chapter 4. Translate these forms on the blank lines.

(א)	פְּלַגוּ	they divided	:	אִפְּלִיגוּ [1]	_____
(ב)	זָבֵינְנָא	I am buying	:	מְזַבֵּינְנָא [2]	_____
(ג)	עָבֵיד	making	:	מְשַׁעְבֵּיד [4]	_____
(ד)	הֲדַר!	go back!	:	אַהֲדַר! [5]	_____
(ה)	אֵיפּוֹק	I will go out	:	אַפֵּיק [6]	_____
(ו)	נְחָתוּ!	they went down	:	אֲחִיתוּ [7]	_____
(ז)	סַק!	go up!	:	אִסְתַּלַּק! [8]	_____
(ח)	לְמִידַע	to know	:	לְאוֹדוֹעֵי [10]	_____
(ט)	לְמֵילַף	to learn	:	לְאַלּוֹפֵי [11]	_____
(י)	יָתֵיבְנָא	I am sitting	:	מוֹתִיבְנָא [13]	_____
(יא)	אָכְלָן	eating	:	מִתְאַכְלָן [16]	_____
(יב)	אֲמַרָה	she said	:	אִיתְאַמְרָה [17]	_____
(יג)	לְמִיבְעֵי	to ask	:	לְאִיבּוֹעֵי [18]	_____
(יד)	תֶּחֱזֵי	you will see	:	תַּחֲזֵי [19]	_____
(טו)	אֲתַאן	we came	:	אַיְיתֵינָא [24]	_____
(טז)	הֲוֵינַן	we were	:	הֲוֵינַן [25]	_____
(יז)	לֵיעוֹל	let him enter	:	לֵיעַיֵּיל [26]	_____
(יח)	קָיְימַתְּ	you are standing	:	מוֹקְמַתְּ [27]	_____

The answers for this exercise are found on page 296.

EXERCISE 2: ANALYSIS OF VERBS FROM THE TALMUDIC
PARADIGMS

Read the following quotations from the Talmud carefully. Each of
the numbered words is a verbal form found in the paradigms in
Chapter 4, and these numbers relate to the exercise on the next page.

(א) בְּעָא‎(1) לְמֵיהֲדַר‎(2) לְאָתוֹיֵי‎(3) מָאנֵיה, וְלָא אִימְצִי. אַקְרְיֵיה,
וְאַתְנְיֵיה‎(4) וְשַׁוְיֵיה גַּבְרָא רַבָּה. (בבא מציעא פד, א אל פי כתב יד)

(ב) נֵיקוּם,‎(5) וְנֵיזִיל,‎(6) וְנֶעֱבֵיד‎(7) עִיסְקָא, וּנְקַיֵּים‎(8) בְּנַפְשִׁין: "אֶפֶס כִּי לֹא
יִהְיֶה בְּךָ אֶבְיוֹן." (תענית כא, א)

(ג) כִּי מְטָא לְמָתָא, נְפַקָא‎(9) דְּבִיתְהוּ לְאַפֵּיה כִּי מִיקַשְׁטָא. כִּי מְטָא
לְבֵיתֵיה, עַלַת‎(10) דְּבִיתְהוּ בְּרֵישָׁא ... אֲמַר‎(11) לַהּ לִדְבִיתְהוּ:
יָדַעְנָא‎(12) דְּרַבָּנָן מִשּׁוּם מִטְרָא קָא אָתוּ,‎(13) נִיסַק‎(14) לְאִיגָּרָא
וְנִיבְעֵי‎(15) רַחֲמֵי! אֶפְשָׁר דְּמְרַצֵּי הַקָּדוֹשׁ בָּרוּךְ הוּא וְיֵיתֵי‎(16)
מִיטְרָא. (תענית כג, ב)

(ד) ... אִיתְּתָא לְבֵי תְּרֵי לָא חַזְיָא,‎(17) אֲבָל מָמוֹנָא אֵימָא‎(18) הָנֵי
מִיפַלְגָא‎(19) פָּלְגֵי!‎(20) צְרִיכֵי.‎(21) (קדושין מג, ב)

(ה) אֵיזִיל‎(22) וְאֶשְׁמַע מִינֵּיה מִילְּתָא, וְאֵיתֵי,‎(23) וְאֵיסַק.‎(24) (שבת מא, א)

(ו) מַאי הֲוָה‎(25) לֵיה לְמֶיעֱבַד?‎(26) (בבא מציעא ו, א)

(ז) וְתִיפוֹק‎(27) לֵיה דְּבָעֵינַן לְמֶעֱבַד הֶיכֵּרָא!‎(28) (בכורות נח, א)

(ח) ... הֲוָה קָא מְזַבֵּין‎(29) אַרְעָא וְזָבֵין‎(30) תּוֹרֵי ... (גיטין נב, א)

In the table on the next page, the left-hand column lists all the
verbal forms that have been numbered in the sentences above. To
the right of that column, five additional columns appear with the
headings ROOT, *BINYAN*, TENSE, HEBREW (translation), and
ENGLISH (translation), respectively. For the first verbal form, בְּעָא,
we have already filled in the spaces under those five headings.
Study the other verbal forms carefully, and fill in the rest of the
table yourself. Since you may want to refer back to the
conjugations of the verbs, their numbers in Chapter 4 have been
printed in square brackets in the root column.

ARAMAIC VERB	ROOT	*BINYAN*	"TENSE"	HEBREW	ENGLISH
בְּעָא (1)	בעי [18]	קַל	Past	רָצָה	*he wanted*
לְמֶיהְדַר (2)	[5]				
לְאַתּוֹיֵי (3)	[24]				
אַתְנְיֵיה (4)	[22]				
נֵיקוּם (5)	[27]				
נֵיזִיל (6)	[15]				
נֶעֱבֵיד (7)	[4]				
נְקַיֵּים (8)	[27]				
נְפַקָא (9)	[6]				
עֲלַת (10)	[26]				
אֲמַר (11)	[17]				
יָדַעְנָא (12)	[10]				
אֲתוּ (13)	[24]				
נִיסַק (14)	[8]				
נִיבְעֵי (15)	[18]				
יֵיתֵי (16)	[24]				
חֲזְיָא (17)	[19]				
אֵימָא (18)	[17]				
מִיפְּלַג (19)	[1]				
פְּלִגִי (20)	[1]				
צְרִיכִי (21)	[3]				
אֵיזִיל (22)	[15]				
אֵיתֵי (23)	[24]				
אֵיסַק (24)	[8]				
הֲוָה (25)	[25]				
לְמֶיעֱבַד (26)	[4]				
תֵּיפּוֹק (27)	[6]				
בָּעֵינַן (28)	[18]				
מְזַבֵּין (29)	[2]				
זָבֵין (30)	[2]				

The answers for this exercise are found on pp. 296-297.

EXERCISE 3: ANALYSIS OF VERBS AND PHRASES IN A TALMUDIC PASSAGE

In the following passage twenty-six items are numbered. For each verb (or pair of verbs connected by a hyphen) please fill in the table on the next page. The beginning of this narrative, which is written in Hebrew in the Babylonian Talmud, has been reproduced here in small print in order to provide the background for the Aramaic portion that contains all the verbs featured in this exercise.

תנו רבנן: מעשה בתלמיד אחד שבא לפני רבי יהושע, אמר לו: תפלת ערבית רשות
או חובה? אמר לו: רשות. בא לפני רבן גמליאל, אמר לו: תפלת ערבית רשות או
חובה? אמר לו: חובה. אמר לו: והלא רבי יהושע אמר לי רשות! אמר לו: המתן עד
שיכנסו בעלי תריסין לבית המדרש. כשנכנסו בעלי תריסין, עמד השואל ושאל: תפלת
ערבית רשות או חובה? אמר לו רבן גמליאל: חובה. אמר להם רבן גמליאל לחכמים:
כלום יש אדם שחולק בדבר זה? אמר לו רבי יהושע: לאו. אמר לו: והלא משמך אמרו
לי רשות! אמר לו: יהושע, עמוד על רגליך ויעידו בך! היה רבן גמליאל יושב ודורש,
ורבי יהושע עומד על רגליו, עד שרננו כל העם ואמרו לחוצפית התורגמן: עמוד!
ועמד.

אמרי⁽¹⁾: עד כמה נצעריה-וניזיל⁽²⁾? בראש השנה אשתקד צעריה⁽³⁾, בבכורות
במעשה דרבי צדוק צעריה, הכא נמי צעריה. תא-ונעבריה⁽⁴⁾! מאן נוקים⁽⁵⁾
(ליה)? נוקמיה⁽⁶⁾ לרבי יהושע? בעל מעשה הוא; נוקמיה לרבי עקיבא? דילמא
עניש⁽⁷⁾ ליה, דלית ליה זכות אבות; אלא נוקמיה לרבי אלעזר בן עזריה, דהוא
חכם והוא עשיר והוא עשירי לעזרא. הוא חכם: דאי מקשי⁽⁸⁾ ליה, מפרק⁽⁹⁾
ליה; והוא עשיר: דאי אית ליה לפלוחי⁽¹⁰⁾ לבי קיסר, אף הוא אזיל-ופלח⁽¹¹⁾;
והוא עשירי לעזרא: אית ליה זכות אבות, ולא מצי-עניש⁽¹²⁾ ליה.
אתו-ואמרו⁽¹³⁾ ליה: ניחא ליה למר דליהוי⁽¹⁴⁾ ריש מתיבתא? אמר להו:
איזיל-ואימליך⁽¹⁵⁾ באינשי ביתי. אזיל-ואמליך⁽¹⁶⁾ בדביתהו. אמרה ליה: דלמא
מעברין⁽¹⁷⁾ לך? אמר לה: לשתמש⁽¹⁸⁾ איניש יומא חדא בכסא דמוקרא ולמחר
ליתבר⁽¹⁹⁾. אמרה ליה: לית לך חיורתא. ההוא יומא בר תמני סרי שני הוה⁽²⁰⁾,
אתרחיש⁽²¹⁾ ליה ניסא ואהדרו⁽²²⁾ ליה תמני סרי דרי חיורתא. היינו דקאמר⁽²³⁾
רבי אלעזר בן עזריה: הרי אני כבן שבעים שנה, ולא בן שבעים שנה. (ברכות
כז, ב-כח, א)

VERB(S)	ROOT	*BINYAN*	"TENSE"	TRANSLATION
אָמְרֵי (1)				
נִצְעַרֵיהּ וְנֵיזִיל (2)				
צַעֲרֵיהּ (3)				
תָּא וְנַעֲבְרֵיהּ (4)				
נוֹקִים (5)				
נוֹקְמֵיהּ (6)				
עָנִישׁ (7)				
מַקְשֵׁי (8)				
מְפָרֵק (9)				
לִפְלוֹחֵי (10)				
אָזֵיל וּפָלַח (11)				
מָצֵי עָנִישׁ (12)				
אָתוּ וַאֲמַרוּ (13)				
לֶיהֱוֵי (14)				
אֵיזִיל וְאִימְּלִיךְ (15)				
אֲזַל וְאִימְּלִיךְ (16)				
מַעֲבְרִין (17)				
לִשְׁתַּמַּשׁ (18)				
לִיתְּבַר (19)				
הֲוָה (20)				
אִתְרַחִישׁ (21)				
אַהֲדְרוּ (22)				
(קָ)אָמַר (23)				

The answers for this exercise are found on pp. 297-298.

A REGULAR ARAMAIC VERB IN TARGUM ONKELOS (SIMPLE)

	אִתְפְּעֵל	פְּעֵל (קל)	פְּעַל (קל)
	PAST		
I	אִתְכְּתֵיבִית	תְּקֵיפִית	כְּתַבִית
you (s.)	f. אִתְכְּתֵיבְתָּ,-ְתְּ אִתְכְּתֵיבְתְּ	f. תְּקֵיפְתָּא,-ְתְּ תְּקֵיפְתְּ	f. כְּתַבְתָּא,-ְתְּ כְּתַבְתְּ
he/she	f. אִתְכְּתֵיבַת אִתְכְּתֵיב	f. תְּקֵיפַת תְּקֵיף	f. כְּתַבַת כְּתַב
we	אִתְכְּתֵיבְנָא	תְּקֵיפְנָא	כְּתַבְנָא
you (pl.)	f. אִתְכְּתֵיבְתִּין אִתְכְּתֵיבְתּוּן	f. תְּקֵיפְתִּין תְּקֵיפְתּוּן	f. כְּתַבְתִּין כְּתַבְתּוּן
they	f. אִתְכְּתֵיבָא אִתְכְּתֵיבוּ	f. תְּקֵיפָא תְּקֵיפוּ	f. כְּתַבָא כְּתַבוּ
		ACTIVE PARTICIPLE	
s.		f. תָּקֵפָא תָּקֵיף	f. כָּתְבָא כָּתֵיב
pl.		f. תָּקְפָן תָּקְפִין	f. כָּתְבָן כָּתְבִין
	PASSIVE/REFLEXIVE PARTICIPLE	**PASSIVE PARTICIPLE**	
s.	f. מִתְכְּתִיבָא מִתְכְּתִיב	f. תְּקִיפָא תְּקִיף	f. כְּתִיבָא כְּתִיב
pl.	f. מִתְכְּתִיבָן מִתְכְּתִיבִין	f. תְּקִיפָן תְּקִיפִין	f. כְּתִיבָן כְּתִיבִין
	FUTURE		
I	אֶתְכְּתֵיב	אֶתְקַף	אֶכְתּוֹב
you (s.)	f. תִּתְכַּתְבִין תִּתְכְּתֵיב	f. תִּתְקְפִין תִּתְקַף	f. תִּכְתְּבִין תִּכְתּוֹב
he/she	f. תִּתְכְּתֵיב יִתְכְּתֵיב	f. תִּתְקַף יִתְקַף	f. תִּכְתּוֹב יִכְתּוֹב
we	נִתְכְּתֵיב	נִתְקַף	נִכְתּוֹב
you (pl.)	f. תִּתְכַּתְבָן תִּתְכַּתְבוּן	f. תִּתְקְפָן תִּתְקְפוּן	f. תִּכְתְּבָן תִּכְתְּבוּן
they	f. יִתְכַּתְבָן יִתְכַּתְבוּן	f. יִתְקְפָן יִתְקְפוּן	f. יִכְתְּבָן יִכְתְּבוּן
	IMPERATIVE		
(you s.)	f. אִתְכְּתֵיבִי אִתְכְּתֵיב	f. תְּקֵפִי תְּקַף	f. כְּתוּבִי כְּתוֹב
(you pl.)	f. אִתְכְּתֵיבָא אִתְכְּתֵיבוּ	f. תְּקֵפָא תְּקֵפוּ	f. כְּתוּבָא כְּתוּבוּ
	GERUND/INFINITIVE		
	(cnstr. אִתְכְּתָבוּת) אִתְכְּתָבָא	(.inf מִתְקָף) מִתְקַף	(.inf מִכְתָּב) מִכְתַּב

268

A REGULAR ARAMAIC VERB IN TARGUM ONKELOS (INTENSIVE)

	אִתְפַּעַל		פַּעֵל	
PAST				
I		אִתְקַדָּשִׁית		קַדֵּשִׁית
you (s.)	f. אִתְקַדַּשְׁתְּ	אִתְקַדַּשְׁתָּא,־תְּ	f. קַדֵּישְׁתְּ	קַדֵּישְׁתָּא, קַדֵּישְׁתְּ
he/she	f. אִתְקַדַּשַׁת	אִתְקַדַּשׁ	f. קַדֵּישַׁת	קַדֵּישׁ
we		אִתְקַדַּשְׁנָא		קַדֵּישְׁנָא
you (pl.)	f. אִתְקַדַּשְׁתִּין	אִתְקַדַּשְׁתּוּן	f. קַדֵּישְׁתִּין	קַדֵּישְׁתּוּן
they	f. אִתְקַדַּשָׁא	אִתְקַדַּשׁוּ	f. קַדֵּישָׁא	קַדֵּישׁוּ
ACTIVE PARTICIPLE				
s.			f. מְקַדְּשָׁא	מְקַדֵּישׁ
pl.			f. מְקַדְּשָׁן	מְקַדְּשִׁין
	PASSIVE / REFLEXIVE PARTICIPLE		**PASSIVE PARTICIPLE**	
s.	f. מִתְקַדְּשָׁא	מִתְקַדַּשׁ	f. מְקַדְּשָׁא	מְקַדַּשׁ
pl.	f. מִתְקַדְּשָׁן	מִתְקַדְּשִׁין	f. מְקַדְּשָׁן	מְקַדְּשִׁין
FUTURE				
I		אֶתְקַדַּשׁ		אֲקַדֵּישׁ
you (s.)	f. תִּתְקַדְּשִׁין	תִּתְקַדַּשׁ	f. תְּקַדְּשִׁין	תְּקַדֵּישׁ
he/she	f. תִּתְקַדַּשׁ	יִתְקַדַּשׁ	f. תְּקַדֵּישׁ	יְקַדֵּישׁ
we		נִתְקַדַּשׁ		נְקַדֵּישׁ
you (pl.)	f. תִּתְקַדְּשָׁן	תִּתְקַדְּשׁוּן	f. תְּקַדְּשָׁן	תְּקַדְּשׁוּן
they	f. יִתְקַדְּשָׁן	יִתְקַדְּשׁוּן	f. יְקַדְּשָׁן	יְקַדְּשׁוּן
IMPERATIVE				
(you s.)	f. אִתְקַדַּשִׁי	אִתְקַדַּשׁ	f. קַדִּישִׁי	קַדֵּישׁ
(you pl.)	f. אִתְקַדַּשָׁא	אִתְקַדַּשׁוּ	f. קַדִּישָׁא	קַדֵּישׁוּ
GERUND / INFINITIVE				
	אִתְקַדָּשָׁא (אִתְקַדָּשׁוּת־ .cnstr)		קַדָּשָׁא (קַדָּשׁוּת־ .cnstr)	

269

A REGULAR ARAMAIC VERB IN TARGUM ONKELOS (EXTENSIVE)

	אִתְפְּעַל		אַפְעֵל	
PAST				
I		אִתְּפְקָדִית		אַפְקֵידִית
you (s.)	f. אִתְּפְקַדְתְּ	אִתְּפְקַדְתָּא,־תְּ	f. אַפְקֵידְתְּ	אַפְקֵידְתָּא, אַפְקֵידְתְּ
he/she	f. אִתְּפְקַדַת	אִתְּפְקַד	f. אַפְקֵידַת	אַפְקֵיד
we		אִתְּפְקַדְנָא		אַפְקֵידְנָא
you (pl.)	f. אִתְּפְקַדְתִּין	אִתְּפְקַדְתּוּן	f. אַפְקֵידְתִּין	אַפְקֵידְתּוּן
they	f. אִתְּפְקַדָא	אִתְּפְקַדוּ	f. אַפְקֵידָא	אַפְקֵידוּ
ACTIVE PARTICIPLE				
s.			f. מַפְקְדָא	מַפְקֵיד
pl.			f. מַפְקְדָן	מַפְקְדִין
PASSIVE/REFLEXIVE PARTICPLE			**PASSIVE PARTICIPLE**	
s.	f. מִתְּפְקַדָא	מִתְּפְקַד	f. מַפְקְדָא	מַפְקַד
pl.	f. מִתְּפְקַדָן	מִתְּפְקְדִין	f. מַפְקְדָן	מַפְקְדִין
FUTURE				
I		אֶתְּפְקַד		אַפְקֵיד
you (s.)	f. תִּתְּפְקְדִין	תִּתְּפְקַד	f. תַּפְקְדִין	תַּפְקֵיד
he/she	f. תִּתְּפְקַד	יִתְּפְקַד	f. תַּפְקֵיד	יַפְקֵיד
we		נִתְּפְקַד		נַפְקֵיד
you (pl.)	f. תִּתְּפְקְדָן	תִּתְּפְקְדוּן	f. תַּפְקְדָן	תַּפְקְדוּן
they	f. יִתְּפְקְדָן	יִתְּפְקְדוּן	f. יַפְקְדָן	יַפְקְדוּן
IMPERATIVE				
(you s.)	f. אִתְּפְקְדִי	אִתְּפְקַד	f. אַפְקֵידִי	אַפְקֵיד
(you pl.)	f. אִתְּפְקַדָא	אִתְּפְקַדוּ	f. אַפְקֵידָא	אַפְקֵידוּ
GERUND / INFINITIVE				
	(־cnstr. אִתְּפְקָדוּת) אִתְּפְקָדָא		(־cnstr. אַפְקָדוּת) אַפְקָדָא	

AN INDEX TO VERBAL ROOTS IN TARGUM ONKELOS

Paradigms of a variety of Aramaic verbs, including all their conjugated forms that actually appear in the Babylonian Talmud and/or Targum Onkelos, have been presented in Chapter 4 (Talmud) and Chapter 5 (Onkelos). In addition, the *complete* (artificial) paradigms of regular verbs in Targum Onkelos, in the six major *binyanim*, have now been added in a compact format (Appendix C).[1] From this material the learner can locate the form confronting him in the text — or at least a form whose pattern can serve as a *model*.

In order to facilitate the identification of the appropriate model verb, the following alphabetical index of all the verbal roots in Targum Onkelos (on pp. 273-288) directs the learner to the most appropriate paradigm.[2] When the best match for one *binyan* of a given verb is not the best fit for another *binyan* of the same verb — as often happens — the listing of that verb is split according to its *binyanim*. For example, the very first root אבד is divided into three: *binyan* קל and the suggested model verb is אזל; *binyan* פַּעֵל with model verb קדש, and *binyan* אַפְעֵל with model verb אכל.

Before undertaking a search for a model root, the learner must first determine the root of the verbal form in question. One should bear in mind that Jewish tradition does not maintain that grammatical roots were revealed at Sinai; rather a *root* is a useful artificial construct invented by human beings. In fact, linguistic scholars have debated for centuries whether Hebrew (and Aramaic) roots are basically *triliteral* (comprising three root-letters) or not. Today the triliteral theory holds sway, and indeed it is relatively easy to identify the three root-letters of regular verbs (שְׁלֵמִים, whose root-letters always remain intact) by deleting standard personal prefixes

---

1   For *binyan* קַל, the verbs כתב and תקף are used, and for the אִתְפְּעֵל, כתב exclusively (p. 268); for the intensive פַּעֵל and אִתְפַּעַל *binyanim*, the verb קדש is used (p. 269), and for the extensive אַפְעֵל and אִתַּפְעַל *binyanim*, פקד (p. 270).

2   For the Aramaic verbs in the Babylonian Talmud, which are much more numerous, this formidable task has not been undertaken. Moreover, many of the basic verbal entries in this author's complete Aramaic-Hebrew-English dictionary of the Babylonian Talmud, which is being prepared for publication, will refer the learner to the appropriate paradigms in this volume.

and/or suffixes of the conjugation. In many verbal forms, however, only two root-letters are discernible, nevertheless the triliteralists insist that even these verbs are to be classified as triliteral — but with a "troublesome" root-letter that is sometimes missing.[3]

The consonants that are most likely to "cause trouble" are:

CONSONANT	SAMPLE ROOT	SAMPLE FORM	TRANSLATION
1. initial root-letter: נ	נפק	אֶפּוֹק	*I will go out*
2. initial root-letter: י (sometimes appears as ו)	יהב	הַב	*give!*
3. initial root-letter: א	אזל	לְמֵיזַל	*to go*
4. middle root-letter: ו	קום	קָם	*he stood*
5. final root-letter: י	חזי	חֲזָת	*she saw*
6. final root-letter of כְּפוּלִים (2nd and 3rd root-letters identical)	עלל	עָלוּ	*they entered*

The following policy has been adopted for this index: The prevailing triliteral theory has been accepted, and thus every root is represented by three letters. However, since in some instances one of the three letters (or occasionally two) is not stable, such letters have been printed in a *gray* color. Furthermore, in order to accommodate the learner who identifies only two prominent root-letters of some Aramaic verbal forms, the index also includes some two-letter combinations (when they were deemed necessary) to serve as cross-references to three-letter roots.

Examples: חס ← חוס   טר ← טור

The three-letter roots in turn refer to the appropriate paradigms and page numbers in Chapter 5 or in Appendix C.

3 For example, see Rashi's use of the term יְסוֹד הַנּוֹפֵל לִפְרָקִים, *a root-letter that is sometimes deleted*, in his commentary on *Bereshith* 17:11. For a discussion of the issue, see Ḥ. Gamliel: "תפישת השורש של רש"י", *Leshonenu*, 71 (5769), pp. 105-129. Even triliteralists concede that there is often affinity in meaning between verbs that have the same two root-letters in common (e.g., roots that begin with the consonants פר: פרד, פרח, פרס, פרע, פרץ, פרק, פרר).

An asterisk (*) that appears to the right of a page number indicates that the relevant verbal form(s) may appear in the *introduction* to the paradigms (or in a footnote) of the specific verb — not necessarily in the paradigms themselves.

The notes that are indicated by numbers (in superscript) are found at the end of the index, on pp. 288-290.

אבד
קל : אזל   173-172
פַּעֵל : קדש   259
אַפְעֵל : אכל   178

אבי
קל : אתי   211-209

אבל
אתפעל : קדש   259

אגר
קל : אזל   172
אתפעל : אסי   114

אזל 173-172

אחד
קל : אזל   173-172
אתפעל : קדש   259

אחר
פַּעֵל : קדש²   259
אתפעל : קדש   259
אַפְעֵל : אכל²   177

אכל 178-177

אלל
פַּעֵל : קדש   259

אלם
פַּעֵל : קדש   259

אלף 180-179

אמר* 176-174

אנח
אתפעל⁷

אנס
קל : אכל   177

אסי
פַּעֵל : אסי   115-114
אתפעל : אסי   115-114

אסר
קל : אמר   176-174
אתפעל : אמר*   176-174
פַּעֵל : קדש   259

אפי
קל : אתי   211-209
אתפעל : גלי³   203

אצר
קל : אזל   173

ארך
קל : אכל   178
אַפְעֵל : אכל   178-177

ארס
קל : אכל   178
פַּעֵל : קדש⁸, ¹¹   259

אשד
קל : אכל   178-177
אתפעל : אכל   178-177

אתי* 211-209

באש
קל (פְּעִיל) : שאל   217-216
אַפְעֵל : פקד   260

בד ← אבד

בדק
קל : כתב   258
פַּעֵל : קדש   259

בדר
פַּעֵל : קדש²   259
אתפעל : קדש   259

בהל
אתפעל : כתב   258

בהת
קל : תקף   258

בור
קל : קום   194

בזז
קל : על⁴   201-200

בזע
אתפעל : כתב²   258
פַּעֵל : קדש²   259

בחן
קל : כתב   258

בחר
קל : כתב   258
אתפעל : כתב²   258

בטל
קל : כתב   258
פַּעֵל : קדש   259

בי ← אבי

בית
קל : קום⁵   195-193
אַפְעֵל : קום   194

בכי
קל : גלי   203-202

בכר
פַּעֵל : קדש   259
אתפעל : קדש   259

בל ← יבל, בלי

בלבל
¹⁰ACTIVE

* Please take note of form(s) presented only in the *introduction* to this verb.

274

גרם
קל: כתב 258

דאת
אַפְעֵל: פקד 260

דב → דוב

דבח
קל: כתב[2] 258
פְּעֵל: קדש[2] 259

דבק
קל: כתב 258
אתפעל: כתב[12] 258
אַפְעֵל: פקד 260

דבר * 155-157

דוב
קל: קום 194

דוך
קל: קום 194

דון/דין
קל: נוח 136-138
אתפעל[1]

דור
קל: קום[2] 193

דחי
קל: גלי 202

דחל
קל (פעיל): תקף 258

דחק
קל (פעיל): תקף 258
אתפעל: כתב[12] 258

די → ידי, נדי

דך → דוך, דכי

דכי
קל: שתי 214-215

פְּעֵל: גלי 202-203
אתפעל: גלי[12] 202-203*

דכר
קל: דבר 153-155
אתפעל: דבר* 153-155
אַפְעֵל: פקד[2] 260

דלי
קל: גלי 202-203

דלק
קל (פעיל): תקף 258
אַפְעֵל: פקד 260

דמי
קל: גלי 202
פְּעֵל: גלי 202

דמך
קל (פעול)[13]

דן → דון, דין

דנח
קל: כתב 258

דע → ידע

דעץ
פְּעֵל: קדש 259

דקק
אַפְעֵל: על 201

דר → דור, נדר

דרך
קל: כתב 258

הב → יהב

הדר
קל: דבר 155

הוי (הי) 212-213

הימן * 218

הך → הלך

הלך 170-171

המם
אתפעל[7]

הני
אַפְעֵל: חזי 204
אתפעל: חזי 204*

הפך
קל: כתב[3] 258
אתפעל: כתב[3] 258

הרהר
ACTIVE[10]

ודי → ידי

זבן 151-152

זהר
אַפְעֵל: פקד[2] 260

זוד
אַפְעֵל: קום 194

זון
קל: קום 193-194
אתפעל[1]

זוע
קל: קום 193-194

זור
קל: קום 193, 195

זחל
קל: כתב 258

זין
פְּעֵל[7,8]

זכי
קל: גלי 202-203
פְּעֵל: גלי 202-203

* Please take note of form(s) presented only in the *introduction* to this verb.

* Please take note of form(s) presented only in the *introduction* to this verb.

חלף
פָּעֵל: קדש 259

חלץ
פָּעֵל: קדש 259

חמד
פָּעֵל: קדש 259

חמם
קל: עלל 201-200

חמע
קל: כתב[2, 3] 258
אַפְעֵל: פקד 260

חמר
קל: כתב[8] 258

חנט
קל: כתב[3] 258

חנן
קל: עלל 201-200
אתפעל: קדש 259

חס ← חוס

חסל
אתפעל: עבד 159
אַפְעֵל: פקד 260

חסן
אַפְעֵל: פקד 260

חסר
קל: דבר[3] 154
פָּעֵל: דבר 154

חפי
קל: חזי 205-204
אתפעל: חזי 204*
פָּעֵל: גלי 202

חפף
אתפעל[7]

חפר
קל: דבר[3] 154

חצד
קל: כתב 258

חרם
אַפְעֵל: פקד 260
אתפעל: פקד 260

חרר
אתפעל[7]

חשב
קל: כתב[3] 258
אתפעל: כתב 258
פָּעֵל: קדש 259

חשך
קל (פעול)
אַפְעֵל: פקד 260

חת ← נחת

חתן
אתפעל: קדש 259

טב ← יטב

טבל
קל: כתב 258

טבע
אתפעל: דבר[12] *153

טוי
קל: גלי[8] 202

טוף
קל: קום 194
אַפְעֵל: פוק 162

טחן
קל: כתב 258

טל ← נטל, טלל

טלטל
ACTIVE[10], PASSIVE[10, 12]

טלל
אַפְעֵל: עלל 201-200

טלע
אַפְעֵל: פקד[2] 260

טלף
אַפְעֵל: פקד 260

טמם
קל: עלל 200

טמר
פָּעֵל: דבר 153
אתפעל: כתב[2] 258
אַפְעֵל: פקד[2] 260

טעי
קל: גלי 203-202
אַפְעֵל: גלי 203-202

טעם
אַפְעֵל: פקד 260

טען
קל: כתב 258

טף ← טוף, טפי

טפי
קל: שתי 215

טפס
אתפעל: כתב[12] 258

טפש
אתפעל: דבר[12] *153

טקס
פָּעֵל: קדש 259

טר ← נטר

טרד
קל: כתב 258

---

* Please take note of form(s) presented only in the *introduction* to this verb.

* Please take note of form(s) presented only in the *introduction* to this verb.

* Please take note of form(s) presented only in the *introduction* to this verb.

מנע
קל: כתב 258
אתפעל: כתב[2] 258

מס׳
קל: חזי[8] 205
אתפעל: גלי 203
אפעל: גלי 202-203

מסכן
[10]PASSIVE

מסר
קל: כתב[2] 258
אתפעל: כתב[2] 258

מצ׳
אתפעל: גלי 203

מר ← אמר, מר׳

מרג
אתפעל: כתב 258

מרד
קל: כתב 258

מרט
קל: כתב 258

מרס
קל: כתב 258

מרע
קל: כתב[2] 258
אפעל: פקד[2] 260

מרק
אתפעל: כתב 258

מר׳
אפעל: על[2] 200
אתפעל: קדש 259

מש ← מוש

משח
קל: כתב 258

משש
פעל: קדש 259

מת ← מו׳ת

נבח
קל: נפק 164

נב׳
אתפעל: גל׳ 202*

נבע
קל: כתב 258
אפעל: נחת[2] 165

נגב
קל (פעול)[13]

נגד
קל: נפק 162-164
אתפעל: כתב 258

נגח
קל: נפק 163

נגף
קל: נפק 163

נד ← נד׳

נד׳
קל: על 200
אפעל: על 200

נד׳
אפעל: נפק[15] 162-164
אתפעל: נפק[15] 162*

נדר
קל: נפק 162-164

נהר
קל: כתב 258
פעל: קדש 259
אפעל: פקד 260

נו׳ח 196-197

נז׳ן
קל: נפק 162, 164

נזק
אפעל: פקד 260

נז׳ר
קל (פעיל): נפק 162, 164

נח ← נו׳ח

נחם
פעל: קדש 259
אתפעל: קדש 259

נחש
פעל: קדש 259

נח׳ת 165-166*

נט׳ל
קל: נפק 162-164
אפעל: נפק 162, 164
פעל: קדש 259
אתפעל: קדש 259

נט׳ר
קל: נפק[3] 162-164

נ׳ ← נ׳י

נכל
פעל: קדש 259

נכ׳ס
קל: נפק 162-164
אתפעל: כתב 258

נכת
קל: כתב 258
אתפעל: כתב 258
פעל: קדש 259

נס׳ב
קל (פעיל): נפק 162-164
אתפעל: כתב 258
אפעל: נפק 164

* Please take note of form(s) presented only in the *introduction* to this verb.

* Please take note of form(s) presented only in the *introduction* to this verb.

* Please take note of form(s) presented only in the *introduction* to this verb.

עסר
פַּעֵל: קדש[2] 259

עוף → עף

עצר
קל: עבד 159

עוק → עק

עקד
קל: עבד 159

עקר
פַּעֵל: דבר 155

ערב
פַּעֵל: קדש[11] 259

ערבל
[10]PASSIVE

ערע
פַּעֵל: קדש[2, 11] 259

ערק
קל: כתב[3] 258
פַּעֵל: קדש[2] 259

עשק
קל: כתב[2] 258

עתד
פַּעֵל: קדש 259
אתפַּעַל: קדש 259

עתק
אתפַּעַל: קדש 259

עתר
קל: עבד 159
פַּעֵל: דבר 154

פגע
קל: כתב 258

פגר
פַּעֵל: קדש 259

פוג
קל: קום 194

פול
קל: קום[8, 16] 133

פח → נפח

פטר
קל: כתב 258
אתפַּעַל: כתב[2] 258

פי → אפי

פל → נפל, פול, פלי

פלג
קל: כתב 258
אתפַּעַל: כתב 258
פַּעֵל: קדש 259

פלח
קל: דבר 154-155
אתפַּעַל: כתב[2] 258
אַפְעֵל: פקד[2] 260

פלי
פַּעֵל: גלי 202-203

פני
קל: גלי[8] 202
אתפַּעַל: גלי 202-203
פַּעֵל: גלי 202-203

פנק
פַּעֵל: קדש[8] 259
אתפַּעַל: קדש 259

פסל
קל: כתב 258

פסק
קל: כתב 258

פק → נפק

פקד
פַּעֵל: קדש 259
אתפַּעַל: קדש 259

פרח
קל: ידע 184
פַּעֵל: קרב[2] 158
אַפְעֵל: פקד[2] 260

פרס
קל: כתב 258

פרע
קל: כתב[2] 258
אתפַּעֵל: כתב[2] 258

פרק
קל: כתב 258
אתפַּעֵל: כתב 258
פַּעֵל: קרב 157-158
אתפַּעֵל: קרב 157-158

פרש
פַּעֵל: קרב 157-158
אתפַּעֵל: קרב 157-158
אַפְעֵל: פקד 260
אתפַּעֵל: פקד 260

פש → נפש

פשר
קל: ידע 184
פַּעֵל: דבר 154

פתח
קל: דבר 154-155
אתפַּעֵל: כתב 258

פתי
אַפְעֵל: גלי 202-203

צב → נצב, צבי

צבי
קל: שתי 214-215

צבע
פַּעֵל: דבר 155
אתפַּעַל: קדש[14] 259

צד → צוד, צדי

צד׳
קל: שתי 214
פְּעַל: גלי 203-202

צה׳ ← צח׳

צוד
קל: קום 195-193

צוח
קל: כתב 258
אַפְעֵל: פקד 260

צור
קל: קום 193
פְּעַל 7,8

צות
אַפְעֵל: קום 195-193

צח׳
קל: שתי 214

צ׳ ← נצ׳

צלב
קל: כתב 258
אִתְפְּעַל: כתב 14 258

צלח
פְּעַל: דבר 154
אַפְעֵל: פקד 2 260

צל׳
קל: גלי 203
פְּעַל: גלי 203-202
אַפְעֵל: גלי 203

צמח
קל: כתב 258
פְּעַל: דבר 155
אַפְעֵל: פקד 2 260

צנע
אַפְעֵל: פקד 2 260

צר ← צור

צרח
אִתְפְּעַל: קדש 14 259

צרך
קל: צרך 8 57

צרף
פְּעַל: קדש 11 259

צרר
קל: כתב 8 258

צת ← צות

קבל
קל: כתב 258
פְּעַל: קדש 259
אִתְפְּעַל: קדש 259

קבע
קל: כתב 258

קבר
קל: דבר 155-154
אִתְפְּעַל: כתב 2 258
פְּעַל: קדש 259

קד ← יקד

קדם
פְּעַל: קדש 259
אַפְעֵל: פקד 260

קדש
פְּעַל: קדש 259
אִתְפְּעַל: קדש 259
אַפְעֵל: פקד 260

קום * 195-193

קוץ
קל: קום 194-193

קטל
קל: כתב 258
אִתְפְּעַל: כתב 258
פְּעַל: קדש 259
אִתְפְּעַל: קדש 259

קטף
קל: כתב 258

קטר
קל: כתב 258
אַפְעֵל: פקד 2 260

קלי
קל: גלי 203-202
אַפְעֵל: גלי 203

קלל
קל: עלי 4 201-200
אַפְעֵל: עלי 201

קלף
פְּעַל: קדש 259

קלקל
ACTIVE 10

קם ← נקם, קום

קמץ
קל: כתב 258

קנ׳
קל: גלי 203-202
פְּעַל: גלי 203-202
אַפְעֵל: גלי 203-202

קסם
קל: כתב 258

קוף ← נקוף, קפי

קפי
קל: גלי 202

---

* Please take note of form(s) presented only in the *introduction* to this verb.

* Please take note of form(s) presented only in the *introduction* to this verb.

רעי
קל : גלי 202-203
אתפעל : גלי 202-203
אפעל : גלי 203

רעם
אתפעל : קדש[11] 259
אפעל : פקד 260

רעע
קל : כתב[2,8] 258

רצע
אפעל : פקד[2] 260

רק → ריק, רקק

רקק
קל : על 201

רשי
קל : גלי 202-203
פעל[8,18] : גלי 112

רשע
אפעל : פקד[2] 260

רת → ירת

שאל *216-217

שאר
אתפעל : כתב[2,14] 258
אפעל : פקד[2] 260

שבח
פעל : קדש[2] 259

שבי
קל : גלי 202-203
אתפעל : שתי[14] 216*

שבע
אתפעל : כתב[2,14] 258

שבק
קל : כתב 258
אתפעל : כתב[14] 258

שבת
קל : כתב 258

שגי
קל : גלי 202

שגר
פעל : כתב[8] 258

שגש
פעל : קדש 259

שד → אשד, שדי

שדי
קל : שתי 216
אתפעל : שתי[14] 216*

שדל
פעל : קדש 259
אתפעל : סלק 167, 169

שדר
פעל : דבר 154

שהי
קל : גלי 202

שוט
קל : קום 193

שוי
פעל : גלי 202-203

שוע
קל : נוח 136-138
אתפעל[1,14]

שוף
קל : קום 193

שזר
קל : כתב[8] 258

שחל
קל : כתב 258

שחק
קל : כתב 258

שחר
פעל : קדש[2] 259

שט → ישט, שוט, שטי

שטח
קל : כתב 258
אתפעל : סלק 167

שטי
אתפעל : סלק[15] 168

שטף
קל : כתב 258
אתפעל : כתב[14] 258

שיזב 223-224

שים
קל : קום[5] 194

שיצי 221-222

שכב
קל (פעיל) : תקף 258

שכח
אתפעל : כתב[2,14] 258
אפעל : פקד[2] 260

שכלל
[10]ACTIVE
[15]PASSIVE

שלב
פעל : קדש[8] 259

שלהב
[10]REFLEXIVE

שלהי
[10]PASSIVE

* Please take note of form(s) presented only in the *introduction* to this verb.

* Please take note of form(s) presented only in the *introduction* to this verb.

תר ⟵ יְתַר, נְתַר	תקן	תן ⟵ נְתַן, תני
תרד	פָּעֵל: קדש 259	**תני**
פָּעֵל: קרב 157-159	אִתְפָּעַל: קדש 259	פָּעֵל: גלי 203
אִתְפָּעַל: קרב [12] 157-159	אַפְעֵל: פקד 260	אִתְפָּעַל: גלי [12] 202*
תרע	**תקע**	**תנן**
פָּעֵל: קרב 157-159	קל: כתב 258	קל: כתב 258
אִתְפָּעַל: קרב 158	**תקף**	**תפל**
תרץ	קל (פְּעֵיל): תקף 258	אִתְפָּעַל: קדש [12] 259
קל: כתב [8] 258	פָּעֵל: קדש 259	**תקל**
	אִתְפָּעַל: קדש [12] 259	קל: כתב 258
	אַפְעֵל: פקד 260	אִתְפְּעֵל: כתב [12] 258

* Please take note of form(s) presented only in the *introduction* to this verb.

Notes

In the footnotes to the index, all references to a Biblical chapter and verse indicate Targum Onkelos to that particular pasuk — not the Biblical passage itself.

1   The paradigms in Chapter 5 do not contain parallels for forms from the אִתְפְּעֵל *binyan* such as: יְתְּדָן, *it will be judged* (*Shemoth* 21:20-21); אִתְּעַר, *he awoke* (e.g., *Bereshith* 9:24); and אִתְּשַׁע, *it was plastered* (*VaYikra* 14: 43, 48), from the "hollow" roots דון, עור and שוע, respectively, whose middle root-letter is ו.

2   When a verbal pattern calls for a *tzerei* vowel immediately before the consanants א, ה, ע or ר — that vowel is usually replaced by a *pathah*. Examples: the participle אָמַר and the past tense אִתְאֲמַר (on p. 175 above) — rather than forms like the standard כָּתַב and אִתְכְּתִיב, respectively.
  Furthermore, when a *hirik* vowel precedes a final ה or ע, the final consonant is vocalized with a "furtive" *pathah*, i.e., a vowel that is written underneath but pronounced before the guttural consonant. Example: the passive participle פְּתִיחַ (*Bemidbar* 19:15) — rather than כְּתִיב.

3   When a verbal pattern requires a *mobile sheva* (שוא נע) for the first root-letter, if that consonant is א, ה, ח or ע — the *sheva* is replaced by a *hataf-pathah*. Examples: עֲבַד and אִתְעֲבִיד (on p. 159 above) — rather than forms like the standard כְּתַב and אִתְכְּתִיב, respectively.

4   The root עלל serves as a model for "geminate" roots, i.e., roots whose second and third root-letters are identical, but it is not a perfect match because its own initial root-letter is the guttural consonant ע. The normal vocalization for the future prefix of geminate roots is a *hirik* followed by a *dagesh* in the first root-letter, e.g., תְּבּוֹז (*Devarim* 20:14) from the root בזז. Since the guttural ע in עלל cannot take a *dagesh*, the prefix letters in its future (and infinitive) forms are

vocalized with the long vowel, *tzerei*, e.g., תֵּעוֹל (p. 201). See note 11 below.

5   "Hollow" verbs (i.e., verbs whose middle root-letter is ו or י) are conjugated like the קוּם paradigm, but in some of them a *ḥirik* vowel (followed by a vowel-letter י) *sometimes* prevails. Examples: מִית in the past tense (on p. 198 above) and נְבִית in the future tense (*Bereshith* 19:2) — rather than forms like the standard קָם and נְקוּם, respectively.

6   The second-person-singular *feminine* form of the future tense (a form missing from our paradigms) does occur: תִּבְעִין (or תִּבְעַן in some editions), *you should request,* in *Bereshith* 30:2, and תִּקְרִין (or תִּקְרַן), *you shall name,* in 16:11 (ibid.) .

7   In many Yemenite editions of Targum Onkelos, the unusual פַּעֵל pattern appears, featuring a *kamatz* under its first root-letter and a middle root-letter without a *dagesh*. It serves as the intensive *binyan* — rather than the common פַּעֵל pattern — especially in the conjugation of some "hollow" roots (חוט, לוט and צור) and some "geminate" roots (גפף, לפף, עלל and ענן). Examples: גָּפֵיף, *he embraced* (*Bereshith* 29:13), and חָטִיטוּ, *they sewed* (ibid. 3:7) — rather than forms like the standard קַדִּיש and קַדִּישׁוּ, respectively. Cf. Morag, (above, p.15 note 8), pp. 221, 244-45.

Similarly, the passive/reflexive אִתְפָּעַל pattern is sometimes found in Yemenite editions instead of the more usual אִתְפַּעַל. Example: יִתְלָפַף, *it will be joined together* (*Shemoth* 28:7) — rather than a form like the standard יִתְקַדַּש.

8   In this *binyan*, the verb appears only in the passive participle.

9   The form אִתְגּוֹלַלוּ, *they were stirred up* (*Bereshith* 43:30), from the "geminate" root גלל, follows an אִתְפּוֹעַל pattern, which functions as a passive intensive *binyan* — like the more usual אִתְפַּעַל. Cf. the other unusual Aramaic *binyanim* described in note 7 and the Biblical Hebrew infinitive form לְהִתְגַּלֵל (ibid. 43:18).

10   This verb is *quadriliteral*, i.e., it has *four* root-letters. Chapter 5 includes the paradigms of four *quadriliteral* verbs from Targum Onkelos — שִׁיצִי, סוֹבַר, הֵימֵן and שִׁיזֵב (pp. 218-24). In addition, the verb שַׁעְבֵּד should also be classified as *quadriliteral* — even though, for pedagogical reasons, it has been presented in our paradigms as derived from the root עבד in the rare שַׁפְעֵל and אִשְׁתַּפְעַל *binyanim* in order to clarify its etymology (pp. 59-62; 159-161). Some of the other four-letter roots used in the Targum (קלקל, טלטל, זעזע, הרהר, בלבל and רברב) seem to duplicate (original) two-letter roots, while others (מסכן, גנדר, רוקן, שכלל, שלהב and שלהי) may be expansions of three-letter roots.

Quadriliteral verbs are conjugated in forms that are analogous to *binyan* פַּעֵל of ordinary Aramaic verbs — either in an *active* sense (e.g., מְהַרְהֵר, *plotting*, *Devarim* 29:17) or as a *passive* participle (e.g., מְהֵימַן, *believed*, in *Bemidbar* 12:7) — or in forms that are analogous to *binyan* אִתְפַּעַל, in a *passive* or *reflexive* sense (e.g., אִשְׁתַּכְלַלוּ, *they were completed*, in *Bereshith* 2:1 and מִתְרַבְרְבַתְּ, *you are setting yourself up as a despot*, in *Bemidbar* 16:13).

11   When the middle root-letter is ר or a guttural consonant, which cannot take the characteristic *dagesh* of the intensive *binyanim*, the previous vowel is often lengthened in compensation for the omission of the *dagesh*, e.g., from a *pathaḥ* to a *kamatz*. Example: the participle מְקָרֵיב (p. 157 above) — rather than a form like the standard מְקַדֵּישׁ.

12   When the first root-letter is ד, ט or ת — the ת from the prefix -אֶת of *binyanim* אֶתְפְּעֵל or אֶתְפַּעַל is deleted and replaced by a *dagesh* in the initial root-letter. Examples: אִדְּבַרַת, *she was taken* (*Bereshith* 12:15); נִטַּפֵּס, *we will consent* (ibid. 34:15) and אַתַּפַּלוּ, *they talked irreverently* (*Devarim* 1:1).

13   Besides the very common פְּעַל pattern of the past tense of the Aramaic binyan קַל and the fairly common פְּעֵיל pattern (e.g., תְּקֵיף, p. 258), a פְּעוּל pattern appears in Targum Onkelos in the verbs דְּמוּךְ, *he slept* (*Bereshith* 2:21; 41:5), and נְגוּבוּ, *they dried up* (ibid. 8:13). Cf. the Hebrew פָּעוֹל pattern, e.g., in the phrase וְלֹא יָכֹל מֹשֶׁה, *and Moshe could not*, in *Shemoth* 40:35.

14   In the *binyanim* אֶתְפְּעֵל and אֶתְפַּעַל, the first root-letter שׁ or ס changes places with the ת from the -אֶת prefix so that the ת is infixed between the initial root-letter and the second root-letter, e.g., between the שׁ and the ב of יִשְׁתְּבַע, *he shall swear* (*VaYikra* 5:24).

Furthermore, because of *assimilation* (i.e., the modification of one sound to resemble an adjacent sound), when the first root-letter is צ (historically, an emphatic *s* sound), the ת becomes a ט (historically, an emphatic *t*). Example: אִצְטְלִיב, *he was hanged* (*Devarim* 21:23). Similarly, when the first root-letter is a ז (a voiced *s* sound), the ת becomes a ד (a voiced *t* sound). Example: אִזְדְּקֵיפַת, *it stood up erect* (*Bereshith* 37:7). For further details, see p. 53 above and especialy note 6 ad loc.

15   The paradigms in Chapter 5 do not contain a verb with י as both its initial and final root-letters that can serve, by itself, as a model for verbs such as ידי. For such verbs, the root ילד has been presented as a model, but — since the final י is also an important factor in the conjugation — the learner should also refer to the paradigm of the verb גלי (on pp. 202-03).

Similarly, with regard to the roots נדי, עני and שדי: Although the learner is referred to the model roots נפק, עבד and סלק respectively, he should also take into account the final י by considering the paradigm of גלי.

16   See the form קים in note 79 on p. 133.

17   However, the third-person-masculine plural of the past tense is רְבִיאוּ, like שְׁתִיאוּ (p. 214).

18   The form מְרַשַּׁן (*Shemoth* 19:13), *permitted*, is the masculine-plural *passive* participle from *binyan* פַּעֵל (parallel to the Hebrew פִּעֵל *binyan*). Other Yemenite versions read מַרְשַׁן, from *binyan* אַפְעֵל (like the Hebrew הִפְעַל).

EXERCISES BASED ON
THE CONJUGATIONS OF THE VERBS

EXERCISE 4: ANALYSIS OF VERBS IN TARGUM ONKELOS
USING THE INDEX

Read the following quotations from Targum Onkelos carefully and
compare them to the Biblical Hebrew passages they are translating.
Each of the numbered words is a verbal form; the numbers relate to
the exercise on p. 293.

תרגום אונקלוס: שמות פרק א

(ו) וּמִית' יוֹסֵף וְכָל אֲחוֹהִי וְכֹל דָּרָא הַהוּא:

(ז) וּבְנֵי יִשְׂרָאֵל נְפִישׁוּ² וְאִתְיַלַדוּ³ וּסְגִיאוּ⁴ וּתְקִיפוּ⁵ לַחְדָּא לַחְדָּא
וְאִתְמְלִיאַת⁶ אַרְעָא מִנְהוֹן:

(ח) וְקָם⁷ מַלְכָּא חֲדַתָּא עַל מִצְרָיִם דְּלָא מְקַיֵּים⁸ גְּזֵירַת יוֹסֵף:

(י) הַבוּ נִתְחַכַּם⁹ לְהוֹן דִּלְמָא יִסְגוֹן¹⁰ וִיהֵי¹¹ אֲרֵי יְעָרְעִנַּנָא קְרָב וְיִתּוֹסְפוּן¹²
אַף אִנּוּן עַל סָנְאַנָא וִיגִיחוּן¹³ בַּנָא קְרָב וְיִסְּקוּן¹⁴ מִן אַרְעָא:

(יא) וּמַנִּיאוּ¹⁵ עֲלֵיהוֹן שִׁלְטוֹנִין... וּבְנוֹ¹⁶ קִרְוֵי בֵית אוֹצְרֵי לְפַרְעֹה יָת פִּיתוֹם
וְיָת רַעַמְסֵס:

(יד) וְאַמַרוּ¹⁷ יָת חַיֵּיהוֹן בְּפוּלְחָנָא קַשְׁיָא... יָת כָּל פּוּלְחָנְהוֹן דְּאַפְלַחוּ¹⁸ בְּהוֹן
בְּקַשְׁיוּ:

(טו) וַאֲמַר¹⁹ מַלְכָּא דְמִצְרַיִם לְחָיָתָא יְהוּדְיָתָא דְּשׁוּם חֲדָא שִׁפְרָה וְשׁוּם
תִּנְיֵיתָא פּוּעָה:

(יז) וּדְחִילָא²⁰ חָיָתָא מִן קֳדָם יְיָ וְלָא עֲבַדָא²¹ כְּמָא דְּמַלֵּיל²² עִמְּהֶן מַלְכָּא
דְמִצְרָיִם וְקַיֵּימָא²³ יָת בְּנַיָּא:

In the following table, the left-hand column lists all the verbal forms
that have been numbered in the texts above. The data for the verbal
forms מִית (row #1) and יִתּוֹסְפוּן (row #12) have already been filled
in – with one exception: The "model-root" column for מִית has been

left blank because the verb (root: מות) is one of those conjugated in Chapter 5 (# 21) and this very form can be found in its paradigm (on p. 200).[1]

The word יְתּוֹסְפוּן, however, does not appear in Chapter 5 (nor in Appendix C on pp. 268-270). To determine its three-letter root, one should ignore the prefix -יְת and the plural suffix וּן- and (for the time being) the "troublesome" letter ו. The two remaining consonants ספ – a combination that qualifies for the "prominent-letters" column – appears in the index (on p. 282) and refers the learner to three roots: יסף, סוף, ספי. Of the three, the best match is יסף because the letter ו which precedes ספ in the word יְתּוֹסְפוּן often serves as an alternate to the initial root-letter י.[2] Now the listing of root יסף in the index (on p. 278) leads to the *model root* יתב in Chapter 5, i.e., to the masculine-singular form יְתּוֹתַב on p. 191 in the paradigm of *binyan* אֶתַּפְעַל – a form that is similar to our plural form יְתּוֹסְפוּן.[3]

1 Note the discrepancy between the Aramaic verbal form (וּ)מְית and the Hebrew word וַיָּמָת that it translates: The -י prefix in Hebrew is characteristic of the "future" tense, and only by virtue of the -ו that precedes it (the so-called "conversive ו") is it understood to have a "past" meaning, whereas the Aramaic verb is a simple past-tense form – with the ו functioning as an ordinary conjunction. The same discrepancy between the two languages is evident in verbs 3 to 7 and verbs 15 to 17 in this exercise.
2 See the list on p. 272.
3 There are two discrepancies between the Aramaic verbal form יְתּוֹסְפוּן and its Biblical Hebrew counterpart וְנוֹסַף:
   A. The Aramaic verb is a "future" form as evident from the characteristic -י prefix, while its Hebrew parallel (וְ)נוֹסַף is a "past" form (from the נִפְעַל *binyan*), which refers to the future only by virtue of the "conversive" -ו that precedes it. The same discrepancy is also found in verbs 11, 13 and 14 in this exercise.
   B. The Aramaic verb is plural, and the Hebrew verb is singular. The same distinction is also found in verbs 10, 13 and 14 because the subject of all of them is the collective noun *people* in the previous verse: עַם in Hebrew, which is treated in this pasuk as singular, versus עַמָּא in Aramaic, which is treated as a plural noun by the Targum. Cf. *Shemoth* 13:17; 32:4.

Please fill in the following table:

TARGUM ONKELOS	BIBLICAL FORM	PROMINENT LETTERS*	ARAMAIC ROOT	ARAMAIC BINYAN	MODEL ROOT	ENGLISH TRANSLATION
מִית (1)	וַיָּמָת	מת	מות	קל	—	*he died*
נְפִישׁוּ (2)						
אִתְיַלַּדוּ (3)						
סְגִיאוּ (4)						
תְּקִיפוּ (5)						
אִתְמְלִיאַת (6)						
קָם (7)						
מְקַיֵּים (8)						
נִתְחַכַּם (9)						
יִסְגּוֹן (10)						
וִיהֵי (11)						
(וְ)יִתּוֹסְפוּן (12)	וְנוֹסַף	סף	יסף	אִתְּפָעַל	יתב	*they will be added*
וִיגִיחוּן (קְרָב) (13)						
וְיִסְקוּן (14)						
וּמַנִּיאוּ (15)						
וּבְנוֹ (16)						
וַאֲמַרוּ (17)						
דְּאַפְלַחוּ (18)						
וַאֲמַר (19)						
וּדְחִילָא (20)						
עֲבְדָא (21)						
דְּמַלֵּיל (22)						
וְקַיֵּימָא (23)						

The answers for this exercise are found on page 299.

* Our index does *not necessarily* present a two-letter combination of "prominent letters" to serve as a cross-reference — when the first two root-letters are not problematic and the third one (i.e., a final י) is apt to "cause trouble" (e.g. בני).

EXERCISE 5: ANALYSIS OF THE TARGUM'S TRANSLATION OF
BIBLICAL VERBS

In general, Targum Onkelos renders Biblical Hebrew into Aramaic
in a straightforward manner, but the translation is not always literal,
i.e., word-for-word — nor mechanical, i.e., grammatical form-for-
grammatical-form. This exercise is designed to give the learner a
taste of translation strategies used by Onkelos. For more details, see
the "Introduction to Targum Onkelos" in *The Ariel Chumash*,
Jerusalem 1997, pp. XVI-XVIII.

Here are seven Biblical passages from *Bereshith* — each one followed
by its Aramaic translation. Underline each of the Aramaic verbs and
the relevant Hebrew word(s) that it purports to translate (some of
which are not identical parallels of the Hebrew), and then fill in the
table on the next page.

בראשית ב:ד אֵלֶּה תוֹלְדוֹת הַשָּׁמַיִם וְהָאָרֶץ בְּהִבָּרְאָם בְּיוֹם עֲשׂוֹת ה' אֱלֹקִים אֶרֶץ
וְשָׁמָיִם.

אִלֵּין תּוֹלְדָת שְׁמַיָּא וְאַרְעָא כַּד אִתְבְּרִיאוּ בְּיוֹמָא דַּעֲבַד ה' אֱלֹקִים אַרְעָא וּשְׁמַיָּא.

ז:יד וְכָל הָעוֹף לְמִינֵהוּ כֹּל צִפּוֹר כָּל כָּנָף

וְכָל עוֹפָא לִזְנוֹהִי כֹּל צְפַר כָּל דְּפָרַח

יב:יא הִנֵּה נָא יָדַעְתִּי כִּי אִשָּׁה יְפַת מַרְאֶה אָתְּ

הָא כְּעַן יָדַעְנָא אֲרֵי אִתְּתָא שַׁפִּירַת חֵיזוּ אַתְּ

יז:א וַיֵּרָא ה' אֶל אַבְרָם וַיֹּאמֶר אֵלָיו אֲנִי אֵל שַׁדַּי הִתְהַלֵּךְ לְפָנַי וֶהְיֵה תָמִים.

וְאִתְגְּלִי ה' לְאַבְרָם וַאֲמַר לֵיהּ אֲנָא אֵל שַׁדַּי פְּלַח קֳדָמַי וַהֲוִי שְׁלִים.

כט:ג וְנֶאֶסְפוּ שָׁמָּה כָל הָעֲדָרִים וְגָלְלוּ אֶת הָאֶבֶן מֵעַל פִּי הַבְּאֵר

וּמִתְכַּנְּשִׁין תַּמָּן כָּל עֶדְרַיָּא וּמְגַנְדְּרִין יָת אַבְנָא מֵעַל פּוּמָא דְּבֵירָא

כט:ח עַד אֲשֶׁר יֵאָסְפוּ כָּל הָעֲדָרִים וְגָלְלוּ אֶת הָאֶבֶן מֵעַל פִּי הַבְּאֵר

עַד דְּיִתְכַּנְּשׁוּן תַּמָּן כָּל עֶדְרַיָּא וִיגַנְדְּרוּן יָת אַבְנָא מֵעַל פּוּמָא דְּבֵירָא

מט:ח יְהוּדָה אַתָּה יוֹדוּךָ אַחֶיךָ

יְהוּדָה אַתְּ אוֹדִיתָא וְלָא בְהֶיתְתָּא

VERB	ROOT	MODEL ROOT	*BINYAN*	"TENSE"	TRANSLATION
(1) אִתְבְּרִיאוּ					
(2) עֲבַד					
(3) פְּרַח					
(4) יָדַעְנָא					
(5) וְאִתְגְּלִי					
(6) אֲמַר					
(7) פְּלַח					
(8) הֲוִי					
(9) מִתְכַּנְּשִׁין					
(10) ˟מְגַנְדְּרִין					
(11) יִתְכַּנְּשׁוּן					
(12) ˟יְגַנְדְּרוּן					
(13) אוֹדִיתָא					
(14) בְּהֵיתְתָא					

The answers for this exercise are found on page 300.

˟ quadriliteral

295

ANSWERS TO EXERCISE 1

(א) they disagreed   (ז) depart!   (יג) to be asked
(ב) I am selling   (ח) to inform   (יד) you will show
(ג) subjugating   (ט) to teach   (טו) we brought
(ד) bring back!   (י) I am placing   (טז) we discussed
(ה) I will take out   (יא) being eaten   (יז) let him bring in
(ו) they brought down   (יב) it (f.) was said   (יח) you are establishing

ANSWERS TO EXERCISE 2

ARAMAIC VERB	ROOT	BINYAN	"TENSE"	HEBREW	ENGLISH
(1) בְּעָא	בעי	קַל	Past	רָצָה	he wanted
(2) לְמֵיהְדַר	הדר	קַל	Gerund	לַחֲזוֹר	to go back
(3) לְאַתוֹיֵי	אתי	אַפְעֵל	Gerund	לְהָבִיא	to bring
(4) אַתְנְיֵיה	תני	אַפְעֵל	Past	הִשְׁנָה לוֹ; לִמֵּד אוֹתוֹ	he taught him (oral law)
(5) נֵיקוּם	קום	קַל	Future	נָקוּם	let's get up
(6) נֵיזִיל	אזל	קַל	Future	נֵלֵךְ	let's go
(7) נֶעֱבֵיד	עבד	קַל	Future	נַעֲשֶׂה	let's do
(8) נְקַיֵּים	קום	פַּעֵל	Future	נְקַיֵּם	let's fulfill
(9) נְפַקָא	נפק	קַל	Past	יָצְאָה	she came out
(10) עַלַת	עלל	קַל	Past	נִכְנְסָה	she entered
(11) אֲמַר	אמר	קַל	Past	אָמַר	he said
(12) יָדַעְנָא	ידע	קַל	Present	יוֹדֵעַ אֲנִי	I know
(13) אָתוּ	אתי	קַל	Participle	בָּאִים	coming
(14) נִיסַק	סלק	קַל	Future	נַעֲלֶה	let's ascend
(15) נִיבְעֵי	בעי	קַל	Future	נְבַקֵּשׁ	let's ask for
(16) יַיְתֵי	אתי	אַפְעֵל	Future	יָבִיא	He will bring
(17) חֲזֵיָא	חזי	קַל	Pass. Part.	רְאוּיָה	fit
(18) אֵימָא	אמר	קַל	Future	אֹמַר	I would say
(19) מִיפְלַג	פלג	קַל	Infinitive	חָלוֹק	(divide)
(20) פָּלְגֵי	פלג	קַל	Participle	חוֹלְקִים	dividing
(21) צְרִיכֵי	צרך	קַל	Pass. Part.	צְרִיכִים	needed
(22) אֵיזִיל	אזל	קַל	Future	אֵלֵךְ	I will go
(23) אֵיתֵי	אתי	קַל	Future	אָבֹא	I will come
(24) אִיסַק	סלק	קַל	Future	אֶעֱלֶה	I will go up

ANSWERS TO EXERCISE 2 (continued)

ARAMAIC VERB	ROOT	BINYAN	"TENSE"	HEBREW	ENGLISH
(25) הֲוָה	הוי	קַל	Past	הָיָה	*was*
(26) לְמֶיעֱבַד	עבד	קַל	Gerund	לַעֲשׂוֹת	*to do*
(26) תִּיפּוֹק	נפק	קַל	Future	תֵּצֵא	*let it be derived*
(27) בָּעֵינַן	בעי	קַל	Present	צְרִיכִים אָנוּ	*we need*
(28) מְזַבֵּין	זבן	פַּעֵל	Participle	מוֹכֵר	*selling*
(30) זָבֵין	זבן	קַל	Participle	קוֹנֶה	*buying*

ANSWERS TO EXERCISE 3

VERB(S)	ROOT	BINYAN	"TENSE"	TRANSLATION
(1) אָמְרִי	אמר	קל	Participle	*they say*
(2) נְצַעֲרֵיה וְנֵיזִיל	צער, אזל	פַּעֵל, קל	Future	*shall he continue to harass him*
(3) צַעֲרֵיה	צער	פַּעֵל	Past (+ suffix)	*he harassed him*
(4) תָּא וְנַעֲבְרֵיה	אתי, עבר	קל, אַפְעֵל	Imp., Fut.* (+suffix)	*come and let's depose him*
(5) נוֹקִים	קום	אַפְעֵל	Future	*shall we install*
(6) נוֹקְמֵיה	קום	אַפְעֵל	Future* (+suffix)	*let us install (him)*
(7) עָנִישׁ	ענשׁ	קל	Participle**	*he will punish*
(8) מַקְשֵׁי	קשׁי	אַפְעֵל	Participle**	*he will raise a difficulty*

*   These future forms have a "modal" sense in Talmudic dialectic and are best translated as *let*....

** These participles have a future indicative meaning and are used in the Talmud instead of the ordinary future tense.

ANSWERS TO EXERCISE 3 (continued)

VERB(S)	ROOT	*BINYAN*	"TENSE"	TRANSLATION
(9) מְפָרֵק	פרק	פַּעֵל	Participle**	he will refute
(10) לְפָלוֹחֵי	קל	פלח	Infinitive	to serve
(11) אָזֵיל וּפָלַח	אזל, פלח	קל	Participle**	he will go and serve
(12) מָצֵי עָנֵיש	מצי, ענש	קל	Participle	he can punish
(13) אָתוּ וַאֲמְרוּ	אתי, אמר	קל	Past	they came and said
(14) לֶיהֱוֵי	הוי	קל	Future	he should be
(15) אֵיזִיל וְאִימְלִיךְ	אזל, מלך	קל, אתְפְּעֵל	Future	I shall go and consult
(16) אֲזַל וְאִימְלִיךְ	אזל, מלך	קל, אתְפְּעֵל	Past	he went and consulted
(17) מַעַבְרִין	עבר	אַפְעֵל	Participle**	they will depose
(18) לְשְׁתַּמֵּש	שמש	אתְפַּעַל	Future*	let one use
(19) לִיתְּבַר	תבר	אתְפְּעֵל	Future*	let it be broken
(20) הֲוָה	הוי	קל	Past	he was
(21) אתְרְחִיש	רחש	אתְפְּעֵל	Past	it occurred
(22) אַהֲדְרוּ	הדר	אַפְעֵל	Past	"they" surrounded
(23) קָאָמַר	אמר	קל	Participle + קָ	he says

* These future forms have a "modal" sense in Talmudic dialectic and are best translated as *let....*

** These participles have a future indicative meaning and are used in the Talmud instead of the ordinary future tense.

ANSWERS TO EXERCISE 4

TARGUM ONKELOS	BIBLICAL FORM	PROMINENT LETTERS*	ARAMAIC ROOT	ARAMAIC *BINYAN*	MODEL ROOT	ENGLISH TRANSLATION
מִית (1)	וַיָּמָת	מת	מות	קל	–	he died
נְפִישׁוּ (2)	פָּרוּ	(נ)פש	נפש	קל	תקף	they became numerous
אִתְיַלָדוּ (3)	וַיִּשְׁרְצוּ	לד	ילד	אתפעל	–	they reproduced
סְגִיאוּ (4)	וַיִּרְבּוּ	(סג)*	סגי	קל	שתי	they multiplied
תְּקִיפוּ (5)	וַיַּעַצְמוּ	–	תקף	קל	–	they grew strong
אִתְמְלִיאַת (6)	וַתִּמָּלֵא	(מל)*	מלי	אתפעל	גלי	it became full
קָם (7)	וַיָּקָם	קם	קום	קל	–	he arose
מְקַיֵּים (8)	יָדַע	קם	קום	פַּעֵל	–	(was) fulfilling
נִתְחַכַּם (9)	נִתְחַכְּמָה	–	חכם	אתפעל	קדש	let's take counsel
יִסְגּוֹן (10)	יִרְבֶּה	(סג)*	סגי	קל	גלי	they will multiply
וִיהֵי (11)	וְהָיָה	(הי)*	הוי (היי)	קל	–	it will be
יִתּוֹסְפוּן (12)	וְנוֹסַף	סף	יסף	אתפעל	יתב	they will be added
וִיגִיחוּן (קְרָב) (13)	וְנִלְחַם	נח	גוח	אַפְעֵל	קום	they will wage (war)
וְיִסְקוּן (14)	וְעָלָה	סק	סלק	קל	–	they will go up
וּמַנִּיאוּ (15)	וַיָּשִׂימוּ	מן	מני	פַּעֵל	גלי	they appointed
וּבְנוֹ (16)	וַיִּבֶן	(בן)*	בני	קל	גלי	they built
וְאַמַרוּ (17)	וַיְמָרֲרוּ	מר	מרר	אַפְעֵל	עלל	they embittered
(דְ)אַפְלַחוּ (18)	(אֲשֶׁר)עָבְדוּ	–	פלח	אַפְעֵל	פקד	they enslaved
וַאֲמַר (19)	וַיֹּאמֶר	מר	אמר	קל	–	(and) he said
וּדְחִילָא (20)	וַתִּירֶאןָ	–	דחל	קל	תקף	they (f) feared
עֲבָדָא (21)	עָשׂוּ	–	עבד	קל		they (f) did
(דְ)מַלִיל (22)	(אֲשֶׁר) דִּבֶּר	–	מלל	פַּעֵל	קדש	he said
וְקַיֵּימָא (23)	וַתְּחַיֶּין	קם	קום	פַּעֵל	–	they (f) kept alive

* See the note on p. 293.

ANSWERS TO EXERCISE 5

בראשית ב:ד אֵלֶּה תוֹלְדוֹת הַשָּׁמַיִם וְהָאָרֶץ בְּהִבָּרְאָם בְּיוֹם עֲשׂוֹת ה' אֱלֹקִים אֶרֶץ וְשָׁמָיִם.

אִלֵּין תּוֹלְדֹת שְׁמַיָּא וְאַרְעָא כַּד אִתְבְּרִיאוּ[1] בְּיוֹמָא דַעֲבַד[2] ה' אֱלֹקִים אַרְעָא וּשְׁמַיָּא.

ז:יד וְכָל הָעוֹף לְמִינֵהוּ כֹּל צִפּוֹר כָּל כָּנָף

וְכָל עוֹפָא לִזְנוֹהִי כֹּל צִפַּר כָּל דְּפָרַח[3]

יב:יא הִנֵּה נָא יָדַעְתִּי כִּי אִשָּׁה יְפַת מַרְאֶה אָתְּ

הָא כְעַן יָדַעְנָא[4] אֲרֵי אִתְּתָא שַׁפִּירַת חֵיזוּ אַתְּ

יז:א וַיֵּרָא ה' אֶל אַבְרָם וַיֹּאמֶר אֵלָיו אֲנִי אֵל שַׁדַּי הִתְהַלֵּךְ לְפָנַי וֶהְיֵה תָמִים.

וְאִתְגְּלִי[5] ה' לְאַבְרָם וַאֲמַר[6] לֵיהּ אֲנָא אֵל שַׁדַּי פְּלַח[7] קֳדָמַי וֶהֱוֵי[8] שְׁלִים.

כט:ג וְנֶאֶסְפוּ שָׁמָּה כָל הָעֲדָרִים וְגָלֲלוּ אֶת הָאֶבֶן מֵעַל פִּי הַבְּאֵר

וּמִתְכַּנְּשִׁין[9] תַּמָּן כָּל עֶדְרַיָּא וּמְגַנְדְּרִין[10] יָת אַבְנָא מֵעַל פּוּמָא דְּבֵירָא

כט:ח עַד אֲשֶׁר יֵאָסְפוּ כָּל הָעֲדָרִים וְגָלֲלוּ אֶת הָאֶבֶן מֵעַל פִּי הַבְּאֵר

עַד דְּיִתְכַּנְּשׁוּן[11] תַּמָּן כָּל עֶדְרַיָּא וִיגַנְדְּרוּן[12] יָת אַבְנָא מֵעַל פּוּמָא דְּבֵירָא

מט:ח יְהוּדָה אַתָּה יוֹדוּךָ אַחֶיךָ

יְהוּדָה אַתְּ אוֹדִיתָא[13] וְלָא בְהֵיתְתָא[14]

VERB	ROOT	MODEL ROOT	BINYAN	"TENSE"	TRANSLATION
(1) אִתְבְּרִיאוּ	ברי/א	גלי	אִתְפְּעֵל	Past	(they) were created[1]
(2) עֲבַד	עבד	—	קל	Past	(He) made[1]
(3) פָּרַח	פרח	ידע	קל	Participle	flying[2]
(4) יָדַעְנָא	ידע	—	קל	Present	I know[3]
(5) וְאִתְגְּלִי	גלי	—	אִתְפְּעֵל	Past	(He) revealed Himself[4]
(6) אֲמַר	אמר	—	קל	Past	He said[5]
(7) פְּלַח	פלח	דבר	קל	Imperative	serve![6]
(8) הֱוֵי	הוי	—	קל	Imperative	be!
(9) מִתְכַּנְּשִׁין	כנש	קדש	אִתְפַּעַל	Participle	(they) would gather[7]
(10) מְגַנְדְּרִין	גנדר	quadriliteral	ACTIVE	Participle	(they) would roll[7]
(11) יִתְכַּנְּשׁוּן	כנש	קדש	אִתְפַּעַל	Future	(they) will gather
(12) יְגַנְדְּרוּן	גנדר	quadriliteral	ACTIVE	Future	(they) will roll[8]
(13) אוֹדִיתָא	ידי	—	אַפְעֵל	Past	you confessed[9]
(14) בְהֵיתְתָא	בהת	תקף	קל	Past	you were ashamed[10]

1. simple past — for gerund (pp. 43-44).   2. verbal form — for wing (noun).
3. יָדַע + אֲנָא (p. 32) — not past tense (See Rashi).
4. revealed — not seen.   5. past — for future with "conversive vav".
6. serve — for walk (See Rashi).   7. customary action (See Rashi).
8. future — for past with "conversive vav" (See Rashi).
9. past — for future.   10. additional verb.

SOURCES IN ENGLISH FOR FURTHER STUDY

1. Mishnaic Hebrew

(1) Bar-Asher, Moshe. "Mishnaic Hebrew: An Introductory Survey." *Hebrew Studies* 40 (1999) pp. 115-151.

(2) —, *Studies in Mishnaic Hebrew*. Scripta Hiersolymitana: Publications of the Hebrew University of Jerusalem, Vol. 37. Jerusalem: Magnes, 1998; Varda, 2010.

(3) Chomsky, William. *Hebrew: The Eternal Language*, Philadelphia: 1964. pp. 157-171.

(4) Kutscher, Eduard Yeḥezkel. "Hebrew Language." *Encyclopedia Judaica*. 1971 ed. Vol. 16, pp. 1590-1607.

(5) —, *A History of the Hebrew Language*. Ed. Raphael Kutscher. Jerusalem: Magnes, 1982. pp. 115-147.

(6) Segal, M. H. *A Grammar of Mishnaic Hebrew*. Oxford: Clarendon Press, 1927.

2. The Aramaic of the Babylonian Talmud

(7) Bar-Asher Siegal, Elitzur A. *Introduction to the Grammar of Jewish-Babylonian Aramaic. LOS III/3*. Münster: Ugarit-Verlag, 2013.

(8) Frank, Yitzḥak. *The Practical Talmud Dictionary*. Jerusalem: Ariel, 1991; Maggid-Koren 2016.

(9) —, *The Comprehensive Talmud Dictionary* (work-in-progress) <http://www.daf-yomi.com/BookFiles.aspx?id=15>.

(10) Jastrow, Marcus. *A Dictionary of the Targumim, the Talmud Babli and Yerushalmi and the Midrashic Literature*. New York: Pardes, 1950.

(11) Klein, Hyman. *An Introduction to the Aramaic of the Babyloninan Talmud*. London: 1943.

(12) Kutscher, Eduard Yeḥezkel. "Aramaic." *Encyclopedia Judaica*. Jerusalem, 1971 ed. Vol. 3, pp. 259-287.

(13) Morgenstern, Matthew. *Studies in Jewish Babylonian Aramaic Based upon Early Manuscript Sources*. (Harvard Semitic Studies). Winona Lake: Eisenbrauns, 2011.

(14) Sokoloff, Michael. *A Dictionary of Jewish Babylonian Aramaic of the Talmudic and Geonic Periods*. Ramat-Gan, Israel: Bar-Ilan Univ. Press, 2002.

3. The Aramaic of the Targum Onkelos

(15) *Comprehensive Aramaic Lexicon*. Interactive Computer Program, <http://call.cn.huc.edu>. May 2009. (Print version not yet completed. Baltimore: Johns Hopkins University Press.)

(16) Cook, Edward M. *A Glossary of Targum Onkelos*, Leiden: Brill, 2008.

(17) Frank, Yitzḥak. Introduction to Targum Onkelos. *The Ariel Chumash*. Ed. Emanuel Feldman. Jerusalem: Ariel, 1997. pp. xvi-xix.

(18) Goshen-Gottstein, M.H. "The Language of Targum Onkelos & the Model of Literary Diglossia in Aramaic," *Journal of Near Eastern Studies* 37.2 (1978): pp. 169-179. <http://www.jstor.org/stable/545142>. Web.

ADDENDUM (to the Aramaic *binyanim* described on p. 20)

SIMPLE		INTENSIVE		EXTENSIVE	
Active	Reflex./Pass.	Active	Reflex./Pass.	Active	Reflex./Pass.
קַל	אִ[ו]תְפְּעֵל	פַּעֵל	אִ[ו]תְפַּעַל	קַל	אִתַּפְעַל

The crucial difference between *binyan* אִתְפְּעֵל (the reflexive/passive of the simple [i.e., the קַל] and *binyan* אִתְפַּעַל (the reflexive/passive of the intensive [i.e., the פַּעֵל] is the "doubling" of the middle root-letter in the latter, which is marked by a "strong" *dagesh*. Since, however, most reliable Talmudic texts do not mark vowels or *degeshim*, it is often difficult to determine which of the two *binyanim* is the more appropriate for a specific verbal form.

Usually, in *binyan* אִתְפְּעֵל the basic form (i.e., third-person masculine singular, past tense) has a vowel-letter *yod* — indicating a *tzerei* or a *ḥirik* between the second and third root-letter, e.g., אִתְכְּתֵיב; on the other hand, in the אִתְפַּעַל *binyan* there is no *yod* and the vowel under the second root-letter is a *pathaḥ* (or a *kamatz* before a guttural), e.g., אִתְקַדַּשׁ. There are *exceptions*, however, in both directions: i.e., the *yod* is absent from some אִתְפְּעֵל forms and the vowel should (probably) be *pathaḥ*. e.g., אִיעֲנַשׁ (Morag, p. 140); and, conversely, in certain אִתְפַּעַל forms the *yod* does appear (indicating a *tzerei* vowel), e.g., אִיכַּוִּין (Morag, p. 153). Therefore, this factor is hardly a foolproof guide for determining which *binyan* is the better fit for a specific form.

But another element is probably more significant, and it explains the aforementioned exceptions: namely, **which active *binyan* of the same verb corresponds to the reflexive/passive form under consideration**: If the parallel active *binyan* from the same root is the simple קַל (e.g., עֲנַשׁ, *he punished*), it stands to reason that the matching reflexive/passive *binyan* is the simple אִתְפְּעֵל (e.g., אִי[ו]תְעֲנַשׁ, *he was punished*); conversely, if the parallel active *binyan* is the intensive פַּעֵל (e.g., כַּוִּין, *he directed*), then the matching reflexive/passive *binyan* is the אִתְפַּעַל (e.g., אִיכַּוֵּין, *he concentrated*).

In fact, for some Babylonian Aramaic verbs, both of these reflexive/passive *binyanim* (and their active parallels) are in use, e.g.,: אִיעֲקַר, *it was uprooted* (the אִתְפְּעֵל, which is parallel to עֲקַר, *he uprooted*, the קַל) and אִיעַקַּר (the אִתְפַּעַל, *he became sterile*, parallel to עַקַּר, *he caused sterility*, the פַּעֵל).